Selected Essays
and Other Writings of
JOHN DONALD WADE

JOHN DONALD WADE

Selected Essays
and Other Writings of
JOHN DONALD WADE

Edited and with an Introduction by
Donald Davidson

UNIVERSITY OF GEORGIA PRESS Athens

❦❧

Contents

Acknowledgements

THE EDITOR of this volume wishes to express his deep sense of gratitude to the relatives and friends of John Donald Wade and to other persons whose interest and generous assistance facilitated and indeed made possible the publication of this collection: to Mrs. John D. Wade of Marshallville, for important information and for access to certain manuscript material; to Miss Anne Wade of Marshallville; to Mr. Richard E. Dodd of Marshallville, for invaluable counsel and encouragement; to Professor Ed Dawson of the Department of English, The Woman's College of Georgia, Milledgeville, for his kindness in giving me the benefit of his own pioneer survey of the Wade material; to Professor Edd Winfield Parks of the Department of English, University of Georgia; and to Mr. Robert G. Benson of New Orleans, Graduate Student at Vanderbilt University, whose bibliographical investigation expedited the collection of material and made possible early preparation of the manuscript.

In capitalization and punctuation the texts of the essays follow the printed originals without change. Whether certain minor peculiarities and inconsistencies in such matters are attributable to various "house styles" or to John Wade's own preferences, the editor does not undertake to determine.

D. D.

❦

John Donald Wade, 1892-1963:

A Sketch of His Life

By John O. Eidson

JOHN DONALD WADE grew up in middle Georgia in the kind of agrarian environment which, as to both place and people, he liked to write about. He was born at Marshallville, Georgia, on September 28, 1892, the son of John Daniel and Ida Frederick Wade. He attended elementary and high school in Marshallville, for a few months attended Peacock's School in Atlanta, and entered the University of Georgia in 1910, graduating with the A.B. degree in 1914. After a year at Harvard University, where he received the M.A. degree in 1915, he spent two years at Columbia University working toward the Ph.D. degree. His education was then interrupted for two years while he served in the U.S. Army as a Second Lieutenant in World War I; in 1919 he became an Instructor in English at the University of Georgia.

From 1919 to 1926, John Donald Wade taught at the University of Georgia, spending, however, some time at Columbia University, and devoting very much time to work on his doctoral dissertation. In 1924 he received his Ph.D. degree from Columbia, and published *Augustus Baldwin Longstreet: A Study of the Development of Culture in the South,* one of the most notable books ever written about the South. By 1926 he had attained the rank of Associate Professor and had become one of the most respected members of the faculty at Georgia.

The year 1926 began an eight-year period during which—with many interspersed visits back home—Dr. Wade was "headquartered" outside of Georgia. That year he was awarded a Guggenheim Fellowship and went to London to do research for a biography of John Wesley. His mother went with him, as she did

Dr. John O. Eidson is Dean of the College of Arts and Sciences at the University of Georgia.

on many of his travels, and they also visited Egypt. After his return Dr. Wade spent a year in Washington as Assistant Editor of the *Dictionary of American Biography,* and in 1928 went to Vanderbilt University as Professor of English. His years at Vanderbilt were among his most active in writing and in stimulating students to write. Vanderbilt was experiencing a remarkable renaissance of creative and scholarly writing, and Dr. Wade played a prominent part in it. He published his *John Wesley* in 1930, his essay "The Life and Death of Cousin Lucius" in *I'll Take My Stand* the same year, and a number of other well-known essays soon afterward.

In 1934 Dr. Wade returned to the University of Georgia as Professor of English. In 1939 he became Head of the Department of English and Chairman of the Division of Language and Literature, and continued in these positions until 1946. In Athens, as he had been in Nashville, he was a powerful stimulant to the intellectual life of the students. Along with his colleague Roosevelt Walker he founded an extremely active group called the Fortnightly Club in which faculty and students met for discussion and debate, often far into the night. Dr. Wade's office was generally filled with students, borrowing and talking books, and discussing everything imaginable. A common saying among students was "You never forget a class with Dr. Wade."

He continued, too, his own writing, contributing to several anthologies and literary histories and to such periodicals as the *American Mercury,* the *American Review,* the *Virginia Quarterly Review,* the *Southern Review,* and *American Literature.* He was one of three editors of the anthology *Masterworks of World Literature,* which was published in 1947 and is now widely used as a college text. He read papers before civic and scholarly groups, taught in the summers at Duke and the University of North Carolina, and served for two years as Associate Editor of the *Sewanee Review.*

In 1947 he founded the *Georgia Review,* a literary quarterly which he made both regional and general and which he edited until his retirement from the University in 1950. The *Review* and his editorials and articles for it form one of his chief legacies to the University and to Georgia.

From 1950, Dr. Wade's chief interests and activities centered around Marshallville. In 1942 he had married Julia Floyd Stovall of Athens, and when he retired from the University, they moved to Marshallville and lived in the old Frederick home, the ancestral estate of his mother. They had one daughter, Anne Treutlen

Wade, who grew up in Marshallville, attended the University of Georgia, and graduated in 1966. After his first wife's death in 1959, Dr. Wade married Florence Lester of Marshallville in 1962. He died on October 9, 1963, and is buried in Marshallville.

In his last years, Dr. Wade was still active and productive. He was writing and lecturing. When he died, he had just finished a major work and was scheduled to give a series of lectures at Mercer University. He devoted himself fervently to bringing a special distinction to the town of his birth. He had set up a Marshallville Foundation for this purpose, and organized a citizens' club for bringing well-known speakers to the community and holding discussions on cultural topics. He planted camellias for several miles along the roads leading into town, founded a boys' club, established a local library, and designed behind his home an extensive arboretum and Garden of World History.

Throughout his life, John Donald Wade brought distinction to whatever he did, wherever he was—Vanderbilt, University of Georgia, Marshallville. What the university students said of his classes, one can also say of him—you never forget Dr. Wade.

Introduction

THE GARDENS OF JOHN DONALD WADE

TO HAVE WIT—and wisdom too, that so much rarer blessing; to have knowledge of men and their ways, and great learning too, much of it very special, and yet avoid the vices of the modern specialist; in temperament and code, as by inheritance and natural inclination, to be a gentleman of the old school (if one may use that term), and yet a skillful modern in alert, practical perception, and so able to bring imagination and insight to any undertaking, small or large; to have religious faith and practice works, without the contemporary separation of the twain; to have the gift of language that, when friends or casual guests are at hand, makes one room an everywhere and one small Georgia town a world garden—how difficult, how all but impossible in the skeptical, self-deluding twentieth century! Yet such were—though still incompletely stated—the talents and virtues of John Donald Wade, some of whose writings are here assembled. This is his book; and never, I think, did any book more emphatically and warmly declare the man and his vision of a world, in the large or in miniature. The very cadence of his voice is here, his gesture, his presence.

Curious inquirers, thumbing books of reference, may often have been puzzled to find John Donald Wade identified as "foundation executive." Whether the designation was fixed by the editor of some work or reference or represents a waggish and maybe very practical notion of Wade's, I do not know. I would suspect the latter. The term is quite correct, but needs explanation. Far back in the nineteen-thirties or earlier John Wade conceived and began to put into effect a scheme that he had devised for beautifying the highway approaches to his native town of Marshallville, Georgia. The plan—as Wade stated it in a pamphlet that I am sure he wrote—was to make this natural sort of beautification a memorial to the founders of Marshallville—those adventurous families that migrated West, *en bloc,* from Orangeburg, South Carolina, in the eighteen-thirties, cleared land, and settled

1

in what has remained to this day one of the choice spots of Georgia and the South. The Marshallville Foundation was John Wade's device for enlisting support from the descendants of the Marshallville pioneers.* In that sense it was an entirely local device, and it worked.

Camellias were planted along the main road entering the town, and crepe myrtles beside them to shade the plants while they were young and to enhance the general effect in later years. I well remember how some of the planting was done during the winter of 1932-33. In that winter, after a year of disaster, my wife, our daughter, and I were in effect "refugeeing," by invitation of Wade and his mother in the "little green house" that adjoined the stately Frederick mansion—which itself had only lately been moved from another site to replace the Wade house, burned some time before. The county "chain gang" were brought in to do some of the digging and planting. Chain gang, yes—but entirely without chains, a jovial and willing group, distinguished from other laborers only by their prisoner's stripes and the presence of an attendant who hardly seemed to be a guard. They did not fit the description that was appearing in the New York papers of those years and that was much groaned and gloomed about in publications like *I Was a Fugitive from a Georgia Chain Gang*.

The memorial idea was serious and important, but actually it was only part of John Wade's long-range intention as "executive" of the Marshallville Foundation. The drift from country to city had already begun. Wade had no idea of joining it himself. What he feared was its centripetal pull upon Marshallville. He aimed to forestall, or at least blunt, that destructive force by making the town a place that people—especially young people—would find pleasant, would indeed love, and so not be lured off to Macon or Atlanta or New York. For thirty years and more the Marshallville Foundation quietly functioned in various ways to that general end. Which is to say that John Wade—certainly much more than a mere "executive"—indeed more like a master gardener—never ceased to think of what next might be planted. But his plantings were not merely horticultural.

All of this was but a part of what the world lamely calls a "philosophy of life." Better say, it was a conviction deeper and warmer than any known philosophy can provide. There was in it

---

Who's Who in America records Wade as "founder and president of the Marshallville Foundation since 1944."

something of the principle described by the historian Toynbee as "withdrawal-and-return"—the withdrawal being made that man may better participate, in a high sense, in the world's affairs. One may think of St. Jerome in his cave, or Horace on his Sabine farm, or Thoreau at Walden. But none of these examples fits John Wade. One might do well to say that Marshallville, with the old plantation country of Georgia around it, became for John Wade the fixed point from which he could view the far too moving, far too changeable world, and from time to time join that world, when joining it would really count.

Among the occasions of world-joining that really counted were Wade's year of graduate work at Harvard and then, after a tour of duty in World War I, his period of further study at Columbia University. Out of his work at Columbia came his Ph.D. degree in American Literature, and, much more important, the publication in 1924 of his first book, *Augustus Baldwin Longstreet,* a massive biography of nearly 400 pages. Wade did not think of this notable volume as just biography. The subtitle gives the clue: *A Study of the Development of Culture in the South.* Certainly it is about Longstreet himself—Longstreet the cantankerous individual American who was born in the late eighteenth century and lasted over, through all his transformations into lawyer, preacher, college president, and writer, into the latter half of the nineteenth century. It is about Georgia too, from frontier Georgia all the way to Henry Grady's "New South" Georgia. By obvious implication and often wide, direct focus it is about the South at large in the times when the South harbored Calhoun, Moses Waddel, L. Q. C. Lamar, and such lesser figures as Georgia Congressman Augustin S. Clayton, whom Wade had conjectured to be the ghost-writer of David Crockett's "autobiography." Since the volume dealt with Longstreet, it also had to deal with education, religion, politics, race relations, story-telling, preaching, fist-fighting and, yes, racing, journalism, cotton, and so on. By somewhat less obvious implication it dealt also with the United States of which, according to Mr. Lincoln, Thad Stevens, and others, Georgia was an inseparable portion. *That* implication, naturally, was not always grasped by Wade's readers.

Naturally? Indeed so! In 1924 and even later a landmark book like Wade's *Longstreet,* for all its superb quality, was more interesting to the relatively small group of American literature scholars than to literary critics in general, or, say, to Walter Lippmann or readers of the *New Republic* or the *New Masses* or even Wade's fellow-Georgians, including Hoke Smith, Bishop Candler, and the rising Atlanta liberals. To the American literature scholars it was exciting—especially as a portrait of Longstreet as writer—indeed Longstreet as humorist, the author of *Georgia Scenes*. In 1924, to tell the plain truth, there were hardly any authoritative biographies of writers who had happened to flourish south of the Potomac or, for that matter, west of the Hudson. Barrett Wendell of Harvard, a famous professor in his day, just about limited *his* history of American literature to the New England worthies. It should have been entitled, said Fred Lewis Pattee (himself a New Englander), "A Literary History of Harvard University, with Incidental Glimpses of the Minor Writers of America." Yet Barrett Wendell, when his student John Wade came to him for a thesis subject, had the good grace to urge Wade to go to Columbia University and work under William P. Trent, who (Wendell confessed) "knew more about Southern literature than *he* knew."

In his pungent and delightful "review" of *Georgia Scenes* written forty years after his first close reading of it, Wade is quite autobiographical:

So there I was at Columbia University, working with Professor Trent, and the year was, in a way of speaking, 1492.

I was from Georgia, said Professor Trent, and there was a subject cut out for me: Judge Longstreet, the author of *Georgia Scenes,* one of the really first "American Books" in the Whitmanian sense of the phrase, the forerunner of many other notable books, even at last, most likely, of *Tom Sawyer* and *Huckleberry Finn*. The date, as I have remarked, was early, and the speaker was in consequence still able to name all these names standing rather than on his knees.*

So it happened that the biography of Writer-Preacher-Lawyer Longstreet, perhaps somewhat to Wade's surprise, had a good deal to do with the vogue, beginning joyously in the nineteen-twenties and lasting pretty well to the present day, of the "humor of the Old Southwest," as it used to be called, and of frontier humor in general. In his article on "Southern Humor," published ten years after the *Longstreet*, Wade rather carefully plays down the frontier boisterousness of *Georgia Scenes*. He finds it hard to distinguish the particular Southern humor in its very essence. But he concludes that one does find it in the social and historical circumstances and occasions that distinguish the South from other

*Georgia Review, XIV (Winter, 1960), 444-447.

parts of the country. Even a somewhat industrialized South, he maintains, cannot think of people as other than human beings with human imperfections. It cannot think of them as made of metal—mere units behaving with mechanical perfection. Out of that deep-ingrained belief comes "Southern humor." Wade's discourse in this vein can be taken as a postscript to the *Longstreet* and a correction of wrong conclusions drawn from it.

All the same, Wade's *Longstreet* is a pioneer work of great importance, highly original in its conception. At the time when it appeared, perhaps only Edwin Mims's *Sidney Lanier* (1905) and Trent's *William Gilmore Simms* (1892), could be nominated as standard biographies of Southern writers—other than Poe. The *Longstreet* evidently stands at the fountain-head of the new studies in American literature that since the Nineteen-Twenties have swelled into a Mississippi. What is more, the book not only opened a "field"; it initiated a method, in fact a style. Although Wade as writer is somewhat impeded in his *Longstreet* by the necessity of authenticating as well as of marshalling his vast array of facts, the subtle dramatic quality of his later prose is already manifesting itself. It is energizing and enriching with oblique commentary what would otherwise be the flat detail of the researchist. What Ph.D. dissertations of those early years would have begun— or been permitted to begin—with a sentence like Wade's first: "Vehemence, old and oldish men fall periodically to telling the world, counts for more than length of years in the matter of how much a man lives"? How many would have ended with a death scene that is pure dramatic art yet also "true" biography? In those times when the study of literature was very often plain philology, it was a surprise—and maybe, to Kittredges big and little, a shock— to find an aspirant for the Ph.D. degree writing like a novelist or essayist, as in this passage that gives the feelings or perceptions of Gus Longstreet, age 10, in Augusta, around 1800:

The town was full of great men, as great, a youngster might think, as one could see anywhere—Governors, Generals, Admirals, Senators, Judges, poets. This was the first time in the history of the world, even the youngest boy knew that, in which the spirit of man had ever been quite untrammeled by despotism. . . . Hope literally washed the heavens. Puritan Massachusetts, unable to rid itself of the idea of man's essential wickedness, could not as yet envision this earthly paradise. Georgia, with fewer preconceptions, accepted Mr. Jefferson's ideas with less resistance, and believed to an amazing extent, it seemed, that the world stood in a fine way of becoming shortly a place of unvarying loveliness.*

In the principle of both prose and idea, this passage reveals the John Wade that we gradually came to know. From this time on, biography was for him the favorite vehicle for what he had to say, and he had much. Biography was both history and art. The economic determinists of the Twenties and Thirties—men like Charles A. Beard and the elder Schlesinger—were saying that history is social forces. John Donald Wade was thinking: history is people.

When Wade came to the Vanderbilt University Department of English in 1928, his pen was already well practiced. While finishing his *Longstreet* he had taught at his alma mater, the University of Georgia. As one of the early beneficiaries of the Guggenheim Fellowships he had journeyed to England to gather material for his *John Wesley*—especially, of course, to look into the British origins of Methodism, the church to which his family had been devoted for three generations. For still another year Wade was a member of the editorial staff of the *Dictionary of American Biography*. To that monumental work he contributed 116 sketches, most of them but not all on Georgian and Southern subjects. The experience of having to write with clipped terseness according to a prescribed pattern and within a strict word-limit undoubtedly affected Wade's style. Among other things he learned how, in very few words, to make an apparently bald statement of fact carry with it a judgment, either through the vocabulary itself or by skilful placement of one factual item in juxtaposition with others. Thus he often secured a subtly ironic effect, perceptible to a close reader but not immediately evident to readers that take large eyefuls and run as they read.

When he first came to Vanderbilt Wade had a good deal to say about this method to his friends and, I imagine, to his best students. It was the old maxim "Waste not, want not" applied with great finesse and vigor to modern prose. I would surmise that Wade used it with deliberate intent in his biography of John Wesley. Perhaps it was, in part, the brilliant, heightened effect thus imparted to his prose that made some of his Methodist brethren uneasy about the book. Almost any page sizzled and sent off sparks like a bomb ready to explode. A fine prose style, yes. But in some circles during those years a fine style might *per se*

---

*Augustus Baldwin Longstreet (New York: The Macmillan Co., 1924), p. 16.

render a book suspect. It might be thought to have something un-Methodist about it—like (in those other, strictly plain days) a preacher in a surplice, a gowned choir, a crucifix in the chancel, the pulpit "on the side."

Here, for example, are some sentences from Wade's examination of eighteen-year-old John Wesley's education at Oxford:

Regard, then, with patience, this boy. Extenuate his envy—recorded in verse—of Chloe's flea, happy because no region of Chloe's frame was interdicted to him. Set not down as malice his gustatory love of apples, praised in letters home to his mother.*

And here is John Wesley wandering about the streets of Oxford:

Handsome and clever, the descendant of Oxford-bred ancestors, he went about those wistful streets, and into those rich rooms and beside that clement river, no intruder.**

And here is Wade in ironic defense of early Methodist practices much frowned upon at Oxford:

All manner of names, ready on the tongues of collegians to subdue any who are incomprehensible to them, were quickly attached to these zealots, violaters of the tradition—wisely arrived at—that any tradition, once it is asleep, must be left lying so. They were named Bible bigots, enthusiasts, methodists.***

In its excellence as biography, *John Wesley* would hardly have a rival during the Twenties and Thirties—unless perhaps Lytton Strachey in England, then at the height of his vogue. But Wade's Methodist brothers and sisters, accustomed to no more lively fare than the *Christian Advocate,* could not find it in their hearts to cherish *John Wesley.* I recall riding a street-car in Nashville with a very prominent superannuated Methodist preacher as my seat-companion, a good friend, long well beloved in my family. I made the mistake of asking if he had read John Wade's new biography. "That man!" he roared. "Why, he's a skeptic—or worse!" I was quick to give reassurance, but dear Brother X (we called preachers "Brother" in those days) was still ruefully shaking his head when he got off the car.

It is easy enough to fathom Dr. Edwin Mims's reasons—very good ones they were—for inviting John Wade to join the Vanderbilt English department. Dr. Mims rightly figured that Wade

---

John Wesley (New York: Coward McCann, 1939) , p. 26.
**Ibid.,* p. 25.   ***Ibid.,* p. 45.

would be the ideal man to head the department's brand-new graduate program in American literature, suddenly boosted from financial poverty to what in comparison seemed like affluence by its share in the University's "Four Million Dollar" campaign. Wade's reasons for accepting are not so readily fathomable. Undoubtedly he expected to have leisure to write, even while teaching; and the Vanderbilt English department encouraged him in that expectation. Whatever his reasons were, Wade's acceptance made a great difference in all that happened next, both for Wade and for Vanderbilt.

Much happened to Wade—more, I imagine, than he had anticipated, and of a surprising nature. He came to Vanderbilt English department when something more brisk than seminars and theses was shaping up. He found himself in the midst of persons, some of them his department colleagues, who were most furiously and incessantly writing—not only about Milton's prosody and Chaucer's medievalism, but about American affairs, old and new, and in defense or criticism of his native South, by no means excluding Georgia, or, in ways that reflected a sense of crisis, on other large flaming subjects, in verse or prose, fiction, history, criticism, and even drama.

Whatever Wade may have thought, at first encounter, about all this, there is no doubt at all that he felt pretty soon the urge to do as his colleagues were doing, though in his own manner and on subjects to his taste. And his colleagues wasted no time in drawing Wade into their councils and pressing him for contributions. From this time on, Wade's writing owes much, surely, to the impetus given by the activities and ideas represented in the symposium, *I'll Take My Stand: The South and the Agrarian Tradition* and to the opportunities offered him through periodicals that his new friends edited or influenced. In April, 1933, Wade published his memorable essay, "Profits and Losses in the Life of Joel Chandler Harris," in *The American Review*, founded by Seward Collins "to give greater currency to the ideas of a number of groups and individuals . . . who launch their criticisms [of the modern regime] from a traditionalist basis." In July, 1935, he wrote for the first number of the *Southern Review*, edited by Cleanth Brooks and Robert Penn Warren, his lengthy review, entitled "Prodigal," of Thomas Wolfe's *Look Homeward, Angel* and *Of Time and the River*. Undoubtedly the articles that Wade wrote for the *Southern Review* and the three symposia of the Thirties (*I'll Take My Stand, Culture in the South,* and *Who*

Owns America?) were solicited rather than volunteered, and otherwise might not have been written just at that time—if ever—in the form that they took.

But Wade was nothing loath. His hopes of checking the arrogant materialism of the newest "New South" might be a shade less bright than the hopes his friends were advancing, but he warmly shared their beliefs about a great many important matters. And the stir and excitement was a spur to composition. So, when asked, he willingly responded, and wrote reviews and articles rather frequently, both for the periodicals mentioned and for others—for instance the *Virginia Quarterly Review,* founded by James Southall Wilson in 1925. To H. L. Mencken's *American Mercury,* then at the height of its influence, he contributed "Jefferson: New Style," his biographical study of Tom Watson of Georgia, one of his most thorough and lengthy articles. This one he wrote—and evidently researched for—while he was finishing his *John Wesley.* All of these are pieces of the greatest distinction, and all bear the marks of John Wade's own genius. No other hand but his could have written them.

For the record, it is interesting to note that Wade's *John Wesley,* Ransom's *God Without Thunder,* and the Twelve Southerners' *I'll Take My Stand* were all three published during the autumn of 1930, when the Great Depression was shaking the seats of the mighty throughout America and indeed the Western world. Each book in its way was a pronouncement, direct or indirect, upon the folly, economic or otherwise, that had brought about this disaster, and, more broadly, upon the cause and cure of maladies that had been noticed by such prophets as Spengler, Julien Benda and Unamuno, not to mention the ancient Isaiah and Jeremiah. Twenty years after their first pronouncement, a few of the Twelve Southerners, when questioned, went on record as regretting that their symposium had not more emphatically stressed religion as the key to amendment of social chaos. Wade had no need for such regret. Already in the Preface to his *John Wesley* he had written: "I remember that like most other religious organizations, Methodism, in its anxiety to grow quickly in strength and stature, has often minimized the necessity of growing also—a more deliberate process—in knowledge of God and man." The central interest of his book, he declares, is in the answer to two far-reaching questions: "Was John Wesley, the acknowledged, the proclaimed paragon of Methodists, aware of the danger of growing in strength and stature at the expense of growing in wisdom? Did he remind his followers duteously, by his life as well as his words, that there was such a danger?"

In his writings of these years it was not the habit of John Wade to worry a topic through by a straight dialectical process to some logically deducted generalization which could then be preferred to some other generalization discovered at last to be unworthy or false. His desire was to grasp the particulars that made a theory or doctrine applicable and intelligible in warmly human terms. Though in the technical sense Wade did not philosophize, there was a good deal of the Platonic in his method. Rarely could he do without a specific place and specific persons. He liked also to make sudden excursions, anecdotal or fictional, and sometimes keenly satirical, but always weighted with meaning that might be stated metaphorically or that hovered on the edge of symbolism and allegory. If the reader—or the hearer, in the class-room or by the fireside—could not catch on, could not make for himself the necessary generalization, so much the worse for that reader, that hearer.

For the Agrarian symposium Wade wrote, not anything directly argumentative, but "The Life and Death of Cousin Lucius," a paradigm or *exemplum* of the agrarian life as known in the South and as illustrated in the person of "Cousin Lucius." The model for "Cousin Lucius" was Wade's own Uncle Walter: Jacob Walter Frederick (1851-1928), the brother of Wade's mother, Ida Frederick Wade. But "Cousin" suggests, of course, the tie of kinship, near or distant, that marks the traditional South. In "Lucius" there is something of the Ciceronian or other classical affiliation that Marshall McLuhan and other commentators attribute to Southern society. It is represented, if only by mere habit, in the ante-bellum predilection for classical names for both plantation master and Negro slave. Lucius Quintus Cincinnatus Lamar—who was Augustus Baldwin Longstreet's son-in-law—is a lavish example of such naming. Such given names carry as definite an aura of Southern associations as do "Preserved," "Ebenezer," "Mercy," "Patience" for New England.

Taken as a narrative woven out of historical threads, "Cousin Lucius" is the life of a Southern rural community from the Georgia frontier of the Eighteen-Forties to the "New South" of the Nineteen-Hundreds or a little later, as that life was experienced by a very alert observer-participant. This man, Cousin Lucius, is firmly and highly loyal to the South's traditional society and is therefore critical of the new order but not unreasonably hostile to it. More specifically, "The Life and Death of Cousin Lucius" is a dramatized history of John Wade's own beloved land of Peach and Macon counties in Middle Georgia from the days when the Fredericks, Rumphs, Murphs, Slappeys, and other still resident families migrated from Orangeburg County, South Carolina, up to the time when the boll weevil and automobile just about simultaneously invaded the cotton-growing parts of the South. In this latter time planters had to choose between sticking with cotton exclusively (at their peril) or diversifying. Cousin Lucius' people, having already invented and developed the famous Elberta peach, had already begun to diversify. They continued to do so and survived as a community.

   The economic thread is only one of the varied threads in John Wade's weaving. He does not over-emphasize it. His method, easy-moving, subtly dramatic, allows him to make sidelong comments on topics and issues covered more directly by others of the Twelve Southerners. He enjoys the advantages that Addison had as Mr. Spectator. Cousin Lucius is his Roger de Coverley, if you want to take him that way. Yet John Wade is not exactly Addisonian, after all, if only for the reason that he skilfully adapts the modern "stream-of-consciousness" device to his purposes. In the vocabulary of the Nineteen-Sixties "The Life and Death of Cousin Lucius" might be called a "profile"—if that term were not ridiculously inadequate. "Fable" would be better. Realistic though "Cousin Lucius" is in referentials of time, place, and circumstance, it becomes in the end one great metaphor. The last scene is the death of a hero, not of any common man:

A little way down one of the rows between the peach trees, Edward almost stumbled upon some quail. And the quail fluttered up and flew straight toward the packing-house.

He heard his father shout at them as they went by, the shout that he remembered as designed especially for sunsets and clean dogwood blossoms. And then there was perfect silence. And then he heard the frantic voice of Anthony: "Oh, Mas' Edward! Help, help Mas' Edward! Mas' Lucius, Mas' Lucius! . . . He ran, and after unmeasured time, it seemed to him, he rounded the corner of the packing-house and saw Anthony, a sort of maniac between grief and terror . . . holding in his arms Cousin Lucius' limp body. "Oh, Mas' Edward! . . . Fo' God, I believe Mas' Lucius done dead!"

He *was* dead. And all who wish to think that he lived insignificantly and that the sum of what he was is negligible are welcome to think so. And may God have mercy on their souls.

Only one other piece in the present collection takes on the

character of fable so completely: "The Dugonne Bust," written during Wade's last years and published quite frankly as a story. In tone it is sharper than "The Life and Death of Cousin Lucius." The narrative—told in the first person by one Dugonne Truman V—presents the dilemma of a man descended from a Revolutionary War hero who at long last finds reason to doubt the authenticity of his treasured portrait bust of his ancestor—presumably sculptured while the subject was still live. At the end the narrator says that his tale is "not history purely, perhaps, nor yet fiction, purely,—a commentary, I hope, upon the comparative value of what-is and what-one-thinks-is, in this world." Yet he disclaims any idea of being "any man's iconoclast." "I am not so much a breaker of images as I am one who calls attention to how plainly useful images can be . . . ."

Large or small, the *exemplum* is always a dramatic essential of Wade's discourses. In one of the best, after puzzling or affecting to puzzle over definitions of "humor," he comes to "Southern humor," his subject, and promptly slides into an amusing autobiographical recital of how, as a schoolboy, he yearned to "punch out the eyes of the northern generals pictured in my textbooks." Further on, he imagines an encounter between "Southern Humor" as a virtual *persona* and various modern programs including the Marxist program. "Come, Lenin," he interjects, as if it were a political barbecue, "and say so if you will—take care when you do lest your beard bob." Further on in the essay are some pages of lively dramatization in which we find "such a group of people as comes together at countless places in the South to celebrate Christmas by heavy eating." Would it do, asks Wade, "for Cousin Julius to talk of Proust's analyses, for Cousin Mary to tell of Epstein . . .?" Oh, never. "Tell a story now, you, that mail-carrying Uncle Jack and Proust-teaching Cousin Julius will both think pointed, that knit-bed-spread-knitter Aunt Susan can endure without fainting. . . . Scour your memory, sir; let's hear from you . . . what were you born for, anyway?" Or in that very serious discourse, "Of the Mean and Sure Estate," for which he borrows a favorite old Elizabethan title and in which he discusses one war out of many wars "that is carried on in America more actively than it is elsewhere . . . the war of the city against the country," Wade lines up *exemplum* against *exemplum* in sharp ironic contrast. He recalls, for instance, a lady whose husband managed a clothing-store in a town of about thirty thousand people—"and his family and hers are removed only by a tragically narrow margin from village origins." She is commenting on a wedding:

The wedding she had attended was in the house of one of her village-dwelling kin, a branch of her family obviously superior to her own. Exclaimed this lady: "Oh, wasn't the wedding beautiful! really beautiful! my dear, nothing whatever small-townish about it!" *God in his mercy send her grace.*

This article was Wade's contribution to *Who Owns America?*, a symposium edited by Herbert Agar and Allen Tate which intended, like Seward Collins's *American Review,* to bring the Southerners into a united front with the English Distributists, the American Humanists, the Neo-Thomists and other conservatives and even had some thought of getting a nose under the then promising big tent of Roosevelt's New Deal. In 1937, a year after the publication of this symposium, Wade set forth with straightforward directness, in "What the South Figured, 1865-1914," some of the reasons why the defecting lady of his anecdote, along with many other Southerners, had been persuaded to adopt the "nothing small-townish" simper. It is harsh social analysis, one of the briefest and most cutting of his essays. Wade was not wholly at ease in direct analysis, one surmises. On somewhat the same subject he had written far better, in fact, in his earlier defense of Robert Lewis Dabney, Albert Taylor Bledsoe, and Charles Colcock Jones, the old-fashioned opponents of Grady's program, who had "held that the impostor gods, Speed and Mass, were really demons." The central portion of his essay—"Old Wine in a New Bottle"—develops into a powerful Swiftian satirical allegory on the ruin that the demons of Speed and Mass will accomplish in the end.

In the large biographical studies of Henry Grady, Joel Chandler Harris, and Tom Watson, Wade is completely at home. The expansive treatment used in these essays suited wonderfully his temperament and the prose style that he had gradually brought to his own kind of perfection. Wade could well have had in mind a "Georgia Plutarch" much more selective and searching than Philip A. Bruce's *A Virginia Plutarch.* His turn for a kind of moralizing—carefully guarded, and definitely in a modern idiom—makes him seem, in fact, somewhat akin to Plutarch. Certainly his portraits are keyed to a far higher pitch than Gamaliel Bradford's more popular kind of sketching—as in *Damaged Souls* and other books. The obvious British parallel is Lytton Strachey's

Eminent Victorians. But Strachey's acid disillusionment—interpreted in the United States as "debunking"—seems the mark of a merely personal idiom. The cause of his grievance is not evident. Wade's large irony derives from the immense, long-enduring tragedy of the Southern states, from the continually renewed dilemmas of Southerners who have had governmental and social patterns forced upon them that in their hearts they believe are alien, destructive, wrong, and yet must somehow live with; and on the positive side from the deep well of faith native to Wade's being and from the steadfast hopes of his Agrarian friends who had refused to take the easy path of the "New" South.

If Wade had chosen to write novels, he might have been an American Cervantes. His humor, his charity, his knowledge of *lachrimae rerum,* no less than his seasoned realism could with little difficulty have found Don Quixotes and Sancho Panzas to put into fiction. But it is more comfortable to think of John Wade as a Southern Thackeray, with Georgia and the South as his Vanity Fair. His voice in prose—or in familiar talk as his friends and visitors knew so well—rings indulgently, even in reproof, and bids us make allowances for frail humanity. So does Thackeray in those famous commenting "intrusions" for which he has been scolded by such admirers of the "objective" technique as Percy Lubbock, but for which Thackeray's loyal adherents count him specially beloved. Could we ever endure a Lubbockized Thackeray? *Absit omen!* And what would John Wade have been like, squeezing himself into some kind of documented laboratory report? Never, surely, the John Wade of the pieces here collected! Of that sort of clog he was free, once the *Longstreet* was done. And was there any loss, either of substance or authority, when he walked forth unclogged? Is there any failure of authenticity when Wade pictures Senator Tom Watson of Georgia, presidential candidate and author, in rueful meditation at the end of his career, after the failure of Populism and much besides?

But who really cared for his anathemas? At last he must have recognized, with his discernment, that in parts of the South other than Georgia, where he had not been present, the current of industrialism flowed on.

The final result of all his labor had been only to annul the primacy which Georgia long occupied in the South. A nimble, inconstant widow, that State had appeared earliest at the grand ball of Reconciliation, on the arm of Mr. Grady. Forced at last by Watson to repudiate the party, she did not by her less enthusiastic attendance halt the twanging of the fiddles.

And could the science of documentation, however undeniably useful in its place, ever beget passages like this, in Wade's representation of Henry Grady as journalist, on the staff of Howell's Atlanta *Constitution?*

Grady was utterly and ecstatically absorbed in his work and in his passage in general through this world. As it had been with him as a child, it was still—he loved everybody, and everybody, unable to think of anything more appropriate to do under the circumstances, loved him in return.

The moral is not explicit as in Plutarch, that dry but assiduous and informative schoolmaster. The writing is vehement—but it is a controlled vehemence. No doubt Wade would have preferred for his heroes to be more heroic, but he had to take them as he found them. If not so great as Odin, Mahomet, Augustine, Luther, Napoleon, they towered high enough for his purposes. Taken as a group, they fill in the vast gaps obviously left by the textbook historians or that the more artful historians of periods and phases, in their documentary reticence, may have tempted readers to think do not exist. How regrettable that Wade has left us only a half-dozen or so of major portraits to add to his Longstreet and Wesley! But these are precious. How could the publishers and editors of New York and Boston have been so sluggish and sleepy-eyed as not to perceive that here was a man they should have solicited to write more? It is matter for wonderment, too, that in all the clamor of argument and critical discussion that has centered on the authors of *I'll Take My Stand* and their ideas from the autumn of 1930 to this day, the distinction of Wade's contribution to that large endeavor has not yet received its full meed of public recognition.

And yet—thinking in quite other terms and remembering with young John Milton that fame is no plant that grows on mortal soil—we should not too blindly regret or blame; and as for wonderment, why, the wonder is that in the crowded, noisily bewildering decade from 1928 to 1938, John Wade could have written so much. At Vanderbilt he carried, from 1928 until his resignation in 1933, a heavy teaching load. Having come to Vanderbilt to direct the new graduate work in American literature, Wade was disconcerted to find that he was expected, in addition, to accept the regular departmental task of a Sophomore course in English literature and a Freshman course in composition. Goodnaturedly, he somehow managed this, though inwardly rebellious. The students and friends who so often rendezvoused at his large office in Calhoun Hall, with its rocking chair and famous rotating bookcase, always found Wade genial, ready to listen, ready to talk, but also likely, many times, to have some piece of writing in hand. If Wade read from it and solicited his visitor's opinion, it might be that the writing was at a stage where criticism was indeed desired; but sometimes it *might* be a tactful hint that the visitor's early departure was just as desirable as his opinion. Then there were the discussions—whether as to strategy or ideas—with his compatriots of the Agrarian group—dicussions that never flagged from the day of his arrival and that were often supplemented by journeys to the home of Andrew Lytle at nearby Murfreesboro or to Benfolly, the home of the Allen Tates, near Clarksville. On many weekends, too, Wade felt obliged to join his mother at Marshallville. There were periods when he was near to being a commuter, back and forth over the 400-odd miles between Nashville and home.

So, all things considered, John Wade wrote much. And he spent much time leading others to write. In those years when Philology had hardly slackened its grip upon the graduate school dissertation, Wade promulgated with great success the biographical thesis and this in many notable instances closed the gap between History and Literature that social scientists seemed to be widening into an unbridgeable chasm. This excellent bridge-work began in 1932 with Richmond Croom Beatty's pioneer biography, *William Byrd of Westover*. It was soon followed by Leota S. Driver's *Fanny Kemble* (1933), Linda Rhea's *Hugh Swinton Legare: A Charleston Intellectual* (1934), Edd Winfield Parks's *Charles Egbert Craddock* (1941) . . . but to name these few is only to mark the beginning of John Wade's far-reaching influence, through precept and example, whether upon those who actually were his students at Vanderbilt and later at the University of Georgia, or upon many who have never known him—and can not now know him as their teacher—in the flesh.

His influence in a different sphere, as founder and editor of *The Georgia Review,* belongs to the middle years of John Wade's life, when he returned to his alma mater to become Professor of English, and soon Head of the Department of English, at the University of Georgia. Close to home now, Wade's thought centered more warmly than ever in Georgia, but that did not

mean exclusion of something called the World, which indeed
from 1934 to 1950 was making itself felt in Georgia even more
thunderously than Sherman's march of the century previous.

The idea of the *Georgia Review*—if I remember correctly
Wade's statement of it to me—was, quite simply, to review Georgia, for Georgians. That primarily—because Georgians needed
some kind of medium of intercommunication and information
more lofty, more dependable, in fact more *Georgian* than the Atlanta newspapers could offer. Or to put it figuratively, Georgia
was a garden that very obviously needed cultivating—by devoted
Georgians especially. Others might help, if they had green
thumbs. That was the meaning of the announcement that Wade
sent me, among others, in August, 1946. In part it read:

> The chief quality desired in anything the *Review* may publish is
> distinction of thought and of statement. In general, the *Review* hopes
> prayerfully to stress wisdom and judgment more than it does knowl-
> edge and information, and vastly more, of course, than it does folly
> and falsehood.
>
> The *Review* will exist particularly to be of use in Georgia. For that
> reason and other reasons it will try to avoid the "shocking" and the
> enigmatic in both vocabulary and point-of-view. Either of those would
> render it ineffective with most of the people whom it would most like
> to reach. The *Review* would like to confirm rather than annul in
> Georgia people any good qualities that may distinguish them from
> other people.
>
> Unless the import of a composition is clearly universal in its nature,
> everything that is published in the *Review* should be of special interest
> to Georgians. All else being equal, an article about the Okefenokee
> Swamp would be more acceptable than an article about Yellowstone
> Park, and an article by the mayor of Ball Ground, Georgia, more
> acceptable than an article by the mayor of Tacoma, Washington. And
> on the theory that a limb of a tree is more nearly related to the trunk
> than to another limb, an article about Plato might seem more urgently
> relevant than an article about Mr. Philip Murray.*

Whether John Wade ever had to choose between articles sub-
mitted by the mayors of such widely separated places as Ball
Ground, Georgia, and Tacoma, Washington, I do not know. The
standard he himself set was high. Those who read Wade's announcement would hardly have deemed it an invitation to submit
articles on the best recipes for Brunswick stew or the right way to
prune peach trees or the sources of Margaret Mitchell's *Gone*

*Wade's reference is to the labor leader, head of the C. I. O.

with the Wind. More in line with Wade's idea were straight-forward articles on the history of Georgia's peach culture by Inez Cumming, on the city of Savannah by William J. Robertson, and on Atlanta by Hal Steed. In early issues these rubbed elbows with highly sophisticated literary criticism by Calvin S. Brown, John Olin Eidson, and W. R. Moses, a discussion of "Lee the Philosopher" by Richard M. Weaver, and a piece on the future of Arkansas by John Gould Fletcher. But the tone of the *Georgia Review* was set by Wade himself in the characteristic "Editorials" that began each issue. Long since, Wade had learned how to be himself, even though cramped into the objective strait-jacket of the D. A. B. sketch. It was easy to adjust his prose idiom to the requirements of a Georgia-born, Georgia-bound quarterly. Forthwith it became evident that the *Georgia Review,* although certainly not so enigmatic as at times the Ohio-born *Kenyon Review* might be, was no more "regional" actually than, say, the *New Yorker*—was even less so. As time went on, more and more writers with green thumbs appeared, Georgian and non-Georgian, and the *Review* was a thriving garden. After Wade retired from teaching, he could and did edit it for a while from his home in Marshallville, stepping out at one moment to supervise the planting of a new camellia by "T. J." (his man Friday), then back to his "office" to take up his pen and by eloquent letter or postal card to seed the mind and heart of some prospective contributor to the *Review*.

From that same "office" in the old Frederick house John Wade's mother, Ida Frederick Wade, had for years managed plantation affairs. In the autumn of 1932 I had heard, many mornings at sun-up, the voices of Negroes calling "Ol' Miss, Ol' Miss" and knocking or scratching at the screened side-porch door of the big house. And while Miss Ida dealt with the Negroes' questions or pleas, I would rise and come from the "Little House" so close by and gather the pecans that had fallen near the doorstep during the night. Thus would begin a perfect day in Middle Georgia.

The Thirties passed by, and when the Forties had all but passed by, John Wade was master of that old house. His wife Julia was surprised that the Negroes should begin to call her "Ol' Miss" from the time of her first arrival as a bride. But she could not escape the tradition that made "Ol'" a term of greatest respect. For John Wade and Julia and their daughter Anne, the town of Marshallville and the immediately surrounding country became more and more a kind of Prospero's island, almost magically preserved from the tempests that so ruinously swept the land at large. So it seemed, anyhow, to friends from the world outside and to the ever increasing number of visitors who came to make acquaintance with John Donald Wade and see the Eden that he had made famous. To these he was very near a Prospero in person, or in more matter-of-fact terms, without question Georgia's foremost man of letters, in truth one of the century's great unique personalities. How very strange it was that the State of Georgia had somehow neglected to do him public honor or even to solicit the service he could no doubt devotedly have given the State in its public affairs?

If such neglect ever darkened John Wade's mind, he gave no sign of it. The Fifties came. He wrote less, these days, but as a labor of love in 1952 finished a history of the Marshallville Methodist Church, from which "On Jordan's April Banks," one of his most charming historical sketches, was excerpted for the *Georgia Review* in the winter of 1953. Meanwhile, the Marshallville Foundation—which was, practically speaking, John Donald Wade—had decided to enlarge the already beautiful gardens, formal and informal, back of the Frederick house. What had been cotton fields, once backed by a row of long-leaf pines, became A Great Garden of World History. One passed through the stately wooden columns (all that remained from his father, Dr. Wade's house) set at the end of a grassy court and came into a large expanse of slightly rolling, carefully mowed ground. Therein Wade had placed structures of his own devising, made of wood and wire and covered with vines to simulate the characteristic architectural forms of Occident and Orient: at one point Stonehenge, at another Gothic arches, a Pagoda shape, a great Crucifix, towering high; and all with plantings about them of a kind suitable to the country of origin. And beyond the Great Garden was John Wade's arboretum, very large and varied already in the Fifties, and constantly increasing. All living things grew well for him, and his knowledge of trees, shrubs, flowers of every kind was minute, exact, and encyclopedic. If the weather were good, the friend or stranger that came to John Wade's house was sure to be invited to walk—or ride—through the Great Garden. There would be much good talk . . ., and a pause to watch the Georgia sunset . . . and, returning, some moments to linger among the roses and hear once more their old-fashioned names. . . .

There were no idle days. He had much to think about, much to do. The Fifties were passing, the Sixties coming on. He had known much happiness and, as is the lot of mortal man, deep sorrow—in the loss of his Julia. Still he had his daughter Anne, the light of his life—and kin close at hand, first and foremost his ever-beloved cousin Florence Lester; and his cherished friends. Once more, though his years were in the sere and yellow leaf, verging upon three-score-and ten, he began a great book—a narrative, fictional in style, historical in content. It looked far back to the colonial past but centered in the long life of his father, Dr. Wade, and his connections. He drew from old diaries, old letters—a rich store and from his own rich memory. Deeply absorbed, he wrote with his old fervor day after day, finished the great book, had the manuscript typed, asked his friends to read it, then revised the typescript. One thing worried him—the title! What should it be called? He had in mind to choose a phrase from some verses of Housman? Should it be "From Yon Far Country"? Or perhaps "The Land of Lost Content?" In the autumn of 1963 he was scheduled to give the Lamar Lectures at Mercer University and planned to draw from this great manuscript for the purpose, as he had most successfully done a year before at the Vanderbilt Literary Symposium. The notes that he sketched out for the Lamar Lectures were the last he made. For then (how sadly but how well Milton could say it!) came "the blind *Fury* with the abhorred shears, And slit the thin-spun life. But not the praise. . . ."

On a bright October day we came again to Marshallville, many of us, kin and friends from far and wide. Flowers were blooming, leaves rustling as of old, and the house was fairer than ever without and within. But the master of the house was not there to greet us, to move among the guests in the way we knew so well. From the church the young men bore him and laid him to rest among his own, as he wished. We stood silent on that autumn day, and all knew that now had passed from us one of the manliest of men, virtuous and brave and most generous of heart, the best of fathers, the best of friends. Let the coming generations remember well John Donald Wade and bring forth his like again if they can.

PART I

Of the Times and the Customs

The Life and Death of Cousin Lucius

HE REMEMBERED all his life the feel of the hot sand on his young feet on that midsummer day. He was very young then, but he knew that he was very tired of riding primly beside his mother in the carriage. So his father let him walk for a little, holding him by his small hand. On went the carriage, on went the wagons behind the carriage, with the slaves, loud with greetings for young master. In the back of the last wagon his father set him down till he could himself find a seat there. Then his father, still holding his hand, lowered him to the road, and let him run along as best he could, right where the mules had gone. The slaves shouted in their pride of him, and in their glee, and the sport was unquestionably fine, but the sand was hot, too hot, and he was happy to go back to his prim station next the person who ruled the world.

That was all he remembered of that journey. He did not remember the look of the soil, black at times with deep shade, nor the far-reaching cotton-fields running down to the wagon ruts in tangles of blackberry bushes and morning-glories. He knew, later, that they had forded streams on that journey, that they had set out with a purpose, from a place—as travelers must— and that they had at last arrived. But all that came to him later. In his memory there was chiefly the hot sand.

What he learned later was this—that in 1850 his father had left his home in lower South Carolina and followed an uncle of his— Uncle Daniel—to a new home in Georgia. His father was then only twenty or so, and when he inherited some land and slaves he decided to go on to Georgia, where land, said Uncle Daniel, was cheap and fresh, and where with thrift one might reasonably hope to set up for oneself almost a little nation of one's own.

The next thing actually in his memory was also about slaves.

From *I'll Take My Stand: The South and the Agrarian Tradition,* by Twelve Southerners. New York: Harper and Brothers, 1930.

In South Carolina, Aunt Amanda, an aunt of his mother's, had lately died. What that might mean was a mystery, but one clear result of the transaction was that Aunt Amanda had no further use for her slaves, and, in accordance with her will, they had been sent to him in Georgia. Their arrival his memory seized upon for keeps. They were being rationed—so much meal, so much meat, so much syrup, so much rice. But not enough rice. "Li'l' master," said one of his new chattels to him, "you min' askin' master to let us swap back all our meal for mo' rice?" He remembered that he thought it would be delightful to make that request, and he remembered that it was granted.

Next he remembered seeing the railway train. There it came with all its smoke, roaring, with its bell ringing and its shrill whistle. It was stopping on Uncle Daniel's place to get wood, the same wood that all that morning he had watched the slaves stacking into neat piles. It seemed to him indeed fine to have an uncle good enough to look after the hungry train's wants. That train could pull nearly anything, and it took cotton bales away so easily to the city that people did not have to use their mules any longer, at all, for such long hauls.

But in some things the railroad did not seem so useful. For when it nosed farther south into the state, after resting its southern terminus for a year or two at a town some miles beyond Uncle Daniel's, the town went down almost overnight, almost as suddenly as a blown bladder goes down, pricked.

Then a war came, and near Uncle Daniel's, where the road crossed the railroad and there were some little shops, some men walked up and down and called themselves drilling. That seemed a rare game to him, and he never forgot what a good joke it seemed to them, and to him, for them to mutter over and over as they set down their feet, corn-foot, shuck-foot, corn-foot, shuck-foot—on and on. At last the men went away from the crossroads, and Cousin James and Cousin Edwin went with them—Uncle Daniel's son and his daughter's son. His own father did not go and Lucius was very glad, but very sorry too, in a way. He did not go, he said, because he could hardly leave Lucius's mother and the baby girls—for somehow two baby girls had come, from somewhere. Lucius thought his father very considerate, but he wondered whether the girls were, after all, of a degree of wit that would make them miss their father very much.—But before he had done wondering, off his father went also.

That war was a queer thing. It was away, somewhere, farther than he had come from when he came first to Georgia. He heard no end of talk about it, but most of that talk confused itself later in his mind with his mature knowledge. He clearly remembered that there were such people as refugees, women and children mostly, who had come that far south because their own land was overrun by hundreds and hundreds of men, like Cousin James and Cousin Edwin, who were up there fighting hundreds and hundreds of other men, called Yankees. They were really fighting, not playing merely. They were shooting at one another, with guns, just as people shot a beef down when time came. But after they shot a man they did not put him to any use at all.

One day he went with Uncle Daniel to see a lot of soldiers who were going by, on their way north to help whip the Yankees. Uncle Daniel said that the soldiers were the noblest people in the world, and Lucius understood why it was that he took his gold-headed cane and wore his plush hat, as if he were going to church, when he went to say his good wishes to such noble people. As the train stopped and as he and Uncle Daniel stood there cheering, one of the soldiers called out to Uncle Daniel, boisterously: "Hey," he said, "what did you make your wife mad about this morning?"—"I was not aware, sir," said Uncle Daniel, "that I had angered her."—"Well," the soldier said, and he pointed at the plush hat, "I see she crowned you with the churn." Lucius wished very much that Uncle Dainel would say something sharp back to him, but he did not. He simply stood there looking a little red, saying, "Ah, sir, ah, sir," in the tone of voice used in asking questions but never coming out with any question whatever.

Once Lucius was with his mother in the garden. She was directing a number of negro women who were gathering huge basketfuls of vegetables. The vegetables, his mother told him, were being sent to Andersonville, where a lot of Yankees the soldiers had caught were being kept in prison. He asked his mother why they had not shot the Yankees, but she told him that it would have been very un-Christian to shoot them, because these particular Yankees had surrendered, and it was one's duty to be kind to them.

Years later he searched his mind for further memories of the war, but little else remained. Except, of course, about Cousin Edwin. He was at Cousin Edwin's mother's, Cousin Elvira's. It was a spring morning and everything was fresh with new flowers, and there were more birds flying in more trees, chirping, than a boy could possibly count. And at the front gate two men stopped with a small wagon.

He called to Cousin Elvira and she came from the house, down to the gate with him to see what was wanted. She was combing her hair; it was hanging down her back and the comb was in her hand so that he had to go round and take the other hand. What those men had in that wagon was Cousin Edwin's dead body. Cousin Elvira had not known that he was dead. Only that morning she had had a letter from him. He had been killed. How Cousin Elvira wept! He, too, wept bitterly, and the wagon men wept also. But Cousin Edwin was none the better off for all their tears. Nor was Cousin Elvira, for her part, much better off, either. She lived forty years after that day, and she told him often how on spring mornings all her life long she went about, or seemed to go about, numb through all her body and holding in her right hand a rigid comb that would not be cast away.

He was a big boy when the war ended, nearly fifteen, and the passing of days and weeks seemed increasingly more rapid. As he looked back and thought of the recurrent seasons falling upon the world it seemed to him that they had come to the count, over and over, of Hard Times, Hard Times, Hard Times, more monotonous, more unending, than the count of the soldiers, muttering as they marched, years before, in the town which had before been called only the crossroads.

He went to school to Mr. and Mrs. Pixley, who taught in town, some three miles from his father's plantation. Both of them, he learned, were Yankees, but it seemed, somehow, that they were good Yankees. And he took with him to Mr. Pixley's his two sisters. There was a brother, too, and there was a sister younger still, but they were not yet old enough to leave home.

One day his mother was violently ill. He heard her cry aloud in her agony—as he had before heard her cry, he remembered, two or three distinct times. She was near dying, he judged, for very pain—but they had told him not to come where she was and he waited, himself in anguish for her wretchedness. That day as she bore another child into the world, that lady quit the world once and for all. He thought that he would burst with rage and sorrow. Wherever he turned, she seemed to speak to him, and he cursed himself for his neglect of her. Surrounded by a nation of her husband's kin, she had not always escaped their blame. She had known that times were hard, well, well; but she had insisted that some things she must have while her children were still young. She had saved her round dollars and sent them to Philadelphia to be moulded into spoons; she had somehow managed to find some books, and a piano she *would* have. Well, she was dead now, and it seemed to Lucius that the world would be always dark to him, and that things more rigid, more ponderous, more relentlessly adhesive than combs are, would drag his hands downward to earth all his life.

It would not do, then, he decided, to take anybody quite for granted. Already he had learned, as a corollary of the war, that *things* are not dependable; even institutions almost universally the base of people's lives could not, from the fact that they were existent in 1860, be counted upon to be existent also in 1865. He knew now that people also are like wind that blows, and then, inexplicably, is still.

He examined his father, coldly, impersonally, for the first time— not as a fixed body like the earth itself. His father had obviously many elements of grandeur. He was honest and kind and capable. He was introspective, but not sure always to arrive by his self-analysis at judgments that Lucius believed valid. By the Methodist church, which he loved, he was stimulated wisely in his virtues and led to battle against a certain native irascibleness. But in that church such a vast emphasis is set on preaching, that the church is likely to be thought of as little more than a house big enough for the preacher's audience. Lucius learned before long that many of the preachers he was expected to emulate might with more justice be set to emulate him, let alone his father. But his father could not be brought to such a viewpoint, and indeed, if Lucius had dared to suggest his conclusions very pointedly, it might have proved the worse for him.

Soon Lucius was sent to a college maintained by Georgia Methodists, and he stayed till he was graduated. The college was in a tiny town remote from the railroad, and it was such a place that if the generation of Methodists who had set it there some forty years earlier had looked down upon it from Elysium, they would have been happy. Whatever virtues Methodism attained in the South were as manifest there as they were anywhere, and whatever defects it had were less vocal. The countless great oaks on the campus, lightened by countless white columns, typified, appropriately, in his mind the strength and the disciplined joyousness that light might come to. His teachers were usually themselves Methodist ministers, like those who had come periodically to his father's church at home, but the burden of their talk was different. The books they were constantly reading and the white columns among the oaks and the tangible memories thereabout of one or two who had really touched greatness, had somehow affected all who walked in that paradise.

In his studies the chief characters he met were Vergil and Horace and other Romans, who seemed in that atmosphere, as he understood them, truly native. More recent than they were Cervantes and Shakespeare, and the English Lord Byron, the discrepancies of whose life one could overlook in view of his inspiring words about liberty. Hardly dignified enough, because of their modernity, to be incorporated into the curriculum of his college, these writers were none the less current in the college community.

Lucius knew many other boys like himself. In his fraternity, dedicated to God and ladies, he talked much about their high patron and their patronesses, and in his debating society he joined in many windy dissertations on most subjects known to man. In spite of all the implication about him regarding the transiency of earth, in spite of the despair evident in some quarters regarding the possible future of the South, Lucius and his fellows and even his teachers speculated frequently and long on mundane matters. They were large-hearted men, in way of being philosophic, and they felt a pity for their own people, in their poverty and in their political banishment from a land that they had governed—no one in his senses would say meanly—through Jefferson and Calhoun and Lee.

Once he went as a delegate from his fraternity to a meeting held at the state university, where an interest in this world as apart from heaven was somewhat more openly sanctioned than at his own college. The chief sight he saw there was Alexander Stephens, crippled and emaciated and shockingly treble. As he spoke, a young negro fanned him steadily and gave him from time to time a resuscitating toddy. That man's eyes burned with a kind of fire that Lucius knew was fed by a passionate integrity and a passionate love for all mankind. He was obviously the center of a legend, the type to which would gravitate men's memories of other heroes who had been in their way great, but never so great as he was.

Many young men whom Lucius met at the state university acknowledged the complexities of that legend when they attempted to follow it; when they rose to speak—as people were so frequently doing in those days at such conventions—they behaved themselves with a grandiloquence and declaimed with a gilded ardor that matched the legend of Stephens better than it matched the iron actuality. But Lucius did not know that. He admired the fervid imitations. He regretted that he could never send a majestic flight of eagles soaring across a peroration without having dart through his mind a flight of creatures as large as they, but of less dignified suggestion. He was sure that he could never speak anything in final earnestness without tending to stutter a little. His virtues were of the sort that can be recognized at their entire value only after one has endured the trampling of years which reduce a man to a patriarch.

When Lucius finally had A.B. appended to his name with all the authority of his college, he went home again. Hard Times met him at the train. For indeed the stress of life was great upon his father. Cotton was selling low and the birth rate had been high. Sister Cordelia was already at a Methodist college for girls, and Sister Mary would be going soon. And behind Mary was Brother Andrew. Lucius's father had married again, his first cousin, the widowed Cousin Elvira. And in the house was Cousin Elvira's ward, her sister's daughter, Lucius's third cousin. Her name was Caroline, and she was nineteen, and she had recently, like Lucius, returned home from college.

It was time for Lucius to go to work, and there was not much work one could do. The cities had begun to grow much more rapidly than in times past, and some of his classmates at college had gone to the cities for jobs. The fathers of some of them were in a position to help their sons with money till they could get on their feet, but Lucius felt that it would be unjust, in his case, to his younger brothers and sisters for him to expect anything further from his father. About the only thing left was to help his father on the farm, but his father was in the best of health, and as vigorous and capable an executive as ever. He really did not need a lieutenant, and the thought of becoming a private soldier of the farm no more entered Lucius's mind than the thought of becoming executioner to the Tsar. While he was still undecided where to turn, he heard one day of the death of Mr. Pixley. Temporarily, then, at least, he could be Mr. Pixley's successor.

So with his father's help he took over Mr. Pixley's academy, naming it neither for its late owner nor, as his father wished, for Bishop Asbury. Instead he named it for the frail man with the burning eyes whom he had seen at the state university, Stephens.

All that fall and winter and into the next spring he managed his academy—one woman assistant and some eighty youngsters ranging from seven to twenty-one. And just as summer came round the year following he married Cousin Caroline.

So life went with him, year in, year out. Children came to him and Cousin Caroline in God's plenty, and children, less intimately connected with him, flocked to the academy. He was determined to make all these youngsters come to something. After all, his lines were cast as a teacher. At least he could make a livelihood at that work, and very likely, there, as well as in another place, he could urge himself and the world about him into the strength and the disciplined joyousness which he had come to prize and which he believed would surely bring with them a fair material prosperity. If the children were amenable, he was pleased; if they were dull, he was resolute, unwilling to condemn them as worse than lazy. When night came he was tired—like a man who has spent the day ploughing; but perhaps, he thought, in a little while the situation would become easier.

After the war, nearly all the owners of plantations moved into town, and land that had formerly made cotton for Uncle Daniel gradually turned into streets and building lots. Lucius felt that the thing he had learned at college, and had caught, somehow, from the burning eyes of Mr. Stephens, involved him in a responsibility to that town that could not be satisfied by his giving its youth a quality of instruction that he, if not they, recognized as better than its money's worth. He organized among the citizens a debating society such as he had seen away at school, and he operated in connection with it a lending library. Shakespeare and Cervantes and the English Lord Byron were at the beck of his fellow townsmen—and Addison and Swift and Sterne and Sir Walter Scott, and even Dickens and Thackeray and George Eliot. Lucius managed to make people think (the men as well as the women—he stood out for that) that without the testimony and the comment of such spirits on his life they would all find this life less invigorating.

He found abettors in this work—his father and Uncle Daniel and others of the same mind—but he was its captain. His school, then, affected not merely those who were of an age appropriate for his academy, and it was not long before he was known almost universally in his village as "Cap"—for Captain.

His father turned over about two hundred and fifty acres to him as a sort of indefinite loan, and he became in a fashion a farmer as well as a teacher. That possibly was an error, for when word of his pedagogic ability and energy spread far, and he was offered an important teaching position in a neighboring city, he decided not to accept it because of his farm. But possibly all that was not an error. An instinct for the mastery of land was in his blood, and he knew few pleasures keener than that of roaming over his place, in the afternoons, when school was out, exulting in the brave world and shouting to the dogs that followed him.

There is no doubt that Lucius was gusty. He shouted not only to his dogs, but to himself, occasionally, when he had been reading alone for a long time, during vacations, on his shaded veranda. And he shouted, too, when the beauty of the red sinking sun over low hills, or of clean dogwood blossoms in a dense brake, seemed to him too magnificent not to be magnificently saluted.

Hard Times shadowed him night and day, thwarting in his own life more generous impulses than he could number. Hard Times also, singly or perhaps in collusion with other forces, thwarted in the lives of his neighbors activities that he felt strenuously should be stimulated. What did people mean, in a land where all delectable fruits would grow for the mere planting, by planting never a fruit tree? His father had fruit trees, Uncle Daniel had, all of the older men, in fact, commanded for their private use, not for commercial purposes, orchards of pears and peaches, and vineyards, and many a row of figs and pomegranates. But only he of all the younger men would trouble to plant them.

Lucius pondered that matter. Of course there was the small initial expense of the planting, but it was very small or he himself could not have mustered it. Of course there was the despair, the lassitude of enduring poverty. He would shake his head violently when talking about this with his father—like a man coming from beneath water—but for all that gesture could find no clear vision.

It seemed to him, as he considered the world he was a part of, that common sense was among the rarest of qualities—that when it should assert itself most vigorously, it was most likely to lie sleeping. The prevalent economic order was tight and apparently tightening, yet the more need people had to provide themselves with simple assuagements—like pomegranates, for example—the more they seemed paralyzed and inactive. The bewildering necessity of actual money drove everyone in the farm community to concern himself exclusively with the only crop productive of actual money. The more cotton a man grew, the cheaper it went, and the more it became necessary to sustain one's livestock and oneself with dearly purchased grain and meat that had been produced elsewhere. Sometimes when Lucius considered these complexities, and ran over in his mind the actual want of money of his friends, and the cruel deprivation that many of them subjected themselves to in order to send their children away to colleges which were themselves weak with penury—at such times he was almost beside himself with a sort of blind anger.

It was lucky that his anger saved him from despair. He was not built for despair, from the beginning, and he was, after all, the husband of Cousin Caroline, and between her and despair there was no shadow of affinity. In every regard he could think of except money, Cousin Caroline had brought him as his wife everything that he, or any man, might ask for.

She knew how to summon a group of people from the town and countryside, and how, on nothing, apparently, to provide them with enough food and enough merriment to bring back to all of them the tradition of generous living that seemed native to them. He often thought that she, who was at best but a frail creature, was the strongest hope he knew for the perpetuation of that bright tradition against the ceaseless, clamorous, insensate piracies of Hard Times. He was sure that the sum total of her character presented aspects of serenity and splendor that demanded, more appropriately than it did anything else, a sort of worship.

Cousin Caroline had religion. She was made for religion from the beginning, and she was, after all, the wife of Cousin Lucius, and in every regard she could think of except money, Cousin Lucius had brought her as her husband, everything that she, or any woman, might ask for. To many beside those two it seemed that Cousin Lucius, because he never quite accepted the Methodist Church, had no religion whatever, that, having only charity and integrity for his currency, he would fare badly at last with St. Peter as concerned tolls. But Cousin Caroline thought better of St. Peter's fundamental discernment than to believe he would quibble about the admission of one who was so plainly one of God's warriors.

Among the best things Cousin Caroline did for him was to bring him to a fuller appreciation of his father. Always fond of him, always loyal to him, Cousin Lucius had never quite understood his apparent satisfaction with the offerings of Methodism. He was affected inescapably when the Methodists presented his father, on his completing twenty-five years as superintendent of their Sunday school, with a large silver pitcher. Most of the people who had helped purchase it were harried by need, and their contributions were all the fruit of sacrifice.

But it was Cousin Caroline's satisfaction, as well as his father's, with the offerings of Methodism that did most to quiet his misgivings in that quarter. Anything that two lofty souls—or indeed one lofty soul, he conceded—can be fain of, must itself be somehow worthy. And if it is worthy, an adherence to it on the part of one person should never stand as a barrier between that disciple and an honest soul who is unable to achieve that particular discipleship. As Cousin Lucius grew older, then, his love and admiration of his father, while no greater perhaps than they had been formerly, were certainly more active, less hampered by reservations. His father, he knew, had doted on him in a fashion so prideful that it had seemed a little ridiculous, but that surely could be no barrier between them, and the two men loved each other very tenderly.

Occasionally on trips to this or that city, he encountered friends whom he had known at college. Most of them were prosperous, and some of them were so rich and eminent that news of them seeped down constantly to the stagmant community that was his demesne. He was conscious, as he talked with some of them, of a sort of condescension for him as one who had not justified the promise of his youth. Friendly, aware soon that the old raciness and the old scope of his mind were still operative, one and another of them suggested his coming, still, to live in a city, where he might wrestle with the large affairs that somebody *must* wrestle with, and that he seemed so peculiarly fitted to control.

He learned pointedly through these people what was stirring in the great world. All of them recognized that the condition of Georgia, and of all the South, was indeed perilous, for acquaintance with Hard Times had taught them that Hard Times is a cruel master, who will brutalize, in time, even the stoutest-hearted victim. Somehow the tyrant must be cast down.

In the meantime Cousin Lucius saw the Literary and Debating Society, with its library, gradually go to pieces. It had lasted twenty years. People could not afford the bare expenses of its operation. He saw men resort to subterfuges and to imitations for so long that they at last believed in them; and he, for one, while opposed to anything that was not true, was too sorry for them not to be in part glad that they could persevere in their hallucination. He saw the negroes, inescapably dependent on the whites, sag so far downward, as the whites above them sagged, that final gravity, he feared, would seize the whole swinging structure of society and drag it fatally to earth. He saw the best of people, identified with as good a tradition as English civilization had afforded, moving he feared unswervably, toward a despair from which they never might be lifted.

A small daughter of his, one day, chattering to him, said a thing that made him cold with anger. She used the word "city" as an adjective, and as an adjective so inclusively commendatory that he knew she implied that whatever was the opposite of "city" was inclusively culpable. He knew that she reflected a judgment that was becoming dangerously general, and he wondered how long he himself could evade it. For days after that he went about fortifying himself by his knowledge of history and of ancient fable, telling himself that man had immemorially drawn his best strength from the earth that mothered him, that the farmer, indeed until quite recently, in the South, had been the acknowledged lord; the city man most often a tradesman. "But what have history and ancient fable," the fiend whispered, "to do with the present?" Cousin Lucius admitted that they apparently had little to do with it, but he believed they *must* have something to do with it if it were not to go amuck past all remedy.

Some of Cousin Lucius's friends thought that the solution of their troubles was to adopt frankly the Northern way of life; and others thought that the solution was to band themselves with discontented farmer sections elsewhere in the country, and so by fierce force to wrest the national organization to a pattern that would favor farmers for a while at the expense of industrialists. On the whole, philosophically, he hoped that farming would continue paramount in his Georgia. He knew little of the philosophy of industrialism, but he knew some people who had grown up to assume that it was the normal order of the world, and he knew that those people left him without comfort. Yet he doubted the wisdom of fierce force, anywhere, and he disliked the renunciation of individualism necessary to attain fierce force. And he observed that in the camp of his contemporaries who relied on that expedient there were many who favored socialistic measures he could not condone, and more whose ignorance and selfishness he could not stomach. The only camp left for him, in his political thinking, was the totally unorganized—and perhaps unorganizable—camp of those who could not bring themselves to assert the South either by means of abandoning much that was peculiarly Southern or by means of affiliating themselves with many who had neither dignity nor wisdom nor honesty.

Cousin Lucius was nearly fifty by now, but he had not yet reconciled himself to the rarity with which power and virtue go hand in hand, leading men with them to an Ultimate who embodies all that our poor notions of virtue and power dimly indicate to us. When he was at college, among the great oaks and the columns, it had seemed to him that those two arbiters were inseparable, as he observed them along the shaded walks. And he had taught school too long—Euclid and Plato were more real to him than Ulysses Grant and William McKinley.

About 1890 one of Cousin Lucius's friends sent some peaches to New York in refrigerated boxes. They sold well. And slowly, cautiously, Cousin Lucius and all the people in his community began putting more and more of their land into orchards. It took a long time for them to adopt the idea that peaches were a better hope for them than cotton. Old heads wagged sagely about the frequent winters that were too cold for the tender buds, young heads told of the insect scourges likely to infest any large-scale production; and every sad prophecy came true. In spite of all, the industry proceeded. Farm after farm that had been sowed to crops afresh each year since being cleared of the forests was set now in interminable rows of peach trees. In spring, when the earth was green with a low cover-crop and each whitewashed stalk of tree projected upward to the loveliest pink cloud of blossom, Lucius was like a boy again for sheer delight. And in summer, when the furious activity of marketing the fruit spurred many of the slow-going Georgians to the point of pettishness, his own vast energy became, it seemed, utterly tireless. What he saw made him believe that the master compromise had been achieved, that an agricultural community could fare well in a dance where the fiddles were all buzz-saws and the horns all steam-whistles.

An instinct, perhaps, made all of Cousin Lucius's children less confident of that compromise than he was. Without exception they revered him; and persuaded, all of them, of his conviction that the test of a society is the kind of men it produces, they could not think poorly of the system that had him as a part of it. But they could not gain their own consent also to live in that system. And one by one they went away to cities, and they all prospered.

An instinct, too, perhaps, made the people of his community restive under the demands he made of school children. He had yielded to the community judgment to the extent of turning his academy into a public school, but he could not believe that the transformation was more than nominal. That is where circumstance tricked him. The people had lost faith in the classics as a means to better living, or had come to think of *better living* in a restricted, tangible sense that Cousin Lucius would not contemplate. And to teach anything less than the classics seemed to him to involve a doubt as to the value of teaching anything. He wondered why people did not send their children to "business colleges" and be done with it. So he was repudiated as a teacher, after thirty faithful years. The times, he thought, and not any individuals he knew, were responsible and he was in no way embittered. It was, of course, a consideration that he would no longer draw his hundred dollars a month, but the farm was more remunerative than it had been since the Civil War. And before long the village bank was reorganized and he was made its president.

Money was really coming into the community, and it was sweet not to be stifled always with a sense of poverty. But sometimes he felt that money was like a narcotic that, once tasted, drives men to make any sacrifice in order to taste more of it. All around him, for instance, many gentlemen whom he had long recognized as persons of dignity were behaving themselves with a distressing lack of dignity. On the advice of New York commission merchants they were attaching to each of their peach-crates a gaudy label, boasting that peaches of that particular brand were better than peaches of any other brand. There were gentlemen who were actually shipping the same sort of peaches, from the same orchard, under two distinct brands. Cousin Lucius was sure that such conduct was not native with them, and he was at a loss to know what they meant. What if the commission merchants had said that such practice was "good business"? Who were the commission merchants, anyway?

Another by-and-by had come round and Hard Times was no longer knocking at the door. Cousin Lucius saw men and women, whose heads had been held up by a feat of will only, holding their heads high, at last, naturally. He thought they should hold them higher still. By the Eternal, these people were as good as any people anywhere, and it had not been right, he believed, nor in accord with the intent of God, for them to be always supplicants.

It made him glad to see the girls of various families with horses and phaetons of their own. When a group of citizens promoted a swimming club, he exulted with the happiness of one who loved swimming for itself and who loved it in this special case as a symbol of liberation. The water that he cavorted in on the summer

afternoons, while he whooped from time to time to the ecstatic
shrieks of a hundred children, plopped no more deliciously upon
his body than upon his spirit. For forty years he and his kind had
wandered through a dense wilderness, with little external guid-
ance either of cloud or fire. He told himself that by the light of
their own minds they had wandered indeed bravely, but he was
unashamedly glad that help had come, and that other men and
cities were at last visible.

His father lived on, hale at ninety. He had become in the eyes
of everybody who knew him a benign and indomitable saint.
Shortly before his death he was in extreme pain and feebleness,
and Cousin Lucius, for one, while he was saddened, could not be
wholly sad to have the old man go on to whatever might await
him. As he ran over in his mind the events of the long life just
ended, one thing he had not before thought of stuck in his memory. His father had continued superintendent of the Methodist
Sunday school until his death, and yet when he had rounded out
his fifty years, though his flock was less hard pressed by far than it
had been twenty-five years earlier, there was no silver pitcher offered in recognition of that cycle of effort. He believed that his
father, too, had let the anniversary go unnoticed.

Yet Cousin Lucius felt that the omission meant something, most
likely something that the people were not conscious of. To all appearances the Methodists were never so active. Like the Baptists—
and as incompletely as he indorsed the Methodists, it truly grieved
him for them to execute their reforms Baptistward—they had re-
placed their rather graceful wooden church with a contorted cre-
ation, Gothic molded, in red brick. Most of their less material defects remained constant. But the church's neglect of his father's
fifty years of service made him know that in spite of its bustling
works, it was bored upon from within by something that looked to
him curiously like mortality. And the most alarming part of the
situation was that the church could not be persuaded of its mal-
ady. People simply did not look to it any longer as to the center of
all their real hopes. He felt that for the great run of men the
church is an indispensable symbol of the basic craving of humanity for an integrity which it must aspire to, if it can never quite
exemplify.

He dimly felt that in its zeal to maintain itself as that symbol
it had adopted so many of the methods of the men about it, that
men had concluded it too much like themselves to be specially
needful. It had become simply the most available agent for their

philanthropies. For its continued services on that score they paid it the tribute of executing its ceremonies, but they believed, in their hearts, if they were not aware that they did, that all those ceremonies were quite barren. Cousin Lucius, too, had felt that they were barren, but rather because they understated the degree of his humility than because they overstated it. It seemed to him that most of his contemporaries, who were in fact, by now, almost all his juniors, felt that those ceremonies needlessly belittled creatures who were in fact not necessarily little at all.

He did not solve those questions, but he held them in his mind, to couple them, if occasion came, with facts that he might run upon that seemed related.

So the new day was not altogether cloudless. Cousin Lucius felt that people were going too fast, that, villagers, they were trying to keep the pace of people they considered, but whom he could not consider, the best people in the great cities. He believed that the people who had represented in an urban civilization in 1850 what his family had represented at that time in a rural civilization were most likely as little disposed as he was to endorse the new god, who was so mobile that he had lost all his stability.

Tom and Dick and the butcher and the baker and others were all shooting fiercely about in automobiles, and Europe was trying to destroy itself in a great war—and then America was driven into the war, too. As a banker, he urged Tom and Dick to buy government bonds to sustain the war, but most of them were more concerned to buy something else. Perhaps the older families in the cities were protesting as he protested—and to as little purpose. And people would not read any more. Well-to-do again, they would not listen to his efforts to reorganize the old Library. They would swim with him, they would set up a golf club, but they would not read Cervantes because they were too busy going to the movies.

That war in Europe, with the clamorous agencies that swung to its caissons, woman's suffrage and "socialism" and prohibition, was a puzzle to him. His knowledge of history taught him that most of the avowed objects of any war prove inevitably, in the event, not to have been the real objects. As for woman's suffrage, despite his fervor for justice, he was sure that the practice of a perfectly sound "right" often involves the practicer, and with him others, in woes incomparably more galling than the renunciation of that right.

Socialism meant to him at bottom the desire of the laboring

classes for a more equable share of the world's goods, and the laboring classes that he knew were negro farm hands. It seemed to him that in all conscience they shared quite as fully as justice might demand in the scant dole of the world's goods handed down to their white overlords.

For many years Georgia had had prohibition, and he had voted for it long before it was established. He believed that it was mainly an expedient for furthering good relations between the whites and negroes. It was not practical for a rural community to command adequate police protection, and he was willing to sacrifice his right to resort to liquor openly, in order to make it less available to persons who were likely to use it to the point of madness.

But national prohibition, involving the effort to force upon urban communities, and upon rural communities with a homogeneous population, a system designed peculiarly for the rural South, seemed to him as foolhardy and as vicious as the efforts of alien New England to control the ballot-box in the South. The law was passed in spite of him, and for a while—stickler as he was for law—he grudgingly abided by it. But he soon learned that he was alone, with scarcely anybody except women for company, and that made him restless. He remembered his initial objection to the program, and reminded himself of the statute books cluttered with a thousand laws inoperative because people did not believe in them, and at last, so far as he was concerned, repealed the national prohibition law altogether and abided by the prohibition law of Georgia only, as he had before abided by it, with wisdom and temperance.

One day he was sitting in his brother's store, and he heard some men—they had all been students of his—talking lustily among themselves out on the sidewalk. "What this town needs," said one of them, "is looser credit. Look at every town up and down the road—booming! Look at us—going fast to nothing. What we need is a factory, with a big payroll every Saturday. Naturally we haven't got the capital to float the thing from the start, but, good Lord! how would anything ever start if people waited till they had cash enough to meet every possible expense? In this man's world you've got to take chances. The root of our trouble"—and here Cousin Lucius listened earnestly. He was president of the bank, and though he had not thought the town was disintegrating, he recognized that comparatively it was at a standstill—"the root of our trouble," continued his economist, " is old-man Lucius.

Fine old fellow and all that kind of thing, but, my God! what an old fogy! I'll tell you, it's like the fellow said, what this town needs most is one or two first-class funerals!"

Cousin Lucius was pretty well dazed. He did not know whether to go out and defend himself, or to hold his peace, and later, when appropriate, to clarify his position as best he could for a race that had become so marvelously aggressive. He was afraid that if he went he would not be able to talk calmly. He had fairly mastered his trait of stuttering, but he felt sure that before any speech he might make just then he would do well to fill his mouth with pebbles and to plant himself by the roaring surf.

He knew well what that bounding youngster had in mind. He wanted, without effort, things that have immemorially come as the result of effort only. His idea of happiness was to go faster and faster on less and less, and Cousin Lucius was bound to admit that that idea was prevalent nearly everywhere. He did not know, for sure, where it had come from, but it was plainly subjugating Georgia, and if reports were faithful, it was lord everywhere in America. He did not care, he told himself, if it was lord everywhere in the hypothecated universe, it should win no submission from him. The true gods might be long in reasserting themselves, but life is long enough to wait. For that which by reason of strength may run to fourscore years, by reason of other forces may run farther. He would not concede that we are no better than flaring rockets, and he would never get it into his old-fashioned head that anything less than a complete integrity will serve as a right basis for anything that is intended to mount high and to keep high.

He would not say all that now. He believed that the peach business would be constantly remunerative, but he remembered that it had been in existence less than twenty-five years, and he knew that many things of longer lease than that, on men's minds, had suddenly crashed into nothingness. For that reason he was glad that his community had undertaken the commercial production of asparagus and pecans as well as peaches and the older dependence, cotton. He did not anticipate the collapse of all those industries. All that he insisted on was that the expansion of his community be an ordered response to actual demands—not a response so violently stimulated to meet artificial demands that it created new demands faster than it could satisfy the old ones.

The peach crop in 1919 was a complete failure—for reasons not yet determined. The fruit was inferior; the costs of production and transportation, high; the market, lax. And in turn other crops were almost worthless. Next year, everybody said, things would be better. And pretty soon it was plain to Cousin Lucius that his faith in the compromise between farming and industrialism had in its foundations mighty little of reality.

He was himself cautious and thrifty and he had not spent by any means all that the fat years just past had brought to him. He had saved money—and bought more land. He blamed, in a fashion, the people who had lived on all they had made, but against his will he had to admit to himself that he did not blame them very much. Gravely impoverished for years, holding in their land a capital investment that in theory, only, amounted to anything, they had toiled to feed and clothe a boisterous nation which had become rankly rich and which had reserved for itself two privileges: to drive such iron bargains with the Southern farmer that he could scarely creep, and to denounce him from time to time for his oppression of the negro. Seeing all that, Cousin Lucius could hardly blame the grasshoppers for flitting during the short and, after all, only half-hearted summer of the peach industry. But he considered that he was weak not to blame them more, and he was torn to know whether he should promise the people a better day, which he could not descry, or berate them about the duties of thrift.

The towns in the peach area which had committed themselves to the looser credits he had heard advocated were in worse condition now, by far, than his own town. The same people who had called Cousin Lucius an old fogy began now to say that he was a wise old bird. And he accepted their verdict to this extent—he was wise in seeing the folly that a farm community surely enacts in attempting to live as if it were an industrial community. While he conceded that no community could in his day be any longer purely agrarian, he felt—when he heard people urging a universal acceptance of the industrial program—that that program was not suitable even for an industrial community if it was made up of human beings as he knew them. He recognized that his wisdom was only negative, that there were basic phases of the question that lay too deep for his perceiving.

The farmer, it seemed to him, was in the hard position of having to win the suffrage of a world that had got into the industrialists' motor-car and gone riding. He could run alongside the car, or hang on behind the car, or sit beside the road and let the car go on whither it would—with destination unannounced and, one might suspect, unconsidered.

The case was illustrated by some towns he knew. One of them had continued to grow cotton exclusively—and the world had forgotten it. Many of them had run as hard as ever they could to keep up with the world, and they had fallen exhausted. His own town had hung on as best it could, and though the industrialists might grumble, it managed not to be dislodged. That was a half victory indeed.

He thought as a matter of justice to the farmer and as a matter of well-being for the world, that that motor-car should be controlled not always by the industrialists but sometimes by an agency that would be less swift, more ruminative. A truly wise bird would bring *that* about, and Cousin Lucius knew that that lay clean beyond him.

One might speculate on these things interminably, but what Cousin Lucius actually saw was that the economic structure of his community was falling down, like London Bridge, or like the little town which, as a child, he had seen burst, bladder like, when the railroad pushed on beyond it. He heard doctrinaire persons, sent down by the government, explain that the trouble lay wholly in the commitment of the people to one crop only. That infuriated him. His community was not committed to a one-crop system; it had four crops. But he found the doctrinaire persons hopelessly obtuse.

Four crops! They had five crops, worse luck, for the countryside everywhere was being stripped of its very forests, so that the people in the cities might have more lumber. That was a chance of getting some money, and one could not let it pass. Woods he had roamed, calculating—as he had learned to do at college—their cubic content in timber per acre, were to his dismay being operated upon in actuality, as he had often fondly, with no thought of sacrilege, operated on them in fancy. It seemed that people could not be happy unless they were felling trees.

One day the young school superintendent began chopping some oaks on the school grounds, for the high purpose of making an out-of-door basketball court. Cousin Lucius had not a shred of authority to stop the young man, but when he found that the persons who did have authority would not interfere, he interfered himself. At first Cousin Lucius reasoned with him calmly, but the superintendent would not be convinced. There was much talk.

"I have the authority of the Board of Education," said the superintendent, concluding the matter. But Cousin Lucius was determined that that should not conclude the matter. "Authority or no authority," said he, flustered, stuttering a little, "you will take them down, sir, at your peril." Then he walked away.

The superintendent knew that Cousin Lucius had no mandate of popular sentiment behind him, but knew also *one* person who did not mean to risk that old man's displeasure. The trees were spared.

The sacrifice of the forests was a symbol to Cousin Lucius, and a sad one. He knew by it how grave, once more, was the extremity of his friends—how fully it meant the arrival once more of Hard Times as their master. Even now they retained a plenty of most things they actually needed, but lacked the means of acquiring anything in addition. Of course they had wanted too much, and had curbed their desires in general less successfully than he had done, and they were consequently harder pressed. But they were a people not bred to peasant viewpoints. Traditionally they were property owners. They worked faithfully, they maintained holdings upon the value of which was predicated the entire economic structure of the nation. Society would not in either decency or sense deny that value, and it never did. What it did—by some process Cousin Lucius could not encompass—was to make the revenues from that value quite valueless—or at least quite valueless as compared with the revenues from equal amounts of capital invested elsewhere.

Once again he saw inaugurated the old process, checked for a while, of people leaving their farms and putting out for the cities. And he observed that those who went prospered, while those who stayed languished. Formerly, the more or less gradual development of the cities made them incapable of offering work to all who came, and many of his younger neighbors kept to their farms through necessity. Now the cities were growing like mad—precisely, he thought, like mad—and most of the old families he knew were moving off, losing their connection with their old home. Some survived their difficulties, but many, after lapsing deeper and deeper into debt, finally turned over their holdings to one or another mortgage firm, and went away. And the mortgage firms turned over the land to aliens, people from here and yonder, whose grandfathers never owned a slave nor planted a pomegranate.

Even the negroes, conscious at last of the insatiate capacity of the new cities, were moving away. The Southern cities had absorbed as many negroes as they could use, but the Northern cities had much work of the sort they felt negroes were suited for. It saddened Cousin Lucius to see them go. Men and women whose parents had come with his parents from Carolina, and who lived in the same houses all their lives, were going away—to Detroit, to Akron, to Pittsburgh. Well, God help them.

The prospect was not cheerful, but Cousin Lucius thought that as a human being he was superior to any prospect whatever. When he preached that doctrine to some of his friends they taunted him with the idea that his particular bravery was sustained by certain government bonds he had, and it was true that he had the bonds. He and Cousin Caroline had not stinted themselves during the fat years all for nothing, and he had kept out a small share of his savings to go into Liberty Bonds. But he told those who mourned, and he told himself, that even if he had not saved the bonds, he would still have asserted his humanity over the shackling activities of mere circumstance.

It was a fine sight to see him early on a summer morning walking the mile-long street between his home and the bank. On one side there were great oaks bordering his path, and the other side was a row of houses. In front of nearly every house a woman was stirring among her flowers, and Cousin Lucius had some words for nearly all of them. "Nice morning, ma'am," he would say. "I hope you all are well this morning." And then he would pass on, and often he would sniff the cool air greedily into his nostrils. "My, my," he would say, "sweet! How sweet the air is this morning!" And when a breeze blew, he would stretch out his arms directly into it—for of all the good things to have up one's sleeve he considered a summer breeze among the usefulest.

The time came round when he and Cousin Caroline had been married fifty years. And they gave a great party, and all their children came home, and people from all that section came to say good wishes to them. Cousin Caroline sat most of the evening, lovely in her black dress and with her flowers, and Cousin Lucius —sure that Cousin Caroline would pay for the two of them whatever was owing to propriety—sat nowhere, nor was indeed still for a moment anywhere. He looked very elegant, as young, almost, as his youngest son, and he was a vigorous, apparently, as anybody in all that company. Cousin Lucius had never lost a moment in his whole life from having drunk too much liquor, but he had always kept some liquor on hand, and he felt that that night surely justified his touching it a little more freely than was his custom. So he summoned by groups all the gentlemen present into his own backroom, and had a toast with them. Now the room was small and there were many groups and that involved Cousin Lucius's having many toasts, but he used his head and came through the operation with the dignity that was a part of him.

Not everybody was satisfied with his conduct. Some of the ladies especially who had men-folk less well balanced than they might have been, thought the situation scandalous. They had been indoctrinated fully with the dogma which says that life must be made safe for everybody at the cost, if necessary, of shutting the entire world into a back yard with high palings, and they believed that somebody prone to sottishness might be wrecked by Cousin Lucius's example. They did not realize the complexities of life which baffle those who have eyes to see, and make them despair at times of saving even the just and wise—much less the weak and foolish.

Those ladies were not shadowed—nor glorified—by a sense of tragic vision, and they were not capable—not indeed aware—of philosophic honesty, but they were good and angry with Cousin Lucius and they went to Cousin Caroline and told her that she should curb him. That lady was not dismayed. The thought of being angry with Cousin Lucius did not once occur to her, but for the briefest moment she realized that she was having to check herself not to be outraged against the little ladies who had constituted themselves his guardians. "Oh," she said, "you know Lucius! What can *I* do with Lucius? My dear, where *did* you find that lovely dress. You always show such exquisite taste. I am so happy to have you here. No friends, you know, like old ones. I am *so* happy."

The next winter Cousin Lucius and Cousin Caroline both had influenza, and Cousin Lucius's sister, who came to look after them, had it, too. They all recovered, but Cousin Lucius *would* violate directions and go back to work at the bank before he was supposed to go. And as spring came on it was evident that something ailed him, very gravely. It was his heart, but he refused to recognize the debility that was patent to everybody else, and went on.

And when summer came, and the jaded people began again to market the peaches they felt sure—and rightly—would be profitless, he, with the rest, set his operations in motion. One of his sons, Edward, was at home on a visit, and early one morning the father and son went out to the farm, with the intention of coming back home for breakfast. Only the negro foreman, Anthony, was at the packinghouse, where they stopped, and Edward strolled down into the orchard, leaving Cousin Lucius to talk over the day's plans with Anthony. A little way down one of the rows between the peach trees, Edward almost stumbled upon some quail. And the quail fluttered up and flew straight toward the packing-house.

He heard his father shout at them as they went by, the fine lusty shout that he remembered as designed especially for sunsets and clean dogwood blossoms. And then there was perfect silence. And then he heard the frantic voice of Anthony: "Oh, Mas' Edward! Help, help, Mas' Edward! Mas' Lucius! Mas' Lucius! O Lord! help, Mas' Edward!" Stark fright slugged him. He was sick and he could scarcely walk, but he ran, and after unmeasured time, it seemed to him, he rounded the corner of the packing-house and saw Anthony, a sort of maniac between grief and terror, half weeping, half shouting, stooping, holding in his arms Cousin Lucius's limp body. "Oh, Mas' Edward! Mas' Edward! Fo' God, I believe Mas' Lucius done dead!"

He *was* dead. And all who wish to think that he lived insignificantly and that the sum of what he was is negligible are welcome to think so. And may God have mercy on their souls.

Southern Humor

LONG AGO, at the sanguine age when one hopes at length to know everything, I had it as my business once to write something about a man who was notable as a humorist. My first obligation seemed to me to find out what humor, after all, was—what its sources were, what its charms. Or, more simply, to find out what makes a thing funny, and why, indeed, we are pleased to have funny things brought to our attention, whether relevantly or not.

I read much, then, on that score, and the result was like most results, not satisfying; I was left for all my effort not much the wiser. Incongruity, contrast, from what I could make out, seemed to be the bed-rock found uniformly by all pundits seeking humor's origin. What bed-rock was found by those seeking its fascination, remains to me this day unknown, as it apparently did to my masters, in spite of their profound method of saying so. What I had been able to reckon for myself, I found after irksome suspense to be what other people also had reckoned. What I had not been able to reckon—why humor is delightful—I found after irksome suspense was a question that other people also had found always beyond them.

Naturally, one hazards guesses, and the guesses about the fascination of humor group themselves for the most part either about the conscientious motive of correction or the quite unconscientious one of escape. To jeer at a person or a state of affairs leads the jeerer, with more or less earnest inimicalness on his part, into satire or irony. But some of us fell short, somehow, of acquiring our just endowment of inimicalness, and we have come to cherish the idea that a mordant earnestness on our part about other people's activities is an impulse to be eschewed. People of this stripe laugh, certainly; they cannot go about sighing always. They

From *Culture in the South*, edited by W. T. Couch. Chapel Hill: University of North Carolina Press, 1934.

regard the story's butt not with detestation, but with affection, and they do not cherish hope of remodeling anybody or anything very speedily—not even themselves.

These by all rules are life's ineffectuals; but their justification in humanity is that without them humanity would take on an aspect too horrible to contemplate, too indubitably governed by dullness or malice for anybody to wish its continuance. And if facts are regarded and not rules, it is these people who bring about for us, all the betterments we ever get.

As for *Southern,* that qualifies Humor in my title, I have put some thought on that for a long time. I learned the word early, and as a child in a Georgia village-school yearned at times to emulate some of my less restrained peers and punch out with a pencil-point the eyes of the northern generals pictured in my text-books. Restrained, I comforted myself by inscribing encomiumistic phrases under the pictures of southern generals. Later I learned better than to wish to occupy myself so barbarously. But I knew by then, and I know still, how to look at a book and without reading it to be aware, somehow, of every word on the pages that remotely looks like *southern.* I conceived it as my duty, once, over many years, to inspect that word every time it occurred on a page and to ascertain the veracity or falsehood of the sentence containing it. Sometimes the sentence said merely that on the southern slope of these mountains the climate is mild —and that was indeed disappointing. But I was powerfully affected if it declared the southern temperament sluggish, or, on the other hand, if it declared it generous.

I rehearse this autobiography in my anxiety to show that the word southern has long had its importance in my consciousness. Has it a meaning, really, other than the geographic one? It has been fashionable to think so for many years, and if the legend which in the beginning ascribed it meaning was at first legend merely, it is not likely by now legend merely, any more. A dog badly named, or well named, for that matter, will justify what is said of him, and a people will doubtless do as much. So in my mind there is a body of notions that hold their hands up and answer present when one says southern; yet to define those notions (since in definition one must be definite) is more than I can do in this essay, or more than anybody could do, I judge, except by implications and overtones and suggestions that nobody in this swift-moving time would trouble to follow, or, indeed, would trouble in the first place to set down.

And now, writing this article, I review in my mind not merely what has been the course of southern humor historically. I wonder what it is, in essence, and whether it is in fact different from any other humor in anything except in its setting and in the types of people it concerns itself with.

The historical phase of my activity need not cost me great effort. The extent of the contribution southern writers have made to the merriment of this nation and of other nations is a matter chiefly of research, and research students here and yonder have unearthed much information about it—with a solemnity that one must pronounce marvelous.

But the essence of southern humor, and the possibility of distinguishing it from other humor (except, as I have said, by perfectly objective tests)—that, truly, is a horse of a different color.

As the earliest of southern humorists, consider William Byrd, that good Briton. Young, he was a debonair blade of a fellow, as familiar in London as in Virginia; old, when sickness had him, and the inevitable knowledge that he would not come to as much as he had hoped to, he was very tragical. He noted the antics of his contemporaries and wrote about them, not as himself an antic-doer, but as one superior, remote. On one side is his sophistication and his fastidiousness; on the other, their ignorance and blundering. That contrast was accidental; it was not a device of his to make the situation more amusing. His characters seemed to him ludicrous enough, himself not ludicrous at all.

Everything of his that has been published waited, in manuscript form till Byrd was a hundred years dead. That late, his writings were no longer capable of proving a literary influence; times had changed so greatly, toward libertarianism in politics, toward finical delicacy in social intercourse, that his writings lay neglected for almost a further hundred years. So much for what he wrote. What he said, in its influence upon people who knew him personally, was almost surely more influential—and that disparity between what was written and what said is interesting not of itself only, but as an early instance in southern life of a disparity that marks all life, everywhere, but particularly, I think, marks life in the South.

After Byrd, there are few echoes of southern laughter for a long time. Laughter there was, doubtless, and gayety enough, but the soberness of Revolutionary times together with the eighteenth-century ideal of decorum, and the widespread influence of evangelicalism, kept most of this gayety vocal, forbade it the dignity of being written. When Revolutionary earnestness had burnt itself out in a scene of incandescent triumph, when the old aim of decorum had slumped before the new democracy, when evangelicalism, in its ardor to save everybody, had lowered its bars to admit everybody, then there was a new day. The old heaven and the old earth of Byrd or of Franklin or of Timothy Dwight had passed away, except, perhaps, in the heart of Washington Irving. And Irving, the stranded soul, put out soon for Europe and ever afterward in general stayed there.

The new country was above all else hopeful. Democracy in politics and arminianism in religion and free land in economics gave it hardihood to set beneath all of its amusement at the grotesque, the assumption that most grotesqueness would soon end. And the same assumption humanized all the jokes because they had in them always the implication that the superiority of the joker was largely accidental, largely a matter of his having shared more fully than his humorous puppets in wholesome opportunities that would soon be open to everyone. The old story tellers are at constant pains to make this clear. I record all this now, they keep saying, because it is so ludicrous, and because soon the very clowns I write about will be behaving as punctiliously as anybody—their children turning out to be—who knows?—perhaps president. From a time as early as 1825 onward till 1900 this song was never silent in American life; and it is not silent yet—though it is audible, now that the twentieth century is a third gone, principally in the success magazines and in the sophisticated weeklies published in New York.

The Revolution was well over. Old colonials and fresh immigrants were pushing westward. And then cotton as a great commercial possibility came to tempt them all southward. Georgia for a moment became the West, and it was soon, thanks to cotton, a West that was relatively rich, relatively well ordered—though retaining the violent contrasts in cultural groups (southerner, Yankee, immigrant, Negro) that make for humorous situations. Funny, all of this, people kept saying; record it now, set it down now; it is so transient (else it would be sad); it will be gone soon; it is, indeed, already gone.

So they set it down—Longstreet with his horse swappings and his eye-gougings, Thompson with his tobacco-spitters, R. M. Johnston, and Sidney Lanier and Bill Arp Smith and Joel Chandler Harris—all in Georgia. Hooper and Baldwin wrote of Alabama, Crockett and G. W. Harris of Tennessee, Prentice of Kentucky,

Thorpe and Opie Reed and Mark Twain of the South bordering the Mississippi. Even Virginia—that urbane place—offered its quota of natural men to be pictured by the romanticized and romanticizing Dr. Bagby. Even South Carolina—that sedate place —offered its quota to be pictured by the robustious Simms and the much less robustious (oh, much!) Mrs. Gilman.

And except for Mark Twain, who had the advantage of having been born later as well as innately superior to the rest of them, they all said very much the same thing. Their literary form: mostly Addison-like essays or fanciful letters, with an increasing deviation from Addison as it became the practice to introduce more and more dialect, more and more bad spelling. Their subject: unsophisticated country-folk (mostly white at first but at last mostly Negro) in contact with a world unfamiliarly urban. Their attitude: enjoy with me, reader, you who are cultivated, as I am, the foibles of these men and women, all of whom, as you and I both know, have hearts of gold beneath their superficial crudities.

Over and over this went on, and people everywhere found it delectable. America had at last come free of Europe's shadow; and this humor was really the humor of the nation at large at the time when the frontier was the nation's dominant interest. So far was it from sectional merely that its reception was equally clamorous in Philadelphia and in Peoria and in Vicksburg; and the fact is that of the eight southern humorists discussed in *The South in the Building of the Nation* (the eight, I mean, who died before 1900) four were bred and born in the North and one was educated there. The victories this humor won were identical in all sections; the rebuffs it met, ineffectual rebuffs such as the disgust felt for it by females and refined gentlemen, were also identical. It went marching on, and if it had more proponents North than it did South after 1860, so much the more demonstrably was it in the current, in the torrent, indeed, of national development.

For it is worth noting that the Civil War and early post-Civil War proponents of the old humor persisted not in the new America that had taken form along the north Atlantic coast nor freely in the new America that had been driven to take form along the south Atlantic coast. It persisted in the western north, and as soon as the western north lost its distinctiveness the old humor languished there also.

Now certainly as early as the 1830's forces were at work which render the South unable and unwilling to float its raft on the broad stream of national development. In the light of that time the democratic theories of 1800, and the arminianism so dear then, seemed less and less tenable. Negroes, it seemed, so far as this world went, at least, were outside that picture; and as the poor whites hardened in their resentment against their betters, becoming less amenable, they also were excluded. The southern oligarchy tended to become logically both aristocratic and Calvinistic. That is what it became *logically*. What it became actually is a different story.

There was a condition to be reckoned with that inevitably rides down, at last, most schedules of what one ought to believe in deference to one's own purely selfish interests. This consideration was that in the South, because it was a sparsely settled, farming region, people in the various classes, white and black, knew one another personally, intimately. Most often, as a result—one can risk saying so—they had a sort of affection for one another; but even if they had instead a sort of hatred, no one sinned so pointedly as to mistake people for mechanisms.

In the great North, the case went by contraries. There democracy and free-will had all the official endorsement they could ever need, but the unofficial, dominating conviction of individuals endorsed far different doctrines. As industrialism proceeded men became specialists, and as population grew denser it became necessary for every man to rule out from his consciousness the ups and downs of most of the people he had contact with. It became necessary, in short, for people to act as if they believed other people made out of metal rather than of flesh and blood.

What prophet could have foreseen this—fuddled as prophets must always be by the stir about them? South, all roads led *from* America, it was said; North, all roads turned back on themselves toward the ideals of the 1776 Declaration, or toward some vague place that was perhaps Heaven, and that was in any case very nice indeed. But as plain as those roads were, the travelers on them arrived, at last curiously—one group in Paterson, New Jersey, let us say; the other, in Macon, Georgia—cities both of which Jefferson might have understood, but only one of which he might possibly have commended.

In the South, the forces likely to break up the old humor were largely theoretical, and any of them that were more than theoretical were broken in upon by the personal intimacies that characterize a rural civilization. Further, any hard and fast program of social stratification that might have dehumanized and standardized society there, crumbled before the spectacle of reconstruction,

with its pulling down of what had been high and its exaltation of
what had been low. When Marie Antoinette (for all her saying
"let them eat cake, then") is forced at last to beg crusts from her
jailer, the situation is so poignantly tragic that the mind cannot
last it out; it must save itself by laughter. So one's very poverty in
the South in the 1870's—and in more years than those—was often
the theme of one's best stories, the nucleus of ten thousand situations calculated to stir merriment.

Reconstruction, then, with its harsh anarchy, made humor
mandatory. Desolate and lacking cheer, one was the more bound
to simulate it—to shun madness, for simple sanity's sake, *bound*.
Reconstruction with its anarchy broadened, also, the *field* of
humor. Cousin Lucius, in his patched breeches, rehearsing Horace; Cousin Mintora, in homespun, fanning herself with jeweled
ivory—both were figures one could not be wholly solemn about.
And the laughter one accorded them, with themselves leading in
it, was not far different from the laughter accorded the rough-
and-ready catch-as-catch-can citizenry of Longstreet's *Georgia
Scenes*. Black Sambo and his lady, the poor white and his, the
colonel and his—each with his valid claim upon absurdity. And, to
make the gamut complete—put in mind of doing so, perhaps, by
the Negro's personification of animals and his humanization of
deity—one recognizes as valid (out of neighborliness if nothing
else) the claims, out absurdity-way, of beasts on the one hand, of
divinity on the other. Uncle Remus' Brer Rabbit and Mr. Roark
Bradford's God join hands indiscriminately with mankind, and
the trio will likely as not, if a fiddle twangs, do some trick steps
worth a body's trying to catch on to.

Even fine abstractions, programs for salvation, sacrosanct now
in so many places, are not likely to meet in the South with much
decorousness of reception. There, there is remembrance still of
a fine program that came to nothing, for all that General Lee
could do to make it prevalent—it was absurd, perhaps, ever to
hope it would prevail—not soon will another program obtain
one's whole endorsement. A lofty pronouncement, as a pronouncement, is a marvelous thing meriting one's admiration. As something more than a pronouncement, as a signal for action, it evokes
less iron resolution that it does skeptical, half-sorrowful, amusement. Life is volatile—the grave running into the comic, the comic
into the grave, each perhaps dependent upon the other for its
being. This ponderous listing of grievances, this meticulous study
of how to rectify them, this deep drumming to organization and

to action—if necessary, to violent action. Are lister, study-er, drummer really quite solemn—more actually solemn than Cousin Lucius with his Horace, than Jesus in Reverend Sambo's praying? (Come, Lenin, and say so if you will—take care when you do lest your beard bob.) *And, besides, Mr. Lenin, I know Cousin Joe—as well as one man can know another,—made his money curiously too, I heard said. But Lord, more than likely he hardly knew what he was up to. And he's mighty kind to all his folks, sir, and I expect that's being kind to half the county—helped me out, personally, more than once. You talk fine, sir, to a fellow down and out like me, but you can see, I judge, how Cousin Joe being in the family, and all, I'd naturally rather look to him for help than to a man outside the family—especially, if you'll excuse me for saying so, to a foreigner.*

Through the last of the eighteen hundreds much of the recorded humor of America ran in the old channels set before the Civil War. In the South, one could observe Bill Arp and Joel Harris, both of them in many ways reminiscent of old Longstreet, —could observe in the West a parallel reminiscence in Mark Twain, as long as Mark Twain stayed in the West, and as long, incidentally, as there was a West, any longer, in the historic sense, to stay in Mark Twain.

A glib man gifted in grimacing and mimicry, touched with sentimentality, did not need capital to insure profits in the South till a time that only yesterday, it seems, became the past. For long years, there, people relished incalculably the yarns of semi-professional funny-men, some of whom, when they were not delivering their hilarious "lectures" (admittance, say, 25 cents), filled in their time acceptably as ministers of this or that evangelical denomination.

They were the court-jesters of a homogeneous culture and they are extinct now not because the culture they represented has crumbled utterly, but because it has grown self-conscious and ashamed, wistful to be cosmopolitan. En route, at it were, to extinction, they lived for years in the smoking compartments of railway trains and gabbed there interminably, to their own joy and with cost to nobody. Cosmopolitanism, with its creed of efficiency and its experience of human depravity, warned all travelers at length with printed bulletins to beware of all other travelers, and Prohibition left those who were warned ready to heed the warning and often half ready to justify them.

But even in 1932, in the effectible privacy and brevity of a newspaper perusal, one can catch (and many are intent to catch) the echoes of that old buffoonery in the comic-strip depiction of one Hambones, true son of frontier America. Except for Hambones, then, and such—like, the old humor is gone—that is, in its professional aspect. In its non-professional aspect it has waned little to this day.

For consider, now, such a group of people as comes together at countless places in the South to celebrate Christmas by heavy eating. There is grandfather first. The mossy marble has these many years been all anybody has seen of grandmother,—but not all that anybody has heard of her. That lady's sayings, her eccentricities (always whispered about), her preferences in dress and food and flowers, are well understood by her descendants regardless of whether or not they ever had the happiness of seeing her. And there is grandfather's friend, invited in for dinner, a retired small-merchant he; grandfather, a retired farmer. Between the two, so far as one can discern, there is one point of congeniality: they are both upwards of eighty. How they enjoy each other!

Besides these two are mother and father (he, a lawyer) and uncles and aunts, wed and unwed, farmers, doctors, merchants, a mail-carrier, a teacher, a knitter of knit bed-spreads. And there are countless cousins, male and female, conventional for the most part, some unconventional—but none so unconventional as not to know better than to offend this agglomeration of good nature. One cousin conducts a gallery of modern art in Chicago; one, Sorbonne trained, teaches French at Vassar. One, absent, is represented by a note from him saying how sorry he is; he for his part is in Russia, finding out for some great foundation or other about the doings of the Soviets.

Here are all these people, gorged at last, and called upon by six or eight stray diners, as diverse as they, from another family. These people are constrained to talk about something, for along with the fundamental prohibitions (don't walk pigeon-toed, don't pick your teeth, child, in public) they were all given a fundamental admonition—keep, oh, whatever you do keep the occasion *moving*. Moving, my dear, lest we think perchance of how weakness comes at last, and pain, to all of us; lest we think too wrackingly of those whom weakness and pain already shove with brutal deliberation to their end, moving, lest a recognition of our own inadequacy—as persons, as a people—sere us here into sighers only.

Would it do, here, for Cousin Julius to talk of Proust's analyses, for Cousin Mary to tell of Epstein, for Uncle Tom to make Bergson clear, for someone else to echo Swift's mordancy, Wilde's glitter? I ask this question unabashedly as rhetorical. It would never, never do.

This is the challenge—tell a story now, you, that mail-carrying Uncle Jack and Proust-teaching Cousin Julius will both think pointed, that knit-bed-spread-knitter Aunt Susan can endure without fainting, that Rabelaisian Uncle Rob can endure without nodding. Scour your memory, sir; let's hear from you; it is your time now, everybody else has said something—what were you born for, anyway? Slash in where you can, echoing that word of Aunt Susie's, giving it an emphasis that she did not mean to give it, making her disclose more than she meant to, covering her with confusion, while the table roars.

"How was it, Dick, that your mother used the field glasses at the beach. . . . Yes, we have most of us heard but Julius hasn't and besides we want to hear it again." "Now father," protests Dick's mother, Emma, "now, *father!*" And Dick tells it again, and they all shout again.

"Now that," says John, "reminds me of what old Mr. Pixley said" . . . "And Lord, Lord," says grandfather, "when have I thought of old Mr. Pixley? Why John, that man died before ever your mother and father got married." "None the less," says John, "I shall tell you about old Mr. Pixley. . . . ." "Wait," says Henry. "Have you all heard about Res biting Tom Johnson's leg?" (There, naturally, everybody knows both characters. Res is short for Resaca de la Palma, a dog-name in the household since the Mexican War; Tom Johnson is an esteemed but emaciated neighbor).

"Actually bite him?" asks Howard.

"No, just snapped at him."

"I'm glad of that," says Walter, "but what odd taste of Res in the first place!"

"But," George exclaims, *"wasn't* Res an unpractical idealist trying to locate it!"

"Now, boys," says Aunt Mattie, "I have the real truth of it. When Res's tooth struck Tom's breeches, it naturally slid off. . . ."

"How was it, Carrie," asks father, "that old black Bella set you straight about the Family when you first married into it and came here from Boston?"

"What was it, Red, the Yankee said when you bumped into

him after coming back from your schooling in England? *I'm sorry,*
you said—what was it he replied?"

"Uncle John," says Red, "the Yankee said 'What fer.' "

"What was it, Andrew, that little rapscallion said when he
encountered for the first time—and too late at that—quinine with
his natural milk?" "Uncle John," says Andrew, "it was like this.
The child's name was Micajah, and when he became aware of the
quinine he made a wry face and said this: 'Pappy,' says he, 'give
me a chaw er baccer, Mammy's been a-eatin' bitter weed.' "

And so it goes, the old Abductor, the old destroyers, torturers,
weakeners, frightened for a moment to other spheres.

Now all of the people at this Christmas dinner know one another, and the fact that they know, already, most of the stories
they hear told does not make those stories blunt for them. Somehow the story itself is not primarily the thing one laughs at. If
that were true a story read or told by a radio-entertainer or by a
boresome man with a good memory would be as amusing as one
heard acceptably. The important part of a story is the effect it
has on the teller, and one must naturally know the teller well to
perceive what that effect is. That is why a funny thing captured
so that it can be drawn forth and exhibited at will by one man as
by another, loses often, all its force.

That is why uninitiated northern persons often find themselves
impatient at the zest with which southern persons—as sophisticated
as themselves, apparently, listen to one Negro story after another,
through an entire evening. They do not recognize how largely
the point of such stories depends upon outside considerations.
When they are aware of those considerations, when they know
intimately the garrulous raconteur and his mannerisms, their
impatience yields readily. For the initiated understand well
enough that the teller, in the telling, is himself the main point of
his story. They know that the southerner is in many ways bi-
lingual, bi-mental, bi (if I may say so) attituded; he speaks his own
language and the dialect, his own thoughts and the Negro's
thoughts; he has a sentiment for the Negro that the northerner
cannot diagnose except as detestation and at the same time a sentiment for him that the northerner cannot diagnose except as
affection. It is the interplay of all these traits that makes the yarn
worth listening to.

The humor of the Negro, too (I mean as displayed by Negroes),
is dependent upon a sympathetic comprehension. The point is

always in what the teller is really, contrasted with what he tells, and contrasted with his relation to the white man whom he placates and with a complete understanding by each of the other, often hoodwinks.

All of this, I think, suggests with some adequacy the present-day, generally unrecorded type of humor current in the South. The South at large represents in its basic economy the persistence of a tradition long superseded elsewhere, and its humor does too. That economy, obsolete in dominant America, stimulated a social tradition that is as yet obsolescent only, and that is indeed not clearly doomed to extinction, ever. It is a tradition which insists that human beings must quite inescapably remain humorous if they are to remain human, and one may well believe that it will reassert itself.

Even New York, for example, as late as the nineteen-hundreds, found itself as greatly amused by tar-heel O. Henry as pioneer Georgia in its time was amused by Longstreet. And most of O. Henry's merits arise from restatements of the old fundamental theme of American humor, which is in 1932 perhaps less fashionable than it has ever been. I think that it will be fashionable again after a while and that O. Henry would be fashionable again also if it were not for the tawdry newfangledness which he proudly affected and which his contemporaries vulgarly admired.

Newfangledness makes slow headway in the South, and humor there is still at base rural, and all the clanging urbanism of Atlanta or of Birmingham has not been able to make most southerners feel quite at home in the brothel of modish slang—with how great a loss to them let him who will figure. For Atlanta and Birmingham are close, still, to the fields and woods surrounding them, and the bright young people of those cities, let them strive ever so faithfully, are rarely able to pronounce "Sez you," for instance, with a conviction deep enough to keep it from proving nauseous. Most of them luckily have a better wit about them than to try. In the main, when they undertake to be mirthful, they behave themselves as much as they can like Andrew mimicking his young Micajah, or like Dick teasing his mother Emma.

But a discernible amount of southern humor such as Mr. Cohen's Slappey saga, has sprung from sections (more social than geographic in boundary) that are in thoroughgoing fashion both urban and industrialized. This, it turns out, has been most frequently indistinguishable from the humor current in, say, Akron,

Ohio,—a humor sprigs of which have been brought South and set
in soil as much like that of Akron as its admirers could possibly
search out.

On occasion another type has sprung up, indigenous, I think
though sophisticated beyond a doubt, and by many tests urban.
Miss Ellen Glasgow, for instance, is almost wholly dependent in
her subject matter upon the sources of humor which I have suggested as being somewhat definitely southern; and it is obvious
that all of the assumptions behind her hard, bright wit are authen-
tically local. Cabell and Frances Newman and even Mencken must
be reckoned with as belonging to the South. Consider those names,
and pair them, not with the names Richmond, Atlanta, Baltimore,
but with Detroit, Cleveland, Omaha. The pairing most manifestly
will not stand. For these people too are country people, who do
not manage to be at home in whirring cities. Cabell's interests are
in districts that are surely not crowded; Frances Newman's were
in a social plane dominated still by the ideas of Miss Winnie
Davis. Mencken's interests are keener in his yokel, apparently,
than in most other things—and particularly in that brand of yokel
(found seldom in greater verdancy than in the South) whose folly
evinces itself most notably in religion. What is more, Mencken
attacks his victim with a stampeding directness which David
Crockett, could he have heard it, would have mightily exulted in,
which is as distant from the knowing, metropolitan Walter
Winchell as if New York and Baltimore were seven universes
apart. And it must not be forgotten that Cabell and Mencken, at
some inconvenience to themselves, doubtless, continue living
where they do, and that Frances Newman, a little while before
her death, came very definitely to the notion that her place was
South or nowhere.

It is properly terrifying to observe that as time runs, the number
of things a man may be merry over is gradually diminished. "The
year is dying," the poet said—and, philosophically—"let it die." So
I say here—this number is diminishing—let it diminish. But the
year passes, the number falls, with results that no degree of
willingness on our part to have them change, can keep from being
in part bad. We can not laugh ever again with a free heart at
physical deformity or at madness as people—and very good people,
too—did everywhere until very recently. Those sources of laughter
are not sources of laughter any longer—they are gone from that list
and will not be put back there, and I should be as unwilling as

anybody else to see them put back. None the less, we laugh less. Ignorance may go off next; next, the "pain" (so hypersensitive we become) Dick caused his mother about the field glasses.

We progress toward a Heaven, it appears, of unrelieved earnestness and propriety. But there are happily many people who would be unhappy at this prospect, and they are probably the same people who would be most upset at the prospect of their having the opportunity again to exhibit kindness. Doubly hard, then, is their lot, for they are, unless all signs fail, sentimentalists—and the sentimentalist, like the humorist without a mission, is an ineffectual, and his only shadow of justification in life is that without him life would be so very little preferable to death that few would prize it.

For such reactionary persons, I think the South a good place. Many contrasts are deeply rooted here, and they promise to stay rooted. Not soon will the industrialized piedmont regions *completely* overlord the lowlands, nor the forces of modern education (which may conceivably be bad education) overwhelm *completely* in the mind of either barber or bishop the notion that white people and Negroes are somehow not identical.

More progressive sections than ours may actually reach, *via* standardization, before the world ends, that Heaven of deadly uniformity which I am apprehensive of. But I am sure that such a Heaven must be very disagreeable, and that no one of cultivated sensibilities would desire it were it not for the gullibility, latent in the best of us, which teaches men to desire anything which calls itself by an agreeable name.

Many of us would find on attaining such a Heaven that the mere name was insufficient. We should want still a tightening of the heart, at times, with pity, or with indignation, a loosening down of the whole structure of our being, at times, with gigantic mirth.

❦

Of the Mean and Sure Estate

THERE ARE MANY wars afoot in the world, the war of the sexes and the war of the classes, and so on; and there is one war that is carried on in America more actively than it is elsewhere. That is the war of the city against the country. It is certain that no conspicuous part of the writing that has been done in England in late years deals derisively or belligerently with the peculiar shortcomings of countrymen. Possibly there are not any countrymen left there to attack. Possibly European sophistication came to the conclusion, somewhat ahead of our sophistication, that its own means of grace were somehow not wholly adequate, and learned a hesitancy to impose those means where they seemed little wanted.

Always and everywhere, life in the country or in villages is less filled with human association than it is in cities. In the densely settled regions of Europe, human association long since came to imply ideas that were not inescapably pleasant. In America, sparsely settled still, though the twentieth century is more than a third gone, human association is still rare enough and the cities are still new enough—like new toys—for many of us to feel that the fascination of them can never fade. We have felt, pioneers and frontiersmen as most of us are by close inheritance if not actually, that we could never, never see enough people, enough of the structures and devices of people to relieve us of the tedium of unbroken forests and of uninhabited prairie. Many a pioneer built his barns in front of his house, square across a lovely vista, for the good reason that it pleased him to see his barns more than it did to see trees or hills or water. It is more pleasing still, to many Americans, to see the building of the Post Office Department in Washington, or any building, in fact, than to see any object in nature.

From *Who Owns America? A New Declaration of Independence,* edited by Herbert Agar and Allen Tate. Boston: Houghton Mifflin Company, 1936.

The cities, then, have testified agreeably to a nation who felt that nature can be insupportably dull, or violent, concerning man's ability to conquer nature. They have testified also concerning a man's ability to be powerful over his kind, and they have exhibited, one after another, the newest trinkets of scientific discovery to a race which, the world over, found those trinkets irresistible. Stupendously rich off the land tributary to them, they have become centers of medical advance, and even of academic enterprise and of art and religion. It was easy to believe that they were the focus of every desirable thing. Strenuously they proclaimed their own merit, and only the brash had any heart to challenge them.

There was a man speaking in 1935. His age was twenty-five or so, and his business was to pull down boxes in a wholesale grocery store in a town of fifty thousand people. All day he pulled down boxes and put them on a two-wheeled truck and rolled the truck to the delivery door. At night he went to movies. Two men from an adjacent village were buying some groceries from his store to use in connection with a barbecue they were giving. The barbecue was to be in the nature of a "rally" to encourage community interest in a huge planting of camellia japonicas and other shrubs along the highways leading into the two men's village. Each of the two men had been to college in this country and in Europe, each of them derived a livelihood from property he had inherited from his grandparents, each of them had traveled considerably and read considerably—perhaps more than was good for them— and each of them (in a small, Southern way) was a man of affairs. Said the grocery clerk to these men: "What are you guys going to do with so much sugar and coffee?" "We are giving a barbecue," they answered, "in Grovetown. You possibly know where it is. We are inviting everybody in the community. There will probably be five or six hundred people. You'd better come down, too."

"Say, fellows," says grocer, "you might not believe it, you might think me nuts, but I'd sure like to come. I always did say that I'd like to go to a country barbecue and just watch how a bunch of countrymen would act." Unfortunately, the young man could not come.

There was a lady speaking, also in 1935, and she said this:—she said, referring to a gubernatorial candidate whom she detested, "Why, he declared himself that he really did not care for the vote of anybody who lived within the sound of a street-car. You can tell by that," she continued, "what kind of a man he is—he simply

showed that he didn't care for the vote of anybody who is intelligent." The lady was not talking her true mind; she was echo when
she said that, only. Happily, she does not herself live within sound
of a street-car, and she is beyond doubt among the most intelligent
ladies who were eligible to vote in that election.

Besides, she spoke with high precedent. For it was in the same
year that another lady made, or was reported to have made, a
parallel deposition. This personage, the occupant of exalted office,
a member of the President's Cabinet and by inference a sort of
priestess of philosophy, manifested a similar point of view by a
statement that was more extreme, and apparently deliberate. She
was at the time passing through Texas, and she was troubled by
the truly unfortunate condition of some Texas share-croppers. As
bad as things are, somebody said to her, these people have at least
the bare necessities of life and a plenty of sunshine and fresh air—
more than they would likely have if they were in New York. That,
the Cabinet lady declared, was not to the point; for subsistence in
such loneliness seemed to her more abhorrent than starvation
in a metropolis.

Still another lady was speaking in 1935, commenting on a
wedding she had attended. Her husband runs one of several clothing stores in a town that offers a patronage of about thirty
thousand people, and his family and hers are removed by only a
tragically narrow margin from village origins. The wedding she
had attended was in the house of one of her village-dwelling kin,
a branch of her family obviously superior to her own. Exclaimed
this lady: "Oh, wasn't the wedding beautiful! really beautiful! my
dear, nothing whatever small-townish about it!" *God in his mercy
send her grace.*

But as late as 1870, in the South, at least, this had not come to
pass. Then, there was an old gentleman pondering on the case
of his wife's nephew, a young fellow whom he deeply loved.
Responsibilities were heavy upon that young man, and he was
abandoning his farm to further his fortunes store-keeping in a
nearby city. It was a lucky move—he grew rich and his grandchildren are rich still. But all of that was not evident in
1870, and the old gentleman, many of whose own grandchildren were ultimately smothered with mortgages, was sadly
distressed over the departure of his nephew—most of all, perhaps,
over the boy's abandoning the life of a planter, which seemed to
him calculated to promote virtue, for the life of a shopkeeper,
which seemed to him at best not, by stark necessity, hostile to

virtues. "My son," said the Squire, "no man more than I deprecates the circumstances which make necessary your departure. The poet Cowper, whose translation of ancient Homer I do not incidentally esteem as comparable to that of Mr. Pope, has sagaciously observed that God made the country, man made the town. That, sir, is a veracious aphorism, and I hope you will not suffer it to pass from your memory."

All of that was long ago. The poet Cowper and the old Squire, and nearly everything that they thought and said, have for many years been compounded with the earth they cherished. The city-dwellers have long looked with sorrow if not with detestation upon the country; and the country-dwellers—too many of them—with envy and imitative yearnings look adoringly cityward.

That much has been accomplished; and if it were written down in any dependable Scripture that because a thing is done it is also wise and irrevocable, there would be little use talking about any of this any more. Or, indeed, about anything any more. Little use, that is, except the unctuous and practically remunerative, if vapid, one of hymming always upon a theme that nearly everybody is already agreed about.

"It is sweet to dance," a poem says, "to violins when Love and Life are fair, to dance to flutes, to dance to lutes, is delicate and rare." And among certain classes of the cities of our time there is considerable dancing. There is dancing in ballrooms, of the now classical jazz type, and something hardly distinguishable from dancing, in museums and picture-galleries and churches, and at dinner tables, and across the front pages of newspapers and the covers of magazines, and, without stretching the word too far, by the side of unclosed graves and at the lying-in wards of vast hospitals. There is much dancing, alert and nervous—dancing that is aware, of something or other. It is agreeable to have one's practices identified with rightness, whether by direct praise or by a lampooning of practices that are alien; and the bards among us, knowing who at last must pay the piper, have been very busy to satirize rusticity in this nation.

They have learned in general that they must praise the metropolis or, if that is too strong a task for them, that they must deride its antithesis. Rusticity does not command the newest capers, whether of ballroom, gallery, or grave-side, and in many instances it does not apparently greatly care. Yet, with all of its backwardness, it is too widely dispersed geographically, too difficult to subdue politically, too residual, somehow, deep in the spirits of most

Americans, for it to be ignored blandly as one ignores the back-ward, or distressingly *forward,* submerged majority in the great cities. Rusticity is a palpable form that may be flayed, for its out-landishness, for the delectation of the dancers.

"But it is not sweet," the poem continues, "with nimble feet, to dance upon the air," and it may be worth inquiring whether or not the contemporary metropolis carries, along with its many manifest and undeniable virtues, any contrary drifts that may be, at the lightest, of the kind that will bear watching, or, at the gravest, plainly disruptive and fatal. If the principle of metropoli-tanism is basically parasitic, that is bad. If it testifies to man that he is paramount in the natural world, it testifies falsely, leading its dupes to a folly too presumptuous to wring tears from any but the most maudlin of angels. If it implies, through an accelerated enactment of humane undertakings, be they never so numerous nor so vast, that the validity of humane undertakings rests in their size and number, and not in their quality, the spirit in which they are performed—in that case, the principle of metropolitanism is, then, again a false witness.

It is at least arguable that any metropolis is largely parasitic in nature. "But so," the urban apologist might retort, "is a great part of all the spectacular distinction up till now in the world's history—it has all been in a sense the fruit of exploitation." Per-haps so, and perhaps distinction must continue to derive its sustenance as of old. In all events, *somehow,* distinction must be striven for—but this is not to say that the exploiter can dare, ever, at the cost of his soul, to be ruthless, or to be uninspired by a pervading humility and by a sense of his obligation to everything that makes his excellence possible.

The main issue here is to know whether or not the American metropolis senses this humility, this obligation. This much is observable: that there is no end of bitter or supercilious metro-politan talk about the nigglingness and dullness and stupidity and cruelty of non-metropolitan existence—no end of it. And this, too, is observable: that there is more bitter and supercilious talk still when it is suggested that there is an obligation upon the cities to help remedy the conditions which seem to them so heinous. They will accede, now, to the building of passable cross-country highways, for reasons hard to think altruistic. They have so far not widely and generously acceded to the establishment, with tax-money, of free medical attention to the rural indigent (and free medical attention to the urban indigent is largely self-protective). Nor have they acceded to the establishment, from the same funds, of rural libraries, or of schools in rural communities as expensively operated (N.B., *expensively* is the word used, not *sensibly*) as schools in urban communities. This is parasitism of a bad sort, indeed, warranted to kill.

It is evident that man should conquer when he can the often inert and impassive and sometimes fierce and aggressive opposition that nature offers to man's best development. He thinks that he has made substantial progress toward that end. But it is in all conscience a slight progress, and the beam of deterministic science by which he has worked his marvels, and which he believes will enable him to work greater and greater marvels in the future, is the same beam that discloses to him, at the end of all his struggles —if it can disclose anything more tangible than star-dust—a dark and dead and icy world, revolving through frozen vacuity and death and darkness only.

Nor is it set forth in the canon that that Close will spare the towers of Manhattan any more than it does the tin roofs of Gopher Prairie. It will not do, then, if man wishes to avoid absurdity, for him to be cocky in the face of nature except within very definite limitations. And it is easier, if one has money, as an intellectual must, and if one will but stay indoors mostly, as one will, to confuse Manhattan with the island valley of Avalon, where climatic conditions are said to be so agreeable, than it is to make the same confusion in connection with Gopher Prairie. If Romance were the order of the day among the metropolitan intelligentsia, the delusion might be thought of as justifying itself. But Romance, it has been remarked, is a vagrant now, on the town pretty definitely; and the firm realist would do well to pack himself off to a place likely to keep him more persistently reminded of the possible pain and certain futility ahead of him. Or if Religion were the order of the day; but Religion . . .

The essential thing about humane endeavor is not how large it is nor how ready nor even how effective. The essential thing about it is how human it is. That is in fact the essential thing about anything. And it is not the business of man to shape his humanity to the mechanical devices that he has often largely by accident brought into existence. That effort, now vigorously undertaken, must be always vain, and unless all signs fail it leads inevitably beyond mere fruitlessness straight to a torture-chamber that can and will swallow-in all of us in a trice. Unless mankind can subject to his humanity the fiendish war engines he has made, there are odds, and high ones, that these engines will not stop till they have annihilated him.

And there is another subjection for him to accomplish—less sensational, but in the long run as important—one more immediately relevant to a comparison of urban and rural attitudes. He must subject to his humanity the moderately effective sociological agencies that his dwelling in congested areas has forced him to set up. These agencies are evil by as much as they are mechanical, and they are largely mechanical.

Mr. Robert Frost has written a poem in which he tells how a field-hand gives over some necessary hoeing he was about, in order to walk over to the roadside and pass the time of day with an acquaintance of his who was riding by and who had stopped to speak to him. The hoeing could have been finished before dark, and there was much work of another sort for the man to do next morning; it distressed him to be obliged to stop. But he felt himself obliged. The hoeing was important, and if immediate efficiency is the ultimate goal, it was most important. But if there is another goal more desirable than immediate efficiency—a constant, undimmed recognition of the common humanity of man and man, which alone can lead to any worthy and lasting efficiency—in that case, the salutation was mandatory.

That recognition *is* mandatory, and it must be kept constant and undimmed. It must be achieved; and a cash bonus hurled across a fence in lieu of it is not adequate. How possible is it to maintain such a recognition in a great metropolis? Is the human capacity in that regard limited, or not limited? Just how many of his fellows, with their individual joys and woes, can any individual burden himself with emotionally and not be crucified? Alas, human capacity *is* limited, and the answer is, not many. If the individuals whom one encounters are day after day after day quite innumerable, it is only the spiritual immunity to human encounter, which automatically develops, that can fend off quite madness. John Doe, dropped dead on Main Street, means half the town out, to condole with widow Mary—and cakes and pies and jams out, for hers and her children's comfort. John Doe, dropped dead on Broadway, is another story. Curses, that in front of *me,* he fell—a minute more and I would have passed—I, who had business to do, and who am late now for the movie-opening. This is necessary; it is sacrilege; it cannot be otherwise.

All of this is pertinent to the countless charts that American sociologists are forever drawing up to show the relative progress, by which they mean merit, of various sections of states or cities. These charts will show, for example, how on a basis of 214 items considered, Detroit, in an arbitrary scale of 100, will rate 89.7293, while Natchez is admonished to be ashamed of itself with its rating of only 21.0063. Now if these figures are to be taken at their face value, life in Detroit is more likely to turn out worthy and happy than life in Natchez—by exactly as much as 89.7293 is greater than 21.0063. But why are the figures to be taken at their face value? There is no partisan of Natchez who would not wish that his town might have more of the 214 items that are thought to be, and perhaps are, so desirable for people to have. But it is permissible to wonder if the deep-laid assumptions of its citizenry are not also properly to be considered in striking any town's true value. Is the assumption of the common humanity of man with man more palpably discernible in Detroit or in Natchez? And if that item should properly be considered, should it be given the weight merely of any other of the new 215 items—like that, say, of the number of automobiles per capita, or the number of *Saturday Evening Posts* subscribed to—or should it be given a weight as great as that of the other 214 items combined? That, perhaps, the sociologists can determine mathematically.

In the meantime, the showing of Natchez must not be set down as finally ignominious. People *must* know people, and act toward them, all—high and low, old and young, wise and foolish—as if they were people and not mechanisms. Association with a limited group of "congenial" persons, however intimate, is no satisfactory substitute for the thing that is mandatory. An association of that sort is an easy snare to fall into in a great city, and a very pleasant snare, but its resolute hinges are forged with provincialism. Nor will it do to limit one's intimate associations—a feat hardly possible in villages—to a group of approximately one's own age. That snare has worked overtime, and surely, among the cosmopolitan intellectuals of New York. Away from home, and *free* and *proud* and *hale* (twenty-five to fifty, say, in age), they fall into the easy course of seeing mostly people like themselves; and they conclude, naturally, and fervently, out of their own experience, that a lack of money is the only thing standing between all mankind and all that mankind could ever wish for.

That is a very stupid conclusion for an intellectual to come to. For there are the impotence and sensitiveness of youth and the impotence and sensitiveness of age, that are doubtless immutable; and there is stifling pain, impregnable in the hearts of most mortal

beings; and there is the hideous snipping-apart of fond relationships by absence and by meant or unmeant cruelty and by im-
placable death. It takes a fool of high order to imagine that money
may mitigate these curses much. Not without symbolic meaning,
nor without the transcendental direction of some brooding deity,
one is half-convinced, are most walls in New York broken across
with a handwriting that is plainly read: WATCH YOUR STEP.

The same warning, of course, might with some, if not with as
much, justification be written at village drugstores and at country
courthouses and crossroads the nation over. The isolation of
country living that has seemed oppressive to many people, the
lack of devices such as electric light and water facilities that seem
to many people more important than any other matter whatever—
these are in our day remedied or in way of being so. It is not now
on these scores, if it ever was, that country people most need to
change their ways.

But if city people have injudiciously pushed the virtue of
alertness into a sort of chronic hysteria, it is also true that country
people have often not cherished that virtue enough for it to
operate among them at its proper strength. And if city people have
pushed the virtue of imagination into an abstractedness of thinking that finds it easier to fix itself upon A.D. 1996 than upon 1936,
and upon a plan for at least continental redemption than upon a
useful and current deed in one's own ward—if this bad thing is
true, it is also true that country people are, from some standpoints,
distressingly indisposed to concern themselves, in public matters,
with a point in time as distant as next year or with a point in
space more distant than their own land-lines. And if the virtue of
tolerance has grown so great in cities that the mere alienage, the
mere newness, of a thing is taken as enough to commend it wholly,
it is also true that in the country the same qualities in a thing are
frequently thought of as enough to condemn it wholly. *Watch
Your Step* is a good saying and though it certainly needs crying
less urgently through the open land than it does up and down the
length of Broadway, it is worth remembering everywhere.

What it most needs to be shouted about in the country is the
present disposition of the country to ape the city—not to take over
in modified form some of the hysteria, abstractedness, and license
of the city, and temper them down into a proper alertness, imagination, and tolerance, but to take those qualities over bodily, to
imitate the city, as nearly as may be, without reservation. That is
not the way of improvement but of degeneration. It entails, what-

ever all the literary henchmen of the metropolis may say, be they novelists, dramatists, or "critics," an active going out after spuriousness and vulgarity. It implies, more basically, the spectacle of independence doing obeisance before parasitism, of sanity turning presumptuous in the face of nature, and of humanity turning infidel to loving-kindness.

To Suit Your Quilt

THERE USED TO BE a proverb, "Stretch your legs to suit your quilt." That advice can be thought mighty craven. Better, one might say, reverse it. Yet in certain moods a man may take it as it went originally.

In any case, the proverb is interesting with a meaning that would be achieved by emphasizing its next-to-the-last word, "Stretch your legs to suit *your* quilt." Very many of us are always busy stretching or shrinking ourselves to suit somebody's quilt besides our own.

A fashion arises in Paris, France, let us say, in response to the needs of life in that famous capital. Consider "Realism," for example—realism, that is, that is hard and bitter, not the full-cycle, ripe, and dropping-from-the-bough type of realism that thinks of itself as beating the arrival-drums of Salvation. That early realism developed as an appropriate response to the decrepitude and cynicism of an ancient and heavily urbanized society. The next news one heard, it was being acclaimed by all the frontiers as precisely the answer to *their* exigencies. . . .

Another instance of our shaping ourselves to fit the necessities of somebody else, a minute but pertinent instance, is the tendency of us Georgians to fall in, these days, with a social usage of people who live in the vast cities. We will look a dear friend straight in the face—Daniel Boone, say, talking to David Crockett—and announce that we are invited "out" for the evening. Out, and nothing more. That is all well enough for Mr. Ward McAllister, or such-like, who have been obliged to abandon even the relics of neighborliness, but for us—fortunately living in X-ton or in Y-ville, or surely rooted for the most part in those precincts—for us to confide to our friends that we are invited "out" instead of

Editorial, *The Georgia Review*, IV, (Spring, 1950), 1-2.

invited to the Does' or Rowes' is somehow either vain or ill mannered or adolescent. For it is certain that our auditor either knows or will know soon about the Does' party; it is certain that we should *assume* his interest, as we do that of people before whom we refrain from whispering; it is certain that if we are adult and within-the-law he will hardly undertake to restrain us from the party, be it at Does' or Rowes'.

Of course the instances of our acceding to fashion rather than to sense are innumerable, but it may be entertaining to name a few more of them. Back of our need for transportation facilities remains obviously the need for something to transport. But the current disposition is to take the commodity for granted, to cherish the means of distributing it—and we have in consequence schools more devoted to methods than to content, we have scholars talking in such a way as to merit the verdict that a country doctor made upon one scholar recently, "plenty articulate, nothing to say."

So, also, in reference to something besides intelligence, people will say that the village, Fort Z, "though small, is lovely, even if it is not exciting." Is the great Louvre Venus, then, less lovely than the Sphinx, being smaller? Was Herrick's Corinna-parish more or less exciting than London proved to the great Nijinsky for the thirty mad and melancholy years he spent there before his recent death? A place is dull or not as one perceives it. A lad from Buffalo once said that he found Georgia interesting because Georgia people could have more fun with fewer gadgets than any other people he had ever heard of. Meant as a mild commendation, this verdict was in fact precious eulogy.

An advertisement in the *Progressive Farmer* says that the razing of thirty acres of slums and the erection of two vast new housing-projects has made 31,000 people happy.—This is fashionable talk. How happy are these people? Will they be happy long? An advertisement in the *New York Times* suggests that racial segregation must be abandoned because it is costly. Costly? Like Education? The current "Polls" regarding all sorts of things are eagerly followed. Yet who will say that they necessarily mean anything beyond the snap-judgments of a number of snap-judges?—unless, of course, it is held that one man's opinion is as good as another's. But perhaps that *is* held.

If it is . . . If it is . . . Who, if it is, need say what?

~§~

A Broader Field of Usefulness

IN OUR TIME, people are obliged to sacrifice much to their specialty. Often they rid themselves in this way of some of the main functions of their humanity, to become mechanisms only— except for interests of racial and individual continuance and of motion-through-space. Even the amateur gardener must, as he relaxes, work *hard* and with one flower alone, insensitive to any other flower. For all the roads of the mind, it is held, should lead to one Rome, and to one part of Rome—to what part does not matter, provided it is one part only. It seems scarcely possible that the moral force requisite for an organized society can persist on such a basis.

It may be unmannerly to think of paradox in connection with a time that has as its chief aim the aim of being direct and free of conflicting impulses. Yet, in the midst of the current ado about *one* goal, there is ado also about cosmopolitanism, catholicity, integration, and centralization. Somehow, under the flag of thoroughness, we even conceive of a specialist whose exclusive business it is to synthesize elements that are wholly unfamiliar to him. Above all, committed to the centripetal, we are fascinated by the idea of a "broader field of usefulness." Poets seem always to be announcing that life is a dusty book or a piston or some other unexpected thing. Possibly in our day life is also conceived to be a funnel, each man holding the little end to himself in deference to concentration (and giving out) and the big end away from him in deference to catholicity (and receiving).

So far as Georgia goes, one of the distressing results of the passion for a "broader field of usefulness" is the chronic migration hence of many good people. Always, of course, it is possible to believe in the happy state of people who are too far away to be

Editorial, *The Georgia Review*, II (Winter, 1948), 375-377.

closely observed. But with us, the disposition to paint with glory every remote thing has proceeded to lengths that are absurd, for all their being sadly effective. The wise do not take part in this baleful business, but plenty of school teachers and preachers 'do, and newspaper people, and so do others, all the way to members of the various Leagues for Social Betterment—if, indeed, any *other* Leagues continue in existence.

One Georgian who long taught at the University in Athens had an experience lately that bore upon all this sharply. In London, where he had been living for a year or so, he chanced one day upon one of his older Athens colleagues, accompanied, if it was not the other way round, by Madame. It was a kind of displaced home-coming for these three, and they decided to have lunch together. There was much reminiscence.

"Please tell me," said the younger man to the older, "please tell me about Andrew Barton—he was a youngster of great promise— do you hear from him at all?"

Madame flung herself well nigh across the table. Said Madame, "Of course we hear—who doesn't? Can it be that you don't know about Andrew?" Her eyes rolled and her long forefinger was held high, and her lips framed a whisper, "Up yonder!" The inquirer was becomingly grave, and he was about to remark on the pity of Andrew's having been cut off so young. But he was wrong. "Detroit," whispered the lady, "yes, sir, Detroit! Oh, what a broad, broad field of usefulness!"

And it was so of Charlie Dawson and Ed Fortson, their Circles-of-Paradise, named, respectively, Akron and Pittsburgh. "Please tell me," the younger man asked the older one—and Madame told. Till at last, "What of George Hudson?"

Madame lifted instantly her hands and her shoulders, and cast down her eyes. She had heard little of George lately—and that little was apparently too much. She conceded that George had seemed also to be a lad of promise—but what had he done, that handsome and brilliant creature, as soon as he got his diploma? He had gone straight back to live in Waycross, where he had grown up, "Yes, sir, Waycross, and you'd have thought Atlanta would have been the *least* thing to satisfy him. So you can see," she continued, "how it is that all of George's really progressive friends feel that he is a kind of lost leader, one who would not walk breastforward, one who turned his back upon his broader field of usefulness."

Now if gold, as Madame surely was, can rust so lamentably, what can one hope for from common metal like Tina, Rachel, and

Hattie? These girls are surely all of them committed to every standard Saint, but they have no illusions about the relative worth of one who rules a city and one who conquers his own spirit, no illusions about escaping conformity to this world and being transformed, by the renewing of their minds, to prove the perfect will of God. For what do all those things have to do with the realistic approach and with the broader field of usefulness, both of which are so fashionable?

Of course, the proper answer is that the Saints have everything to do with both realism and capaciousness, as well as with the opposites of those things and all matters intermediate. And all these are as rightly pertinent to George Hudson in Waycross, Ivan Johnson in Dalton, and Karl Lawton in Thomasville as they are to Mr. Winston Churchill in London—and it is those three, and the likes of them, who must more than anybody else justify, if they are to be justified at all, not only the University in Athens but every other educational agency in these parts.

All Will Be Well

COUNTING ON the future has immemorially been man's most delightful sport. For a long time, most hopes as to this earthly life were limited to small matters like apple pie for dinner, and so on. Truly heroic delights, of the universal-love, golden-harp sort, were thought of as far off indeed, beyond a Crevasse nobody would tackle till he was obliged to. In that far, fair land, everything was reported as to the heart's desire, but anticipatory reports were overwhelmingly more numerous than reports based on observation.

Now our particular era is one that is proudly committed to the principle of observation, checked and checked and checked. This fact would seem to make us wary of unsustained pronouncement based mainly on sweet hope, especially in view of our knowledge that Tuesday's sweet hope is very often different from Monday's. That is how it might seem to make us, not how it makes us.

As things go, our own Tuesday, like all foregoing days, weaves its fantasy at will, and weaves it boldly for a coming day this side the Crevasse referred to. That is, for a Wednesday that may well be subject to observation, tomorrow, or on the other side of the Time-Curve. Boldly? Brashly, perhaps, as to how Wednesday will really turn out, and more brashly still as to how Wednesday's children may themselves yearn to turn out.

What is possibly Tuesday's best justification for such exercises— that they may keep Tuesday less painfully mad than it would be without them—nobody of course mentions. That is surely all right. Mentioning it would manifestly break down a spell that is practically useful. In the same way, it would break down something useful to dwell much upon the idea that Corporal Brown is in nearly every regard superior to Lieutenant Smith.

For all that, in a certain highly respectable way of thinking,

Editorial, *The Georgia Review*, II (Fall, 1948), 261-262.

Brown does top Smith immeasurably, whatever may be their rank-ing. On this dangerous but diverting plane of thought, all people who are by way of being grown people are bound sometimes to travel. There, one may on occasion wonder about some of the bright new approaches that are periodically acclaimed. Do they not perhaps run wholly counter to the old and monotonous ap-proach that is the only one known to be open throughout to traf-fic, or even likely to be open, ever?

For example, suppose that the National Association for the Ad-vancement of Coastal Places should decide to promote a Bee-Line Causeway between Savannah and Lisbon, with adequate draw-bridges. Surely such a thing should be, and to think less might well be craven! It is almost possible to hear the oratory about this mighty project, about its long existence as a dream only in the head of a seer of a scientist, about its eventually capturing the invincible imagination of Man! The British may perhaps prove timorous about the effect of all this upon the ocean currents and consequently upon their climate. But great undertakings are for the stout-hearted and the daring, and this undertaking *must* be accomplished.

Certainly such a Causeway, if only its well-wishers will not pro-mote it too rapidly, thus stirring stupid and ignorant fears and prejudices, certainly such a Causeway—in response to the slow but sure processes of Evolution and Education—must almost imper-ceptibly within the next few years arise, arise like an exhalation from the vasty deep or fall like a Raleigh-coat from the cosmos, all to the end that the Queen of Portugal and General James Edward Oglethorpe may be quickly married, the lucky things, to live to-gether happily forever and ever afterward! And who can say that that would not be nice?

Or, for another example, suppose . . . suppose . . .

꧁ ꧂

Cats and Queens

THERE IS a current fashion of talking much about planning, and very specially about over-all planning. Little is said about wise planning, about the once-extolled lamp of experience, about projecting a line from the past through the present to determine the future. But it is not foolhardy to suggest that poor planning may be worse than no planning at all, and that for the dim-sighted, a numerous category, poor planning is the easier to fall into as the areas considered become vaster. And it is troublesome to remember that much of the heroic planning devised by people whom we have endowed with power, on the theory of their being not dim-sighted, threatens often to turn out grievously.

An example of all this is the American colleges. Set up to promote clear and discriminating thought, they have recently led the pack in something that all sorts of people, from the common ant upward, have historically deprecated—a disposition to assume an end forever to all rainy days. So far as anybody can tell, the colleges seem to have anticipated a ceaseless horde of G.I. students who would be more and more wildly gluttonous for all of the colleges' offerings. Surely the colleges do not seem to have been sufficiently alert as to the contrary possibility.

Until lately, everywhere one looked in our interesting newspapers, there were numerous pictures with a legend somewhat like this: *Mr. and Mrs. Joe Veteran and their three children, Joe, Jennie, and Eleanor—Mr. Veteran is a first year pre-medical student— pose at the steps of their trailer residence on the campus at Shangrila. Mrs. Veteran plans to help support the family by growing vegetables on top of their trailer. . . .* But the newspapers are not carrying such pictures any more. Now a smart cat could have told a foolish Queen all along that all this would grow tiresome soon,

Editorial, *The Georgia Review*, III (Spring, 1949), 1-2.

and that then, surely without reference to sensible or stupid, Mr. Veteran's family would go about their devices elsewhere—and that Mr. Veteran's successors would likely save themselves altogether the trouble of a stop at that particular "concession."

And now that we are nearly half way in the century, as Lord Byron reported concerning Waterloo, we have hurrying-to-and-fro, gathering tears, tremblings of distress, cheeks all pale, and so forth. The G. I. tuition fees are mitigated, oh, mitigated, and London Bridge is falling down over all America—in the South, of course, but throughout America even beyond the South, where people have no immunity for fallen bridges; and that is indeed something to talk about.

Plainly, none of this is spoken in disparagement of Veterans. They are young and in many cases beautiful and charming, and they have been generally held, very recently in their lives, much in need of direction—so much, actually, in need of direction that the nation set up laws for them, with teeth, to tell them whether they should or should not at all go into the armed services. The Veterans, then, are not to blame. Possibly nobody is to blame. After all, most of us in this world are tarred with the same stick. And it *has* been a good party!

The main people to blame are the people who confuse their bills for high living with those that stem from an over-generosity to pious causes. The first, hard way to escape blame is to be honest in one's own mind, to examine narrowly everything that is contrived by earthly men and proclaimed by them to be wise and powerful. That is what the colleges are first of all supposed to teach, and if they will do that, they will do a great good part by the world, whether or not they receive all the recognition from the world that, as human entities, they naturally wish for.

‿§§∾

A Bet on the Bottom Man

HENRY ADAMS once said there was no reasoning with a Congressman, that a Congressman was like a hog, to be affected only by a lick on the snout. That was sharp talk, true enough and picturesque enough to be remembered. What Henry the Great said and thought about the Presidents of this Republic and about its countless ordinary citizens may never have been so crisply stated. Possibly that fastidious arbiter felt it more prudent, in view of the laws against obscenity, not to loose his aphoristic faculties too freely always. This likelihood has been little reckoned with. It has suited us of late to think poorly of Congressmen, and we have chosen bright sayings to sustain our mood. But there is surely another side to all this.

When one of the best of people, one of the best people one knows at all, opens his lips and says something senseless, there is not a great deal to do about it. For example, a man reports that an elderly shock-victim suddenly began to rehearse in detail a long forgotten episode of his childhood. "Nothing strange about that, whatever," says one of the man's best-of-people; "it is easy to explain that—that was only a natural manifestation of how the mind under stress turns back upon its past." As though that explanation explained anything!

It is marvelous then—or not, according to one's attitude—that in the largest affairs, over great reaches of time and space and through every order of society, there will be a season when all the winds of the mind will blow one way preponderantly, and another season when they will blow another way. In one area, they will blow hard and fast, and in another area lightly. But in both areas they will be moving, in general, at the same time in the same direction.

Editorial, *The Georgia Review*, II (Spring, 1948), 1-2.

During the 1920's and 30's, following the war that was to make us safe for Democracy, we began to feel that however safe we might be for *it,* Democracy was of all things the one least likely to be safe for us. So we—we, that is, the common run of western-society earthlings—apparently felt without any very clear reference to our having autocratic or democratic backgrounds, to our depending upon Moscow or Berlin, or upon London or Washington.

For if dictatorships became increasingly the rule in Europe, certainly we in America, for all our beating of the tom-toms about Democracy, leaned far with the prevailing wind in our disposition to center more and more power in fewer and fewer men. We came to think of every laudable thing, in no matter what realm of activity, as having been with the highest skill contrived and made operative by one Great-Strong-and-Virtuous Man for the benefit of the small-weak-and-virtuous men at the other end of the line— this, in spite of all that could be done by the average-strong-but-vicious men in the middle. Observe the zeal of all of us in pursuit of this mania, particularly the zeal of those seraphim, the colleges and the press, in their persistent effort through press-bureaus, the abracadabra of mass psychology, etc., to build up and transform any workaday midget of their choice into a legendary redeemer.

Observe, in the realm of politics, our reverence for the unique Executive as our champion and our contempt for the more populous, and accordingly, one might think, more democratic, Congress. And as though this impulse were not already strong enough, we have seen it intensified in our day by a renewed muttering of some old, nearly forgotten "charms" that were invented —usefully, long ago—to curb a Congress that itself threatened to become obsessive.

So, in our current world that talks vigorously, if not with consistent stress, of liberty, equality, and fraternity, it has come to be thought that there is no vocation so despicable as to be a representative of the American people in Washington. For even a still damp, young graduate will tell you, if you will give him the chance, about his last year's instructor—"I forget the little fellow's name, but he was a swell guy, and nearly finished his Ph.D."—who purely doted, purely and utterly doted, on baiting Congressmen, "making fools of them, see?"

Fallen, fallen, fallen, oh, John Randolph; Now that is indeed one dark and sullen, mean, deep, hidden lake to lie prone upon, despised and derided, year in, year out, forever!

What the South Figured: 1865-1914

WHEN THE Civil War ended, practically everybody in the South was violently embittered toward the North, and the Reconstruction of the next few years made that bad state of affairs worse. Most people did not justify their emotion on any lofty grounds. They knew only that many a boy who had been alive was securely dead. Drunk from the standard propaganda of war, they frantically repudiated the equally standard propaganda that had maddened the enemy. They hated, and they focused their hatred upon the tangible agency of their discomfort, namely, the government and people of the United States. It was a simple and ardent hatred; they would cherish it, they said, until they died, and pass it down as a master heritage to their remotest descendants. So much passion, so little reasoned out, was, of course, bound to spend itself.

For Southerners are not after all gratifyingly distinguished from the universal breed of worldlings. They find it difficult to concern themselves faithfully about anything that is not tangible and present. One item that *was* tangible and present at the close of the War, and that has continued so these seventy years, was the fact that about half of the Southern population was black. That fact all Southerners have been obliged to reckon with for a long time. It has effectively blocked all programs of either friends or enemies of the South for making the South uniform with the rest of the nation, and its effectiveness in that regard must still be acknowledged—whether gladly or sorrowfully.

If the negro had not been among us, if the War had disposed of the racial issue as it did of the slavery issue, the complete Americanization of the one-time Confederacy would undoubtedly have proceeded more rapidly. The discrepancies between South-

From *The Southern Review,* III (Autumn, 1937) , 360-367.

ern and national conviction about most other matters have tended
to disappear with the passing of time. These discrepancies were
based most generally upon an abstraction or upon something
which was daily more and more remote in point of time, upon
things, in short, that the mass of Southerners were not equipped
to perceive as sharply relevant.

The people, the great mass of them, are scarcely *ever so*
equipped—no matter where. Not a great beast, surely, as one
notable American branded them, the people are nonetheless not
Aristotle. It is as well to concede everything at once and to say
that the mass of people in the South have been, always, in certain
regards, not merely worldlings, but American worldlings. As such,
they grew weary of and quickly discarded the hard doctrine of a
group of native prophets that the South must continue odd and
peculiar, because of some abstruse ethics. As such, they grew weary
of and gradually discarded the soft doctrine of a group of Southern
patriots that the South must continue odd, no matter how far
into the future, because of things that happened years and years—
and many years—ago. As such, they united to repudiate those
politicians, the Populists, whose denunciation of the South's
oppressor, Wall Street, did not compensate for other qualities of
theirs which Southerners could not stomach. But when the Southern promoters came into prominence in the 1880's, the South
embraced them eagerly, let prophets and patriots wrangle as they
would. How else was a people, broken by poverty and sick of
surliness, to receive the Redeemers who came promising the gain
of so much, the loss of so little?

The full rancor of hatred, almost universal in 1865, soon
proved too heavy a burden for the ordinary man to sustain. What
most Southerners felt, or came to feel, was that they were desperately poor, while the North was becoming almost desperately
rich. They wanted to be rich too. For a long time they had
ascribed all of their wretchedness to the Federal Government. If
that government was both omnipotent and immutable, the implications of thinking it also inexorably hostile, were too dispiriting
for endurance. Inimical it certainly seemed to be—what with the
tariff, and all; and all. But Lowell, though he felt obliged to
snub the Virginian Gildersleeve in Baltimore, when they fell to
talking about the War some years after it was over, had persuaded
himself that he might without obloquy eulogize in poetry the
Virginian Washington. Perhaps, then, there might be magnanim-
ity in the North after all. Gradually, the wounded and weakened

South, for the first time in many years, found itself ready to tolerate the ordeal of self-criticism.

Benjamin Franklin had been a mighty name in Carolina as well as in Pennsylvania, and the Southerners connected very closely in their minds the idea of virtue and the idea of prosperity. It was not comforting to a people so minded to compare the tax returns of their region with those of the country at large. Perhaps the old ways were not good ways, after all; surely the section following the new ones was being more opulently rewarded. Perhaps they should change their ways, as a matter of moral duty. And besides, the very idea of change has its unvarying fascination. In any case, though reconditioning requires capital, the Southerners of the 1880's changed considerably. They learned to build the stylish but disagreeable houses of the period. They uprooted much boxwood and gardenia. All agreed that talking was cheap, but that it took money to buy land, which was to say—so strong is tradition even in a progressive's heart—that it took money to get the thing one must have to be really a man, to be at all self-respecting and happy. And all of that, extended, came to mean that with money anybody could be all that one could care to be, without it, nobody could be anything. Perhaps the decision was a just one, but thinking so involves the discrediting of such history and of most sages.

There was no lack of protest against the new impulse. For not even at the very close of the War did all of the Southern dervish-whirlers whirl only for the comfort that movement at the moment offered them. A few of them, prophets, in a sense, actuated by regrets and fears of a cosmic order, executed figures too intricate to be widely understood or valued. Intoning the names of Jefferson and Calhoun, moving to the rhythms of a remorseless logic, they were fatefully out of unison with their fellows. They thought that the proper basis of hatred lay not in the fact that they had suffered deprivation of life and prosperity. Such considerations were ephemeral. These men believed that, in spite of all they could do, a treachery had been accomplished against what America had been supposed to stand for, and against the future of mankind. The late war had seemed to them a test between the strength of men and the strength of things, between a spiritual philosophy and a materialistic philosophy; and they were convinced that the result of it would be the extinction of everything they valued. They felt that more-and-more and not better-and-better was the inevitable motto of the new order, and they be-

lieved that such a premise was compatible only with the standardized and the un-polite, the essentially un-human.

Through the arbitrament of battle (how they loved that
phrase!) had gone against them, they would not in their minds
yield to blasphemy. If that course only remained open to them in
their traditional home, they would move on—to Brazil, or Australia, or where-not, to the ends of the earth, to set up there anew
a nation to their desire. The old Jerusalem had fallen, but in
some green and pleasant land they would build another. Counsel
to this effect they gave freely, but there was little mood in the
South of 1866 for either chariots of fire or for mental fight. The
folk loyalties to home were too strong, the folk aggressiveness too
weak, for the counsel to be widely followed. They were sincere
prophets beyond a doubt, and whether their doctrine was wise or
foolish did not surely play much part in the South's final rejection
of it. It was a hard doctrine, one that assumed an energy of mind
and body and a willingness to combat the trend of the world that
ordinary men are not likely to command.

But well into the 1890's one or another of these prophets, most
notably C. C. Jones, of Georgia, kept thundering from time to
time, with pertinent citation of his reasons, that he did not like
what was happening. A patriarch, outmoded sartorially and in
the rigidness of his social and literary habits, Jones occupied a
position that was even in the South hardly any longer tenable. It
was a position held and defended at times by Edmund Burke and
Cobbett and Carlyle and Ruskin, by Jefferson and Calhoun, by
Emerson and Lincoln. It was not the position of Jeremy Bentham
nor of Lord Macaulay nor of the economist Francis Walker nor
of Jay Gould. It implied a doctrine residing somewhere in the
neighborhood of the philosophic absolutes, which was easily
forgotten in a welter of tangibilities. Emerson and Lincoln had
forgotten it in their agitation over slavery, and had thrown their
weight into the battle on the side to which they were inherently
hostile. If *they* were confused, what of the common citizen? He was
fuddled utterly; and besides, *one* phase of the doctrine that came
clear to him—namely, that it is impossible both to have cake and
eat it—he would never accede to.

The prophets of Jones's stamp found few disciples, but the
patriotic organizations of men and women, formed shortly after
the War and still operative, have very clearly impeded the full
Americanization of our continent. These societies, formed to
perpetuate the memory of those who had died for the Confeder-

acy, would not abide anything that suggested error on the part of their lost saints. They expressed themselves with trembling voices and sometimes went so far—very far indeed, it was thought —as to desire to be excused from Heaven, when their time came, if Yankees were to be among the residents. But sentiment and reminiscence inspired these patriots' every utterance, and those qualities, as things went, were fated for eclipse. The canon which told of the survival of the fit and of perfection through evolution does not greatly exalt either sentiment or reminiscence. And, to tell the truth, the rituals of the patriots *were* monotonous. The gentlemen who uttered them were aging, and the ladies who uttered them were, when all was done and said—though God bless them—ladies. They were all entitled to veneration, and let nobody doubt it, but the common citizen could with equanimity fancy in his heart, if not openly, how life might be if the old rituals were shifted, or even silenced.

The Populists were not essentially either old or feminine or sentimental or reminiscent. They counseled salvation for the South, not as the prophets had done by geographic or at least cultural withdrawal, nor, as the patriots had done, by cultural withdrawal merely. They offered to save the South along with the West by the brash expedient of forcing the nation to have regard for those two dominions in the shaping of its economics. But if the demigod Calhoun had failed in that aim, it was hard to prophesy success for Tom Watson or Ben Tillman. Hope deferred makes the heart flaccid. And if the Populists were really intent, by curbing Wall Street, to help the South, it was remarkable that they were as likely as not to come from Springfield, Illinois, a place which, suggesting Abraham Lincoln, was not inescapably more sympathetic with the South than another place which suggested, say, Horace Greeley. Worst of all, the Southern Populists were by and large poor and ignorant and humble—humble, many of them, in that final stage of humility which is cockiness. They were tenant-farmers and such-like, long trodden upon and at last turning—radicals. Hope deferred had made their hearts brass, for a moment. And nobody could endorse brass. The Southern people were determined to be nice—surely, if they kept well and if it didn't rain, and if nothing happened.

Sidney Lanier was nice, and Henry Grady was too. Cable and Walter Page were in their way also nice. All of them loved the South passionately, and wished it well. They were the promoters of the South. Lanier's testimony, given, mostly, before the smoke had fully cleared from Atlanta and Columbia, was that he admired a slow-moving society and believed the North had been right in the late war, that he adored the spiritual and abhorred the commercial, and did not see how, without wealth, a society could come to anything. Cable was as intense, and as logical, if not as prescient as the ululating and ineffectual prophets. He did not want merely a new South. He believed, if the territory below the Potomac and the Ohio was to be redeemed, that everything which the *idea*, the traditional *concept*, of the South had stood for must be obliterated. He wanted a no-South, did that clerk, a world quite neatly standardized. It was a drastic position, not mollifying to patriots, but as long as he talked of *ideas*, the people at large were not greatly ruffled. When he grew specific with reference to the negro, advocating not racial equality merely, but racial amalgamation, the people at large felt that something very bad indeed had happened, and that they were no longer under obligation to be nice at all. They were very harsh; and Cable shifted his residence to New England.

There are not many examples in history of a man more fortunate than Henry Grady. Beautiful and charming and benign, he had an intelligence superior enough to activate his contemporaries without being so profound or original as to baffle them. And he was born at precisely the right place and time. The old prophets he could not placate; Jones, in his own Georgia, deprecated him. But even Jones—very old by Grady's time, and an acknowledged "pessimist," incomprehensible to Grady and to most others—even Jones he could dismiss graciously. To everybody except the prophets he seemed celestially glamorous. He offered a moral justification to his countrymen for the abandonment of animosities that had become burdensome; he told them that it was evil rather than virtuous—as evil as it had become irksome—to hold themselves alien to a good world that was surely growing better. Not to believe it growing better was unthinkable. He said that the Lost Cause and God and the spiritual life and home and all ladies and the supremacy of the white race were and should forever be sacred. He said that much of the world's trouble grew out of the malfeasance of capitalists, but that capitalists were not by definition Northerners—though, for that matter, he would be the last man to condemn *any* wealth accumulated by thrift rather than by pillage. He promised his countrymen prosperity—the gathering of innumerable fat crops and the whirring of quite countless spindles.

In the South that Walter Page dealt with, the ancient prophets, Jones and all the rest, were dead and their voices turned to fainted echo; the Populists, never really Southern, lay forgotten under an avalanche of national complacency; the Confederate veterans, if not dead, were nearly dead; the Daughters of the Confederacy had left off their weeping and turned themselves to things that count. Page could, with impunity, speak slightingly of all that all of those groups had essentially represented. But he knew that it would not do to dismiss lightly in the South either God or the negro. Possibly he thought that neither of them mattered very much, but the people he wished to influence were not yet so convinced; and he was a good strategist. He was persuaded that the thing for the South to do was to be like the North, which fundamentally seemed to him, around 1900, as delectable a place as one might reasonably wish for. He thought that education was the means to this end. The North was, in the sense of the word he meant, educated. He had lived in the North for a long time, and he had gathered there from what he saw, apparently, that education carried with it not only wealth and happiness but both individual and social integrity. He had as a young man been a student of the classics, and he professed always to preserve his liking for them. But he had come to know about science, and he was a thoroughgoing optimist.

He knew that the course he was urging upon the South was the course not only of Great America but of all the Western world. To confute the idea that that course might not be a wise one, it was only needful to remember that, in view of its popularity, to doubt it was unthinkable. To most Southerners this logic seemed adequate. Scarcely any of them were ready to exalt to their own status the status of the negro, and only a few were ready to lower to their own status the status of the Deity. Whatever might be the fashions, that was a degree of equalitarianism they would not accept. But perhaps the old rumors of a North, and of a Europe, reconciled to materialism and mongrelism, had been unfounded. With their attitude on this score understood, then, the Southerners too were prepared, if they could be received on such terms, to lend themselves to the great, swift current that they had heard, and could with their eyes see, was moving on, and carrying with it all of the Western world. That current was bound for the future. Accordingly, it seemed necessary to believe in the conscious mind at least, in spite of all misgivings, in spite of occasional weird promptings, that it was destined to lead to sunnier and sunnier skies, past islands that would prove more and more ambrosial, till, possibly—by 1914, say—it would be swirling alongside an ever-extending panorama of always increasing loveliness.

PART II

Of Georgians and Others

✥ஃ✥

Profits and Losses
in the Life of Joel Chandler Harris

AS A YOUNGSTER, Joel Chandler Harris was hard-favoured both in appearance and in circumstance. His mother was of a good family (she was born *Harris*), and she proved to be an excellent woman, but in 1848, without conventional reasons she had left her home in a neighbouring community and come, insolvent, to live in Eatonton. Her mother and her quite new son, Joel—both empty handed—arrived that winter almost simultaneously to keep her company.

Joel grew up slight, short, and red-headed—in a day when red hair was not esteemed. He stuttered and he was very shy and very poor. Yet in that town, a sort of capital of Virginia emigrés, he does not seem to have felt himself oppressed. At school, where a benevolent neighbour paid his tuition, he was bright but not studious, bending his energy as boys' energy is bent normally.

The Georgia county of which Eatonton is capital had in 1850 something over ten thousand people, three-fourths of whom were slaves. The lands were already sadly exhausted, but commercial fertilizers were being introduced, and a cotton factory had been built to employ a hundred labourers. People knew there that the entire system of slavery was being violently assailed the world over, but they remembered the prowess in Washington of Mr. Cobb and Mr. Stephens and Mr. Toombs and thought it unlikely that those gentlemen would let anything happen to Georgia's disadvantage.

There were many people of Northern birth living in Georgia—notably more than in any other Southern state—and they, one noted, tended readily to fall in with Southern ways, abandoning their school-teaching and their merchandizing as soon as they

From *The American Review*, I (April, 1933), 17-35.

found money enough to buy land and slaves. Occasionally one met the contention that Yankees were universally a bad lot; one prominent and wealthy planter had long gone unshaved, and would remain so, he said, till Georgia seceded from the accursed Union once and for all. Ordinary citizens were incapable of such definite conviction; and besides, American anti-monarchist as they were, they believed that there was one king remaining whom Divinity still definitely sponsored: namely, cotton. Even New Englanders would have more discretion than to deal with that King too lightly. On the whole one found one's self more scandalized over the new-fangledness of the Governor, in banning wine from his table, than over the goings-on of W. L. Garrison.

For all young Joe Harris could tell, he was in as stable a world as ever turned. From time to time one heard murmurs of the possibility of a great slave insurrection; but the negroes Joe knew were kindly—the women fetched out cakes for him and the men took him hunting—and above all, there was the statement about racial antagonisms made by an important man in Eatonton. People who are kind to their negroes, this man had been accustomed to say, have no cause ever to be afraid of them.

Joe had no reason to suspect the weakness of that dictum as a solution, and the fact that it was considered a solution is itself interesting. In his innocence the gentleman who promulgated it could not conceive that he might suffer at the hands of someone *else's* slaves—whom, manifestly, he could never have injured. The fact that an individual might identify himself so thoroughly with one class (or race) as to condemn and hate all individuals in another class (or race) seemed to him preposterous. He did not himself do that for the white race, and he could not believe any human creature steeped, that far, in perversion.

The essential gathering of Joe's boyhood, then, concerning human relationships, was that if people make other people love them the world will somehow hold together. All this was instinctive with him, and his experience had strengthened his instinct. He knew it so well that he was hardly conscious of it as a conviction. That is why it governed him wholly, and why also at the age of thirteen, it did not keep him from going to the village post-office and reading news out of other people's newspapers. While he was there, one day, he saw a batch of papers that was unfamiliar to him—the first edition of *The Countryman*, published by Mr. Joseph Addison Turner, on his plantation eleven miles from Eatonton. Mr. Turner advertised that he wanted a young fellow to learn printing and to help him with *The Countryman* and to live during the process at *his* house. That was Joe's opportunity. He took it.

Mr. Turner with his brother owned a large plantation, Turnwold, and many negroes, and a hat factory, and two pretentious houses stocked with a well-selected library of about four thousand volumes. He had been a member of the Georgia legislature, and his brother had written a novel, *Jack Hopeton,* which had appeared first serially in the *Southern Field and Fireside* (Augusta) and later in book form in New York. He thought that lawyers were a curse, and that the great trouble with the South was that too great a proportion of its best minds went into politics. In that field they did as well as people from other sections, but concessions won by them for their districts could not hold unless the people at large in those districts developed a well-rounded civilization and so justified the concessions.

Personally, Mr. Turner was an original. He proved himself conventional in part by consciously lowering the tone of his paper, after a while, to increase his subscription list, but he refused to compromise himself by taking into Eatonton for sale the hats made at his plantation factory. He had the hats, all right—fine beavers, wool hats, rabbit, and mixed hats, but whoever wanted one could come to his plantation for it if he wanted it keenly enough. "I am not going to turn peddler," he warned in his paper, "and haul hats backward and forwards to Eatonton. You have already imposed too much upon my good nature. *Quousque, tandem, abutere, Catilina, patientia nostra.*"

He was persistently a sort of grandee. "It is entirely foreign to the nature of gentleman," he wrote once in his paper, "to advertise himself or to drum for subscribers. I have got my consent to advertise, but to drum, never! I could not under any circumstances ask men to subscribe for my paper. It is not genteel to do so."

The time Harris spent with the Turners (from the time he was thirteen until he was seventeen) and in their library and with their negro slaves, was fateful. Fateful for the country, of course: those were the years of the War, but fateful also for the youthful Harris— he left them knowing that he was going to be a writer; and no bombastic writer either, but one, he thought, like Mr. Goldsmith.

After leaving Turnwold, Harris worked for a while with the *Macon Telegraph,* and with the *Crescent Monthly* in New Orleans. "Nursing a novel in his brain," he returned to Georgia at nineteen (1867) and took a position in Forsyth on the *Monroe Advertiser.* Here he knew a town character, an old negro called Uncle Remus, but that was incidental. His main interest was in his newspaper work, particularly in the bright, incisive little comments he stuck here and there between articles of more length and seriousness.

Those paragraphs made a name for him, and in 1870 he went to work in Savannah, at what seemed to him the handsome salary of forty dollars a week. His new job was with the *Savannah Morning News,* edited by Colonel W. T. Thompson, himself a humourist of considerable fame in the forties and fifties. An upcountry bumpkin of twenty-two, stunted and pale, Harris did not seem prepossessing to his colleagues on that prime daily of the state in that serene, coastal capital. Was the critter Colonel Thompson had brought in, they wished to know, human or not human—had he been caught in a fish trap or in a net?

But his clever paragraphs palliated them—for example: "The coloured people of Macon celebrated the birthday of Lincoln again on Wednesday. This is the third time since October"; "There will have to be another amendment to the civil rights bill. A negro boy in Covington was attacked by a sow lately and narrowly escaped with his life. We will hear next that the sheep have banded together to mangle the downtrodden race."

In 1873 Harris was married to Esthel La Rose, daughter of a French Canadian who owned shipping interests in Savannah and who lived there part of each year. She was a Catholic, and a very lovely and lovely-looking girl. His life with her then, and until his death, was romantically happy, and it was on account of her safety and that of their two children that he fled from Savannah in the yellow fever epidemic of 1876, and went to Atlanta. In the midst of that grimness Harris, gilded by his glittering era and too thoroughly a good newspaper wit, *would* have his joke. He registered at the Kimball House: "J. C. Harris, one wife, two bow-legged children, and a bilious nurse."

Coming from Savannah to Atlanta in 1876 meant a great deal. It meant Chicago instead of New Orleans, railways instead of river-traffic, Henry Grady instead of Colonel Thompson, Chester A. Arthur instead of Thomas Jefferson. It would not mean that Harris's pithy comments, which had already made him one of the best known editors in the state, must be stilled. It would mean that he would hardly again, as he had vigorously done in Savannah, oppose a national collusion of Southern Democrats and Liberal Northern Republicans such as the one that had furthered Horace Greeley.

The flight from Savannah had been temporary, but the desolation after the plague there made it impossible for the *News* to pay as liberally as it had done formerly, and Harris settled in Atlanta, with Evan P. Howell and Henry Grady on the *Atlanta Constitution*. Howell was at the time in his late thirties, Harris twenty-eight, Grady twenty-six. The men and the occasion had met, and the *Constitution* under them became perhaps the most influential journalistic force so far seen in the South.

Sitting round his camp after Appomattox, L. Q. C. Lamar, that Georgia-bred Mississippian, had heard despondent talk, indeed, from his fellow officers. Many of them planned to abandon the South—some to go North, some to quit America entirely. Even Jackson's chaplain, the Reverend Richard L. Dabney, was of that mind. Let the geographic South be abandoned, he urged, but let the spiritual South at all hazards be perpetuated—and the way to do that was to effect a wholesale migration of Southern people to Brazil. Lamar spoke very nobly then against all such doctrine— the Dabney talk was visionary—and as for abandoning the South, he would not do that; he had helped involve it in its difficulties, and he felt himself impelled to help extricate it. Not everybody took that exalted attitude. Pickings were better North, people told themselves, and North they went, some to blot out whatever Southern implications they retained (until those implications became fashionable in the next generation), and others to recoup themselves there in hope of returning later—exiled for the moment by poverty. A number of people went from Georgia, most notably the authors Richard Malcolm Johnston and Sidney Lanier. ("You are all so alive up there, and we are all so dead down her," Lanier had written to a Northern friend.) Harris himself had considered going, though he should with regret, he said, give up ruralizing.

But at last the South seemed to be taking hold again, and Atlanta was reaping the rewards of the New Order, if any Southern city was. It had been burned, but it was finer now than before (witness that bright jewel, the Kimball House), and it was natural for the beneficiaries of the New Order to formulate their thesis. This thesis was a mixed one, and so, likely to fare far. It was that Southern men before 1860 were the finest men ever seen anywhere, but unfortunately quite wrong in all their conceptions except that of private virtue—which they really need not have worried about since *that,* somehow, could be trusted to look out for itself. That was its thesis. Its program was, while speaking reverently, always, of the past, to repudiate that past as rapidly as ever one might—with one exception, that the nigger be kept to his place. That was a rock that was to bottle many bays, but somehow the New Order planned to over-leap it. The plan seemed logical, and promised wealth and strength for the hallowed Southland. It met with response in places beyond Georgia's borders, even in New York.

In Georgia, perhaps, it had more resounding names to sponsor it or to seem to sponsor it than it had elsewhere. There were General Longstreet, Governor Brown, Alex Stephens (vaguely), and Benjamin H. Hill. In Congress Lamar had furthered conciliation by his eloquent eulogy on Sumner and, if one were of a disposition to take poets seriously, one might consider young Sidney Lanier, at that time writing for the Philadelphia Exposition poetry that was full of talk about the sacredness of the Union.

The pulpit, too, had its influence. For the grave-minded Bishop Atticus Haygood argued persuasively that without *any* progress, one achieves nothing better than extinction. "If you can't fly," he quoted from an early idol of his, without a full recognition of spiritual implications, "run; if you can't run, walk; if you can't walk, crawl; if you can't crawl, worm it along." And for the less grave-minded, the Reverend Sam Jones epigrammatized the new and increasingly general sentiment. "I am tired," he said, "of singing always *The Sweet Bye and Bye;* let's sing *The Sweet Now and Now* for a spell."

"Worm it along," Bishop Haygood had said. Well, many did, and many would, and many do—just how nearly literally the good Bishop probably did not know. Hardly anybody knew—least of all Grady and Harris. America was a very phenomenal thing however one looked at it; fortunes had grown here at a rate unprecedented in History, and generally, one held, as a work of God's favour. Surely one could not doubt the extension of that favour to a man who, like Commodore Vanderbilt, had given under the auspices of a Methodist Bishop, a round million dollars for Southern education.

An occasional Jeremiah uttered doleful prophecies. As late (or might one better say *as early?*) as 1891, Colonel C. C. Jones of Augusta set his mind forth about the matter in one impassioned sentence. "Under the absurd guise of a new South," he thundered, "flaunting the banners of utilitarianism, lifting the standards of speculation and expediency, elevating the colours whereon are emblazoned consolidation of wealth and centralization of government, lowering the flag of intellectual, moral, and refined supremacy in the presence of the petty guidons of ignorance, personal ambition, and diabolism, supplanting the iron cross with the golden calf, and crooking

> . . . the pregnant hinges of the knee
> Where thrift may follow fawning,

not a few there are who, ignoring the elevating influence of heroic impulses, manly endeavour, and virtuous sentiments, would fain convert this region into a money-worshipping domain; and, careless of the landmarks of the fathers, impatient of the restraints of a calm, enlightened, conservative civilization, viewing with indifferent eye the tokens of Confederate valour, and slighting the graves of Confederate dead, would counsel no oblation saving at the shrine of Mammon."

But sentiments like this were vain in that day; the very axis of the world inclined otherwise. People in general did not recognize how widely large-scale corruption was diffused. The sinister aspects of urbanization, the sundering of actual human relationships in corporate industry, were beyond their imagination. For Harris, cheerfulness was in the air, youth was in his heart, Henry Grady in his office.

But the *Constitution* staff was not blind. Grady spoke and Harris wrote through those years (both through their respectable Democracy—no populists they) with as much clarity and force as ever Tom Watson did against the abuses of their time. In their romantic bravado they could not believe that any system could persist in its unethical phases despite the concerted will of human beings. In their simple loftiness of spirit they could not believe that human beings, once aware of an unethical manifestation, would fail to exercise their concerted will to crush that manifestation. They placed the blame, then, on certain developments of the industrial order in the North; but they thought those malign developments not inherent in industrialism, and they invited industrialism South, feeling that here all that was evil would be extirpated. Given good men, no system can behave badly in their hands.

It is a doctrine that to this day has its forceful advocates. And Grady (and Harris with him) did want to see the South strong—

strong, strong—and swift. If he had a hundred thousand immigrants to bring to Georgia, Grady said, and he wished he had, he would send five thousand to Atlanta, twenty thousand to the farms, and seventy-five thousand to the factories. He looked forward to the time when no Georgia river could reach the sea without turning in its progress ten thousand spindles—"for look you, in my lifetime I shall see our country with a hundred and fifty million people."

From 1886, when he made his famous speech in New York, till his death in 1889, Grady was one of the most prominent figures in America. When he died, great men sent messages and poets poetized and divines moralized and many simple people who had not seen him, wept. His friends in Atlanta put forth as a memorial to him a substantial volume containing a great part of his writings, and some other material ranging from a commendatory notice of the *Constitution,* through many testimonials of Grady's virtue, to a memorial sermon in which the Reverend DeWitt Talmadge argues that though great, a man may be a Christian. The biographical sketch in this volume was Harris's.

Clearly, it seemed to Harris that one of the major luminaries of time had suddenly gone out. "From that time," he says, speaking of Grady's first appearance in New York, "he knew that his real mission was that of Pacificator. There was a change in him from that day forth. He put away something of his boyishness; his purpose developed into a mission." But the King was dead, now, and Harris must have known, in spite of his sincere and perpetual modesty, that the King of *all that,* in Georgia, now, was himself. And he was not made for kingship; his mind was full, always, of modifications.

A modern historian inquiring how it was that Southern leaders were so intent to effect the grand Reconciliation, will doubtless prove before long that they were actuated by economic motives. And he can sustain his case by specific reference to Grady's speeches. A fact one can sustain also, but more by general acquaintance with Grady than by reference to isolated statements of his, is that he wanted reconciliation because he was a generous and lovable human being who winced always under any manifestation of surliness.

That was Harris's case also. He could swear well that in his heart he was not surly, for instance, about the Negro, and he knew hardly anybody else who was surly on that score. It provoked him to observe the constant clamour in Northern newspapers about his and his friends' being governed wholly by impulses which they indeed rarely recognized. He believed that those imputations were founded in an evil passion that had in all conscience lived past its just day, but he thought the accusers sincere, if ignorant, in fact, of what motivated them.

His Uncle Remus sketches, undertaken at first as part of his newspaper work, exhibited his actual attitude as he lived, surely the reverse of surliness. When it was apparent to him that they were being read everywhere and that he as their author had been elevated, despite his protests, to a forum as influential as almost any in America, he must have worked consciously to make those stories propagandist in nature. He must have realized after a few years that his propaganda, through Uncle Remus, had proved effective, and he could tell himself with all justice that much sectional rancour had evaporated before that old man's wit.

These sketches had shown, by implication, the kindliness that had existed in the ancient South between masters and slaves—and that is what, in the North, had been most seriously in doubt. He had tackled that rancour, too, in his *Constitution* editorials and in the numerous non-dialect essays he had published in Northern magazines. Sweetness and light were his weapons, Matthew Arnold one of his chief smiths. To the South, he said this: Treat Negroes as you would like to be treated in their position and don't make yourself equally criminal with irresponsible Yankees by getting angry when they upbraid the Southern attitude about Negroes. To the North he said this: First ask yourself if what you are angry about really happened—then ask yourself if you might not have acted similarly under similar conditions. To both he said: Remember that the other fellow is human only, and above all (oh, above all) that you are also; pity him for his error, help him to avoid it, do not abuse him.

He determined at last to show the kindliness which had existed in the ancient South among white people toward one another—the direct personal kindness that makes affection—which *had* existed, and which existed still among country people. For country people, he explained (writing when America was already almost preponderantly urban—*he could not believe it*) are really the *typical* Americans. So he wrote much to this end, stories and novels which never achieved the popularity of the Uncle Remus material, but which are none the less valid. He spoke oftenest of of one Billy Sanders, most properly placed, as a character, as a lower middle-class white man, considerably better than a cracker—

no polished gem, but a shrewd, shrewd brother, only more kind than shrewd. As to geography, Billy was placed in Georgia, circulating between two actual villages—Shady Dale and Harmony Grove. But to Harris's great distress people in Harmony Grove protested against his making sport of them by using their town's name, and shortly afterward in very shame, re-christened the town (if one may say so) *Commerce.*

The doctrine of Progress had caught hold in Georgia vengefully; the cities grew and the country dwindled. In 1880 hardly a tenth of the people lived in towns; in 1900 more than a fifth did. Atlanta, with a population of about ten thousand in 1860, had about ninety thousand in 1900—the largest city between Baltimore and New Orleans. Atlanta was like the rest of America now— let men hope, for the better. In Savannah, still, one did not have to run to catch a street car. That seemed quaint to Harris in 1900, a reminder of the distant past.

His personal affairs, except in money (he never made a great deal), had advanced as rapidly as those of his city. Learned gentlemen the world over wrote to him about his contributions to folklore. Mr. Robert Louis Stevenson and Mr. Sam Clemens wrote to him, and Mr. Cable wrote, and at times he visited such gentlemen. President Roosevelt wrote to him often, and at last coaxed him to visit the White House. And once at a banquet in Atlanta Roosevelt reminded people that in having Harris they had incomparably a bigger lion present (though a very meek, benign lion) than they had in having *him,* who, as a mere President, was doomed to something like oblivion. Presidents, he had said, come and go, but Uncle Remus stays put. So the world stood with Harris in his early fifties.

Now, whatever are the compensations of being fifty, there are certain difficulties before a man then that he has not had to reckon with formerly. In Harris's own mind, these difficulties were grave. So many people he loved were dead, and much harder of access than so many people he did not love. And these was the matter of his body, pudgy, leaden when it approached staircases. He had money now to deck that body out in good clothing, and to keep his hands immaculate. But to what purpose? Let him groom himself ever so carefully in anticipation of a visit with Mr. Walter Page, Mr. Page only went away to marvel at his unkempt appearance.

But all of that was superficial, and did not satisfactorily explain

the sense of futility that, glowering at him, at first, from around
unexpected corners, came at length to sit beside him often and
boldly, when he had been feeling happiest. He was out of accord
with so many things that people about him seemed to set store by.
People seemed so prone, after for a long time repudiating a good
idea, to accept that idea, nominally, and contort its meaning to
their own convenience. Grady had said: "Put business above
politics." That was wholesome enough as a doctrine of work,
and as a deflation for incompetent people who had been elevated
to high political office for sentimental reasons only. That catch-
word had worked; business was above politics at last in Georgia
too—and let nobody doubt it—but not in a way any righteous man
would have designed.

And that troubled him. An individualist, he could not reconcile
himself to a highly complex and paternalistic government. Corporations were individuals; and yet he abominated the abuses of
corporate monopolies. A countryman, he was fretted by so much
talk about it all—and so much and so much. He only wanted
people to do right.

He was, in short, for all his talk of realism, a romanticist, and
he was mainly ignorant of the teeming world of cities and not at
home there. And he believed that men had hearts still as they had
had long ago in Eatonton, and he believed that people should let
the kindest dictates of their hearts actuate them always. But he
was a realist, too, and he observed that all this was not happening.

Could it be that in teaching the hard lesson of *sectional* sympathy he had been ambushed, as it were, by forces destructive of
the personal, human sympathy which he had somehow taken for
granted? Could it be that in their blundering way the old irreconcilables had been accidentally half-right in their denunciation
of the North? He was himself not of a disposition to denounce
anything, and he did not believe the irreconcilables had been
capable of much discrimination in their thinking; but if by the
North they had meant the new way of life, he was himself at last
a sort of rebel again. It was a swift life, standardized, efficient,
pushing, hard, firm, isolated, viewing with equal warmth of
affection (because the sum in each case was precisely zero) one's
fellow Georgians and the residents not only of Boston but of
Burma.

All of this, too, was bewildering, and he sought solace where
he could. He spent much time in his garden; Snap Bean Farm, he

called it. He marvelled incessantly at birds. He speculated about religion. And slowly he resolved to follow his wife into the Catholic Church.

Atlanta was strong, now, and swift—God knows how swift. Not Mr. Grady's home, nor the like of it, was the center of social life there, as it had once been, but some club was, with gentlemen nibbling caviar and planning to squeeze out their competitors; with ladies opening with a brisk prayer some meeting calculated to strengthen them in their snobbery of blood or ancestry, or of some other thing. Oh, it was scheming *now,* and organization, and the devil take the hindmost—except, that is, if the hindmost knocked at some *appropriately* remote door, as for example, that of some Community Chest. And what those gentlemen needed, and those ladies, was neighbour-knowledge, an actual personal contact with people, who, less competent than they, less glittering, (perhaps only less fortunate) were none the less in the one transcendent item of humanity, identical.

There was need, indeed, that the mocking birds sing valiantly now, and that Snap Bean Farm fruit and flower well, and that Mother Church swing her censers faithfully. And they all did. And the somewhat canonized Uncle Remus smiled valiantly, if wistfully, and proclaimed his world the best of all worlds possible.

In 1900, he resigned from the *Constitution* to devote himself to pure letters, but in 1906 he again ventured into journalism by establishing a monthly periodical devoted to literature and current topics. He wanted it named *The Optimist,* but his promoters persuaded him to call it *Uncle Remus's Magazine;* the trade value of that title, they explained, was too great for it to be neglected. Here he re-enunciated his old program—his and Grady's of 1880— in favour of a broad understanding, and of sweetness and light brought to bear upon every question arising between North and South or between nation and nation.

But his instinct recognized more accurately than his intelligence that those principles did not at that time require the prime emphasis, and what he actually talked of most was the necessity of *individuals'* knowing one another and loving one another, at whatever cost, at however great an apparent waste. It was really not so hard for a man in Atlanta to keep his ire and his rapaciousness down in regard to Boston, Massachusetts; his more immediate task was to keep them down in regard to his neighbour, and the best way for him to do that was for him to know his neighbour. It was hard in 1906 for one to do that, and he, Joe Harris, had perhaps furthered the conditions that had made it harder, and perhaps he and Henry Grady had been misguided in their guiding; no, not Grady—let his lips be sealed before he would say that! Perhaps, then, *he* had been misguided. Then, let him qualify his old teaching—and so he did qualify it, romanticizing about old colonels, who though still hot against Sherman, yet whittled charmingly for children; about the birds, over and over; about his collards, which grew sedately and would not be speeded up by advertising programs; and about young creatures who somehow, absurdly wise, value people more by what they are than by what they have or do.

When he died in 1908, his family set these appropriate words of his on his grave stone. They are beautiful words and they testify to a lovely though no longer ebullient spirit:

I seem to see before me the smiling faces of thousands of children—some young and fresh and some wearing the friendly marks of age, but all children at heart—and not an unfriendly face among them. And while I am trying hard to speak the right word, I seem to hear a voice lifted above the rest, saying: "You have made some of us happy." And so I feel my heart fluttering and my lips trembling and I have to bow silently, and turn away and hurry into the obscurity that fits me best.

Jefferson: New Style

TOM WATSON'S people were middle class farmers. Once Quakers but finally Baptists, they moved to Georgia about 1750, after living for a while in Pennsylvania and North Carolina.

He was born in a proper time for the Civil War to do its work for him. It shattered and impoverished the social system he was part of, and killed this one and that one of his relatives. His father, wounded twice in body, suffered in spirit something little short of annihilation. He quit his newly bepillared house, and gave over his hereditary will to plant things for the joy of his progeny—apple and grape and quince. Thenceforth, he would plant only what he could sell. Then he left his farm, opened a restaurant, gambled, and offered himself as steady dupe for all sharpers.

This father young Tom thought was one to avoid—but his mother was adorable. He was at school, and he was taking music lessons. There were books for him to read; there was a fiddle for him to play, and an alarming knife for the menacing of objectionable school-mates. For the rest, he acquired freckles to match his hair, walked in his sleep, and developed an enduring habit of keeping journals. Soon it was time for him to go away to college, so that he might the better advance himself in the world, and to a Baptist college so that his mother might be the better assured of his advance in worlds more considerable.

His time at Mercer University went chiefly in prodigious reading, and in debate and declamation and dispute. But he could not argue away his poverty. People recognized him for a man of promise, but the recognition could not be drawn upon at any bank. It was soon plain that the poor pay he had for a Summer's teaching, augmented by the sale of his sister's gold watch and his

From *The American Mercury*, Vol. 18 (September-December, 1929) , 293-300 grandfather's silver cup and his own books (value: six dollars), would not hold out further than his second year.

The sober fact was that he had to go to work, and in the Georgia of 1874 there was not much work to be had. He looked about here and there, vainly, and at last journeyed to a convention of rural Baptists, hoping that some deacon there, perhaps, would point him jobward. But the deacons' counsel was mainly celestial, and the boon he craved was immediate. Desperate, he went to a place near a little town named Sylvania, and there, after much canvassing, set up a school with himself as master.

It was a wretched land and it had brought to the ruin of the Civil War a population already ground under by economic shifts. The people had found a philosophy for their necessities. They were kindly, loyal, and in their way aspiring; and Watson's association with them taught him that they were worthy. He was a passionate soul, and he resolved then that something must be done to relieve the abuses they were subjected to.

But school teaching and altruistic impulse did not wholly engross him. He studied law, entertained himself desultorily with a Sylvanian nymph or so, wrote poetry, and played busily on his fiddle. Soon he was an out-and-out lawyer. Living with a former school-mate of his who was a candidate for the ministry, he considered applying for a temperance lectureship, but ended, teetotaling satyr that he was, by acquiring a reputation for immorality.

In November, 1876, he went back to live in Thomson, Ga., where he had been born in 1856. The town itself had changed little since his childhood, but in the State at large much was happening—particularly the movement for the organization of farmers—to give a young lawyer something to think about. As yet Watson thought chiefly of himself. He inaugurated what was to become an extremely successful law practice, married the foster daughter of a seldom-do-well doctor, and assumed more and more, as time went on, the support of any of his relatives, or his relatives' relatives, who found their own support more than they could manage.

Above all, he was pointedly concerned to have it known that he could not be imposed upon. The boy who toted a knife was the father of a man who toted pistols, one of which he at length used to shoot a rival barrister. The victim, Watson said, was trying to destroy him, and he retaliated by wounding him in the hand.

To the satisfaction of both prosecutor and defendant, an accommodating judge arranged to have the case dropped.

Then arose a circumstance nobody had anticipated. The farmers of the community muttered that such a shooting match among farmers would never have been silenced so easily. Soon afterward the accommodating judge came up for reelection by the Legislature. Watson himself, running for that body, was opposed by an acknowledged partisan of the judge. If he would only declare against the judge, he could command almost the entire vote of the farmers. But that declaration against a man who had so recently befriended him was a little more than he could achieve. So he said that he was not against his benefactor at all, but promised that if elected he would exert his influence in the matter of the judgeship, precisely as directed by his constituents.

Another phase of his candidacy had to do with his winning the support of the Negroes. Hard put by his opponent, who also sought this prize, he so far committed himself as to be generally, if falsely, accused of having compromised with Republicanism.

Already master of an exceedingly practical brand of politics, he won the race by a satisfactory margin. And he took with him two things that lasted. One was a definite respect for the political power of organized farmers, and the other, a reputation of being ready for his own ends to endanger the sacred Democratic unanimity.

II

In the Legislature he exerted himself, ineffectually, it proved, in the interest of temperance, tenant farmers, tenanted convicts, and Confederate veterans. The veterans had already the blanket right to peddle anything whatever, but they constituted a formidable political group, and he thought they should have specifically granted to them the right to peddle sewing-machines.

During the session he worked to have that body elect to the United States Senate J. C. C. Black, a resident of Augusta, the metropolis of his congressional district, and incidentally one of the lawyers who had volunteered to defend him when he was arraigned for shooting. Black's opponent was thought of as a kind of second-degree renegade. As Governor, he had granted high political favor to a Georgian who was believed to have sold out to the Yankees. But for all Black's being identified with the Old Order, and for all Watson's likening him to the "redoubtable and chivalrous Henry of Navarre," he was defeated. He could not prevail against the magnanimous— or submissive—programme of Henry Grady, which demanded that all bloody shirts be put under ground with as much speed as was consistent with proper ceremony.

Between Watson and Grady personally there was no bloody shirt whatever. Following Black's defeat, they celebrated at Grady's house, with several other gentlemen, the victory of Grady's candidate. It was a mighty meeting. There was much food and much drink. Grady graced it all with his customary all-enveloping genialness, and Watson, responding with a protracted playing of his fiddle, was awarded, as a gift for his wife, the lovely table decoration, a violin made of tuberoses.

There was no doubt by now that he was a man to be reckoned with. He was diminutive and scrawny, and his voice was often distinctly treble, but all this, he knew, weighed little against him in a State that had lately deified the shrill dwarf, Alex Stephens. Speaking, he was irresistible, swinging his audiences delightedly down the dizzy transitions he made from impalpable illusion, to stories of a man who could smell the gravy and know the sex of the hog—and then back up again to what seemed the final citadel of erudition.

One day his plea might be for temperance; the next for the acquittal of a crony who had regrettably shot down and killed a man; the next, before his *alma mater,* for a revival of the ancient faith which had characterized Southern youth before they turned up smeared with cynicism. There was a plea to be made also for Grover Cleveland, and one for a low tariff, and again and again and again a plea for the advancement of Tom Watson, who would not let himself be imposed upon.

But he was inescapably a Southerner, and by all his associations, a farmer, and both Southerners and farmers were imposed upon. And he was also a father who had been robbed lately of a child whom death took in spite of all his weapons and all his frantic bribes. Fathers, also, it seemed, were imposed upon—by Someone whose identity he could never be quite sure about. Clearly some Power not to be held friendly, a Power whom thinking of somehow set an itch in one's trigger-finger. It was not, evidently, the Person so extravagantly esteemed by churchmen. But who that Person might be was also a mystery—apparently quite beyond pistol-reach.

Other enemies were more tangible. The same North which oppressed the South was identical with the industrialism which oppressed the farmer. The West, daily more powerful, was, as fate had it, as much the natural enemy of industrialism as ever the South was. He burned to effect a treaty between those sections against their common tyrant. The defunct Granger movement, reborn as the Farmers' Alliance, had already done something toward accomplishing that purpose. Even in Georgia politics, complicated by racial and sectional animosities, it had shown itself potent.

The specific move for him individually to make was to go to Congress. The expedient thing for him to do in order to be elected was to affiliate himself, locally, with the cause which he wished truly, in his heart, to see triumph nationally. His campaign, then, was made in all sincerity, and with no touch of personal antagonism for his rival. He was hardly arrayed *against* anybody. The negative aspects of his outlook yielded to his advocacy of principles historically associated with agrarian interests. Everything, in his mind, went down before the advocacy, including the sacred Democratic unanimity. After all, he told the Georgia Legislature in the Summer of 1891, he would give a prize to anybody who could point to any real distinction between orthodox Democrats and orthodox Republicans. For his part, he was a Democrat still, but a Farmers' Alliance man in addition. He was running, in short, it seemed to stanch party men, with the hare and the hounds. They lost no time in declaring him fraudulent.

But he was elected in spite of them. The Farmers' Alliance had already named a Governor, and in the Fall of 1891 Watson established in Atlanta the *People's Party Paper,* a weekly calculated for the needs of his rural followers.

In Congress he worked valiantly, and actually accomplished the legislation which established the rural free delivery of mail. The House, largely untrustworthy, he announced, and too frequently drunk (a charge not sustained), could never, he told his fellow members, make him into a scapegoat. He wanted them to understand that never while he lived would he, a Georgian, be bulldozed by any representative from New York, nor forget the usages which had immemorially obtained among gentlemen.

All of that undeniably sounded grand in Georgia ears, but it could not placate the Democratic organization for his acknowledgedly writing propaganda for another organization than their own. The author of the People's Party Campaign Book, 1892, seemed to all good Democrats to be imperatively in need of extermination.

They gerrymandered his district, summoned J. C. C. Black, the redoubtable and chivalrous, to run against him, and at length defeated him, after a campaign of unprecedented tumultuousness, marked most memorably by Watson's protecting against a mob one of his Negro wardheelers, and by the bright voice of Watson's lady supporters, piping, to the tune of "The Bonnie Blue Flag," "The Young Wife's Song," lately composed by their most versatile captain—in a mood more fiscal than connubial. Watson held always, with a force that time promises to accentuate, that the election was unfairly maneuvered against him. He remained, however, in politics, issuing a daily paper in supplement to his already existing weekly, appealing to Methodist cohesiveness in behalf of one of his candidates, and stumping all Georgia as a sort of messiah of Populism, more Luther, he told himself—and thanked God—than Erasmus.

He ran again for Congress in 1894, and was again defeated—again, he said, dishonestly. But a run-over election held soon afterward, on his demand, gave the same result.

In 1896, against his will, he was the Populist candidate for Vice-President of the United States on a ticket headed by Bryan of the Democratic ticket, but substituting Watson for Bryan's Democratic running-mate. This candidacy involved arduous campaigning in many parts of the country, and when it failed Watson apparently took stock of himself and decided to abandon Luther a while, and try Erasmus, to be a little less Jackson and a little more Jefferson.

He retired from public life and took sanctuary in his home in Thomson. There, using as a nucleus a "Story of France" which had appeared first in his weekly, he determined to write a more voluminous story which should make evident for everyone the force of his doctrines. This work, running well over 2000 pages, was published by the Macmillans, after much of it had been deleted as too radical, in 1899. It was received with great favor in Europe as well as America, and it holds some of its force to this day.

III

While he was writing it, he set himself to do next a popular history of the United States, and after that perhaps a life of Lee, but the wide endorsement of the "France" influenced him to undertake a life of Napoleon. This work, running over 700 pages, appeared in 1902. The product of a somewhat slackened exhaustiveness of preparation, it was nevertheless a commendable piece of work.

"The Life and Times of Thomas Jefferson" (1903) and "Bethany" (1904) a sentimental, structureless novel of Civil War Georgia, deal with subjects nearer their author than ever Corsica was, or Rheims. They exhibit an author immeasurably less detached than the author of the "France," and less able to put down his old irascibleness, which too often, in Thomson or at the Augusta Fair, armed itself, and went menacing.

In 1904, the Populists made him their candidate for the Presidency. Watson himself had advocated Hearst for that office, but he accepted the nomination and conducted a vigorous and able campaign.

During the Summer he went to New York upon the summons of Arthur Brisbane, who wished him to become an editor for the Hearst papers. The proposal somehow did not suit him, but the trip resulted in his meeting the promoter of two magazines, the *Smart Set* and *Town Topics,* and in his determination to edit a New York magazine himself. This publication, a monthly, *Tom Watson's Magazine,* ran from March, 1905, to September, 1906. For a while Watson himself lived in New York, but soon, in consideration of "his interests and local attachments," he went back to Thomson. From that fastness he continued to edit the magazine, assisted by an editorial board, among whom was his twenty-four year old son. Maxim Gorky, Theodore Dreiser and Edgar Lee Masters were among his contributors. He himself, beside his regular editorials, began in the June number his "Life and Times of Andrew Jackson," a work more irascible than his "Jefferson" by as much as his house in Thomson, "Hickory Hill," followed the pompousness of "The Hermitage" more than the dignity of "Monticello."

Soon he decided that in connection with the New York magazine he had been taken in by a promoter whom he should have recognized from the first as a Yankee sharper. The breaking off of their relationship, accompanied by a profuse crackling of incriminatory sparks on both sides, should never, he determined, deprive him of his pulpit as editor. The *People's Party Paper* had been abandoned since about 1900, and it was necessary to begin anew. The *Jeffersonian,* a weekly published first in Augusta and later in Atlanta, appeared in October, 1906, and *Watson's Jeffersonian Magazine,* a monthly published in Atlanta, appeared in

January, 1907. The editor himself remained at his home in
Thomson.

It was in connection with this absentee editorship that he
formed a relation with his executive lieutenant, Mrs. Lytle. An
unattached woman some ten years his junior, her physical mas-
siveness and her aggressively capable mind put her in pointed
contrast to the demure frailness of Mrs. Watson. That lady, now
that she was no longer bearing children, had subsided into the
position of a revered wraith, highly useful as an object of romantic
illusion in his speeches, and as one to frighten away from his win-
dow the birds that distracted him at his writing.

Under Mrs. Lytle's régime the entire publishing activities of
her master were transferred to Thomson. She too moved down as
part of the equipment, first to a residence near the master's, and
soon—past the concrete fountains reminiscent of Versailles—into
the elysium of "Hickory Hill" itself. Watson's publications were
rarely carried on by sufficiently business-like methods. If money
due was collected, and if a proper amount of advertising was
secured, it was Mrs. Lytle who was to thank. Her uses to him became yearly more indispensable, and personal. When he died, it
was she and not Mrs. Watson who attended him, and he made
provision for her support.

She could talk in such a fashion as not to set men snoring when
they came down from Atlanta to "Hickory Hill" to learn from
the sage who ruled it the things they must do if they really wished
to be Governor. She knew also, consummately well, how to mix
the drinks which the sage found more and more necessary for his
happiness and the happiness of his guests.

In the Fall of 1904 Watson officially started his campaign for
the disfranchisement of the Negro, to the end, he said, that white
voters, freed of a Negro balance of power, might safely exercise
individual independence in their politics. When Hoke Smith,
aspiring for the governorship, endorsed this programme, he
gained Watson's vigorous support. Elected, Smith brought about
the promised change, as well as a regulation of both railways and
liquor, by measures Watson had long advocated. The two of them
were then for a long time hand in glove. But finally, because
Smith would not, out of friendship for him, commute the sentence
of a criminal whom he had unsuccessfully defended, Watson
turned violently against him. His desertion of Smith, he maintained, could not be explained on such a basis. But the conviction
that it was mainly personal was not diminished when in Smith's

campaign to succeed himself, he was defeated, largely through Watson's efforts, by a politician whose philosophy was vastly more remote from Watson's than Smith's was.

Again the Populist candidate for President in 1908, he had brought home to him a knowledge that the party was moribund—that its one-time members had repudiated the only agency likely to offer them relief. What served as an even more damaging commentary upon the wisdom of his followers was his delivery of their vote, in the recent Governor's race in Georgia, to a man whom he instinctively believed a Tory. The exigencies of politics could scarcely have held up before him a more nauseous irony. The whole world, he concluded, and publicly advised, often and fervidly, was plunging hell-ward.

And as with the other angels he went hurtling head-long to perdition, he could think of no occupation possible under the circumstances better than that of pinching and tweaking the most refulgent of his fellows—they, it seemed to him, had evidently in the past been most predatory. These galling inflictions he brought about chiefly through his weekly newspaper, which had largely superseded his monthly. Among the brightest of these spirits, doomed with him, were various ecclesiastics, particularly Catholics, and those Protestants who busied themselves with foreign missions. He would not give any of those brethren any rest. His Catholic animosities, indeed, soon blazed into an obsession, the prosecution of which cost him, before all was done, some $200,000. Tried for alleged indecency in his lampoons against Holy Church, he was acquitted. Upon being threatened with a change of venue to some place out of Georgia, he sent word succinctly to the authorities in Washington that he would await upon his doorstep, with pistols, any extraditionary officer sent for him.

He also swept violently into a celebrated law case of 1913-15. A Jew convicted of murder in the Georgia courts was being aided in his efforts for a reversal of verdict by some rich Jews resident in New York. The circumstance seemed to Watson only another instance of Yankee intrusion into Southern affairs, and he was furious. Had he not often warned those Philistines that he would brook no impertinence from them? The fact that fusillade against the Yankees in the affair would inescapably set loose an unreasoning racial hatred, and that it would in great likelihood result in a violation of Georgia sovereignty graver than any Yankee violation, did not check him. He took that risk unblenchingly, and the hatred he released, along with a little hemp rope, did the rest.

And he looked upon his work and—for all he ever said to the contrary—found it good.

Anybody who opposed his undertakings, especially any Georgian, brought down on himself a swirling cyclone of denunciation, made up not only of what Watson thought of him, but of any damaging rumor Watson had heard of him— from a friend who had it for his part also from a friend, who had it, if one's recollection could be trusted, from a Tennessee lady visiting friends of his last Summer. One most flagrant case of this sort was publicly exposed by an opponent of Watson's in Atlanta. But Watson's followers felt, with him, that he was always in danger of being persecuted, and the net result of such episodes was not a remitted loyalty for their chief but an intensified dislike for his foes.

Except among these followers, whose virtues, however numerous, were beyond contest homely, the world everywhere ran less and less to his desire. The election of Wilson to the Presidency was especially bitter to him. The man seemed to him clearly a traitor to the South—as he had repeatedly pointed out on many of his pages while Wilson was still at Princeton. For the South to endorse Wilson now rather than its sons who had proved faithful, was quite unthinkable.

Then the War came—a bad war, he would swear—and did swear; and then the draft law—a bad law, an indefensible law, he would swear—and did. And that, for a time, was the end of all his testifying. His paper was quashed, and the fact that he continued publishing indirectly was small comfort to him. It was as if he had been emasculated.

IV

He was racked by asthma. In the Summer of 1917 his daughter died; and in the Spring of 1918 his son, his sole remaining child, slipped actually from his arms, beyond life, with dazing unexpectedness. And the dark world which was left had utterly topping it, the one man whom he loathed most unreservedly. Torpor seemed the only thing left for him.

He had come, he said, to the end, and it was a sorry mess of mockery that was offered to one who had set out from a Baptist college with such lofty notions. Beyond any question he had sincerely labored for his farmers everywhere, and for his South, and particularly for Georgia.

That was why long ago he had opposed Henry Grady's man for

the Senate. It had seemed to him that Grady, with his blandishments, was imposing upon Southern farmers, and through them upon Southern culture at large, a more drastic defeat than Grant had done with a bludgeon. It was not possible to attack Grady personally; his error was clearly one of judgment only; he was true and lovable—and what was most important—he was dead. But as sure as every gun was iron the thing Grady furthered was calculated to impose upon the South that final defeat which is a defeat of viewpoint.

To beat the North at its own game, as Grady's logic seemed to counsel, involved beyond any escape a necessity that the South become a party to that game. It seemed to Watson a bad game from start to finish, industrialism, and he believed that it would entail consequences subversive to the development of such men as he found admirable. That was to him a fact, and no amount of reservation on the part of bland new-Southists could prevent an industrial society from breeding industial men to run it. As for him, if a choice were necessary, he preferred poverty, which patently is within endurance, to a prosperity founded on assumptions he thought fatal to all dignity and completeness of living.

His aim had been to save the conditions that had made possible such a man as Lee. But all the scores were marked against him, and most of the men one could look to as potential Lees were by plasmic provision sharp enough to read the scores, and to adjust their games accordingly, even at the sacrifice of potential Leedom.

He had set himself to check the entire current of the Nineteenth Century, and he had been forsaken in his effort by the very men whom he was most anxious to keep inviolate from that stream. Those men were with that current now, floating blithely and making money briskly as they floated, and denouncing him—when they could snatch from their enterprises a poor moment for public matters— as a very grave menace indeed.

Against the large force of their current he was not very gravely dangerous after all. In the eagerness of his opposition he received as allies persons whose sole qualification was their like mindedness with him in this one regard. The result was that his army took on the appearance of a mob generalled by an autocrat, who, to retain his power, was capable of expedient concession to the mood of his supporters. Rather than be linked with such an organization, many valid men who were essentially with him in his fear of industrialism were led to disavow all his works. It seemed better to them, on the whole, to endorse the opportunism of their own kind than to endorse alien men whose identity with them in this one matter could not compensate for their general reputation in other matters.

What Watson wanted, along with many others, was a South that should be prosperous without being mechanized. It probably did not occur to him that he was ordering out the moon for a pancake. He must have known that his wish was incalculably more difficult of achievement unless he could have wise men to help him. They would not help. At last many of them proceeded from a passive resistance to the new order to something that could not be distinguished from acquiescence in it. Very well, then, he would do the best he could without them. That best, arrived at with so little worthy cooperation, is what much of the South learned to think most richly delectable.

Undoubtedly, some admirable people, whose antagonism to the new order overshadowed all other considerations, continued to follow him. The rank-and-file of his forces, when not governed by the narrowest self-interest, were controlled chiefly by the impulse which brands as evil anything that is unfamiliar.

With such aid, he in fact threw up here and there some firm dykes. But dykes must be maintained, and only skillful engineers were equal to that task. The inducements offered such labor by agencies concerned to have the dykes broken were continually more irresistible. And who could think that common workmen, unguided, or maliciously guided by spies, would not go about their business in such a way as actually to hasten the crumbling of their defenses? Things having run on in that fashion so long, was it sensible, anyway, by 1900, to hope for an agrarian party that one might look to for any good—to expect intelligent action from a group whose natural leaders kept always deserting to the enemy?

Who were those dastards, that he might read them his anathema? Rich men, generally urbane and urban—in short, most men he would in general most have delighted to have as friends. But who really cared for his anathemas? At last he must have recognized, with his discernment, that in parts of the South other than Georgia, where he had not been present, the current of industrialism flowed on.

The final result of all his labor had been only to annul the primacy which Georgia long occupied in the South. A nimble, inconstant widow, that State had appeared earliest at the grand ball of Reconciliation, on the arm of Mr. Grady. Forced at last by Watson to repudiate the party, she did not by her less enthusiastic attendance halt the twanging of the fiddles. That was indeed contrary to one's expectations.

Somehow, inexplicably, he had been imposed upon all along—perhaps to the quite cosmic extent of having all his dearest purposes thwarted by the very concessions he had himself admitted into his programme, as regrettable but unimportant corollaries. Had the food he had been giving out been really no more than moon-cake, fit in a world like ours not to nourish but to impair his people? Had the really vulgar devices he had resorted to to make them eat it, forever demolished in his own heart the gusty largeness and the classic dignity he had hoped to make jealously regnant there? He would not suffer these things to be. But what can terrorize inexorableness, or whip it into discipline? Such thoughts, moving straight toward madness, constituted an insolent intrusion, more than he could endure—or would,—even as a bewildered man in a world bound at large straight hell-ward.

V

Suddenly he entered the race for Congress. Defeated, he as usual contested the election—vainly.

Next, he put himself up to be named as the person Georgia Democrats would make the nominee of their party in the presidential race of 1920. He was unequivocally against the League of Nations. After a heated campaign he obtained a plurality of votes, but his attempt to seat his delegation in the Democratic Convention was not effective.

He had spun about so long and so orgiastically in political affairs that he could not be still. There was a place in the Senate to be occupied, and he had as well run for that too. So there was another campaign, tumultuous as always, carried on by means of ceaseless tours over the State, always along with the man who was then his choice of the candidates for Governor—a man whom he had loved long since, but most belligerently opposed a while, before taking him again to his heart. These oratorical pilgrimages were most taxing to him. Weighted with grief, broken with illness, he went everywhere, storming, unreservedly worshipped by his supporters, and unreservedly decried by nearly all people to whom he was truly kin.

One night when he was tired, and dizzy for a little sleep, some youngsters in a hotel where he was stopping maintained their boisterous hilarity in spite of all his pleas. At length, into the midst of those youngsters' card-game, came crashing a huge book, and huger imprecations, hurled with deft aim from an over-hanging balcony, by a scrawny old man in underclothes. It was a symbolic deed—proving beyond cavil the ancient taunt of his enemies that he would stop at nothing to bring about his desire. For the Revelation he hurled with such impious hand was a his-tory of the United Daughters of the Confederacy.

But wickedness may for a moment flourish, and the apostate in this matter was gathered up into the Senate which he desired.

There he spoke stringently, as aforetimes, of banks and bankers, demanded the refund of taxes collected on cotton during 1865, disapproved of making reparations to Colombia for America's activities in Panama, and denounced, among other things, the American Legion, Prohibition, and Coca-Cola. And most sensa-tionally, in charges not sustained in any part—like former charges of his in Washington—he declared that American officers in France were often vindictively barbarous toward American en-listed men.

During all of this time he was unwell, and in the latter part of September, 1922, it came to him that he had preferred his last charge, that with no chance of doubt he had reached his finish. He rememberd, perhaps, that Daniel Webster, lying in Wash-ington, like him far from his interests and local attachements, had also recognized that he must be gone. Like Webster, then, to those about him he gave assurance: I am not, he said, afraid to die.

But the sure meaning of those words is beyond anybody's ever laying hold of it. Whether piety or nihilism would do better to cherish them is a thing that only pietists or nihilists may decide with any degree of certitude. Never in words did he question ultimate divinity, but he was under an impression, apparently, that it was extremely ultimate—hardly conscious of preposterous clerics mumbling its name as a talisman—hardly aware of the thousand yarns spun to chronicle its alleged preposterous activities.

There was one thing, he said once, he wanted written on his grave—that he was the enemy of tyrants, priests, and trucklers. The request has not been honored, and it begins to seem that his most enduring monument is the truly excellent watermelon hawked by his name through the revolving Summers.

Henry W. Grady

EVERYWHERE IN the United States, many people go about in their automobiles aimlessly; but nowehere do Americans give themselves to this pursuit with more satisfaction than in the South. There, people ride and ride and ride. Let's ride, one says—and the automobile is off, without ever an inquiry as to destination. Ride where? Ride around; and around. And that is enough. Good Americans, the riders drunken themselves with the illusion of action; good Southerners, they mollify themselves with the substance of inaction. Nothing could be better.

The little towns go by swiftly. "Speed Limit, 8 miles," the warning says, "Law Strictly Enforced." Lordy me! . . . There is Dad's Place, with Chicken Dinners advertised; and Babe's Place. "You Want It?" says Babe's sign, "We Got It." That Babe is a hot one. But one slows down for a coca-cola at last at a crossroads store branded H.G. BROWN, GEN. MERCHANDISE.

Mr. Brown himself opens the coca-cola bottles and hands them out. Mr. Brown is forty-seven years old. He was born in January, 1890, the first of his parents' five children. A month before his birth there were two names held in storage for his arrival. One was Stephen, after his father; the other, Mattie, after his mother—this last in a sort of reserve-storage, to be used only if the worse came to the worst. But also, in December, 1889, on the twenty-third, Henry Grady died in Atlanta. "Mattie," said Stephen Brown to his wife—"Mattie, if it turns out be a boy, we'll name him after Henry Grady. We'll *save* "Stephen,' won't we, Hon?" Well, there the store is, H. G. Brown, General Merchandise.

"I believe, sir," says one of Mr. Brown's coca-cola patrons to him, "that you and I have the same name. My initials too are H. G., H. G. Bates of Ithaca, Georgia."

From *The Southern Review*, III (Winter, 1938), 479-509.

"I'm pleased to know you, Brother Bates," says merchant Brown.

"Well, that is curious," says Patron II, "I have a brother named H. G.—we call him that, H. G., flat."

The trade is ended. The automobile pushes on. In Timmonsville a sign: H. G. Terrell, Banking Company. And out of Timmonsville, beyond it, as up to date as tomorrow, "Mamye's Place" ... Will there never in this newest of New South, turn up a truly MODERN "H. G.'s Place" to proclaim that *whatever* one may want may be there obtained? What kind of world is it that leaves the palpable namesakes of a great progressive either conservatively respectable or a little musty, a little threadbare, never quite dapper like Dad or Babe?

Henry Woodfin Grady was born in Athens, Georgia, May 24, 1850. His father, William Grady, was born in the mountains of North Carolina in 1821, and lived in that section till he was grown. Then he migrated to Athens. There he prospered greatly as a merchant, characterized, as a fellow-townsman remarked later, by the familiar western Carolina thrift and shrewdness that make an elaborate culture perhaps unnecessary. He married into a substantial Athens family—Anne Gartrell was the girl's name—and, by the time of the Civil War, had become a devout Methodist, fathered four children, and shifted his residence repeatedly—each house more substantial than the former—till at last he lived in a sort of Parthenon. Here, there were massive white columns with giant oaks in front of them, and much golden air, through which casual pigeons in the most approved fashion fluttered often down to the veranda floor.

In this Parthenon, situated appropriately in Athens, which was the site of many another such domestic-temple, Henry Grady grew up. Athens was rich, and as the home of the state university and of an exceptionally distinguished citizenry, it was in a rather noble way "cultured." Here Henry thrived, a stocky child, dark-haired, black-eyed, rosy-faced, indigenous, witty and yet tender, as full of life as any egg ever was of meat. He loved everybody, did Henry. There were stupid people, whom one could not surely blame; and malicious people, who were surely stupid if all were known of them; and misguided people, who were in a way stupid too, if that were not to ugly a word to brand them with. And all of those people were likely to be wretched, as, one saw, the beautiful, the true, and the good were likely to be also. It was as well to make a clean sweep and love everybody—his papa and his mama and the other children, and his young friends and all of their folks, and his black mammy and all of the little niggers, and Mr. Cobb who was so powerful, and old Dr. Church, the Vermont-bred president of the University, who was so wise, and Mr. Rattle-Dollar who was so rich and Mr. No-Penny who was so poor. He loved all of those people and a lot more, and they, unable to think of anything more appropriate to do under the circumstances, loved him very cordially in return.

In 1861 William Grady went to war to defend the Southern Cause, equipping at his own expense a company made up of stout Piedmonters from Georgia and the Carolinas. Heavy with a presentiment that he would die, he nonetheless went promptly. Then Henry was in a way master of the White Parthenon. There was schooling for him, of course, at Miss Church's and there were numerous exciting visits to Captain Grady, later Major Grady, off at the war in Virginia. To his father he would go with a black slave, loaded with provisions; to his home he would come back with many messages and a head full of High Romance. There was a job for Henry in the one book-store of Athens; and Romance was nudged the higher. Romance and Sentiment played at stately and beatifying joust across his mind, which was dedicated with ascending fervor now to Scott, now to Dickens, now to Victor Hugo. There was a little printing-press for Henry—and from it issued his paper, *The Monthly Skeedaddle.*

And then, in 1864, Major Grady was shot down at Petersburg, gravely wounded. They started home with him, his black man attending him with unreserved solicitude. They got him as far as his brother's house in Carolina, Greenville, and there the major after three months of galling pain went down to death. There was High Romance in 1864 and Henry Grady was fourteen years old, and he was a part of it. There he was, the head of the House of Grady, and there his mother was, and there were Brother William and Sister Mattie; and there of course was God, in Athens just as much as he was in Heaven. And all of those things were things to think about.

He did not think of them so hard that he was unable to swim fast and far in the creeks pouring into the Oconee River near Athens, or that he could not find time to be coached during the fall of 1865 for entrance into the sophomore class when the University should reopen, after years of inaction, in January, 1866. And he was not unaware in the golden air—little else was gold in Athens, then—of the fresh charm of his contemporary and friend,

Julia King, the daughter of Dr. King.—The Kings were such undoubtedly nice people and all, said Anne Grady, his mother.
Nice, they were naturally pious; and in 1866, at an authentic
revival meeting, Henry Grady and Julia King felt the strange
warming of the heart John Wesley talked about so often, and
joined the Athens Methodist Church.

Henry stayed in the University till he graduated in 1868. Several things that he did there are in a sense important. He read
prodigiously, forming a habit that remained with him always.
He became a charter member of the Chi Phi fraternity; he made
a reputation as a boy orator; he greatly impressed an important
newspaper editor with the correspondence-notes which he occasionally sent to the editor's journal in Atlanta.

As an enthusiastic Chi Phi, he was for a while saturated with
the medieval ritualism that is perennially dear to the American
male. He repaired to dark and secret rendezvous with his brethren; he defended one of them once in a foray which was really
a practical joke, but which, so far as he was informed, might well
have been Armageddon; and surely as a member of his Order he
took solemn vow to hold his honor dearer than his life. All of which
was very well for a youngster. To Grady it continued always to
seem good indeed. He was at the time of his death national head
of the Chi Phi Fraternity, and he belonged to many other orders
of like nature.

At his graduation, Grady, representing his college literary society—also secret—made an oration on the subject that Dreamers
are the Best People. Everybody who heard him was transported;
and it was agreed that he should go to the University of Virginia
to see what laurels might be won there by one who recalled so
agreeably the triumphs of Demosthenes and S. S. Prentiss. So he
spent the next year in Charlottesville, taking only those courses
which attracted him, working at them only as seriously as he was
minded to. He roistered a good deal, quite attractively, and, to
the wonderment of beholders, stimulated only by the strong liquor
of his own nature. Stone sober so far as other liquors went, he
was the least sober man at most gatherings.

He was consistent and industrious about his oratory. He hoped
to be elected class-speaker as he had hoped in Athens, but in the
end, as had been the case formerly, he failed of election by one
vote. That election over, Grady came home to Athens.

He was in Athens, casting about, well-to-do for those times,
better off than most young gentlemen are at any time. He was the

son of the hero Major Grady, who had been a marvelously successful merchant, and he was, besides, the fair-haired boy of circumstance. The editor of the Atlanta *Constitution* remembered him
for his bright correspondence-notes, and the editor invited him,
about then, to go round the state with a number of other people
on a newspapermen's Excursion. He wanted Grady to report the
Excursion for the *Constitution,* and it was then Grady got his first
taste of journalistic blood. He reported the trip better than anybody else, and everybody knew that he did, including Grady; and
his fate was fixed. His reports of that trip were signed King
Hans—Hans, for his own name, Henry; King, for that Julia King
who was the personification of all beauty, all purity, all loveliness,
and so on and on and on—Elaine and Juliet and Helen and all the
others.

Soon Grady went to Rome, Georgia, to edit a newspaper called
the Rome *Commercial.* He had not been there long, learning to
know people, examining with interest the mountain-wolves which
farmers occasionally brought into town tied under their wagons,
before he encountered another type of wolf extremely repugnant
to him, a political Ring menacing the virtue of Roman politics.
He denounced the Ring in an editorial for his paper, but the pro-
prietor of the paper would not suffer the editorial to be printed.
Galahad would not be denied. He bought out of hand the other
two papers of that city, consolidated them, and editorialized as he
would with his own presses. And in 1871, he went back to Athens
to marry Julia King in the Methodist Church. Then to Philadelphia for a honeymoon. Then back to Rome.

Marriage is said to do many things for a young gentleman. Early
marriage, Grady particularly thought highly of. If a young man
will only not gamble, and not drink, and marry early, he wrote at
the age of thirty-four, good things innumerable, and no bad things,
will spring up about him all his life long. Grady was himself a
specimen of what that counsel will do for one. His marriage was
romantically happy till he died, but whatever it did for him at
start—or later, for that matter—it did not convince him that he was
in any way older than his years. His conduct of his new paper was
casual. He worked on it when he was disposed to, and then it was
among the best papers in the state. He abandoned it when he chose
to, to its foreman, while he, for his part, went on excursions to the
mountains—once with a new acquaintance of his, a fellow newspaperman, Joel Chandler Harris. Under such a whimsical editor the
paper succumbed promptly. Mr. Grady was paying for his educa-

tion, a little dearly, perhaps, but none the less pertinently.

Returning to Rome one day, after a brief visit to Athens, he missed his connection in Atlanta and put up for the night at the resplendent new Kimball House. He was brooding mighty matters. He and Bob Toombs—a sort of January and May partnership— had recently considered buying part interest in the Atlanta *Constitution*. That plan had fallen through, but he retained some money, and he was ready to act. At the Kimball House he came upon his friend, Robert Alston, a Carolina low-coast Bourbon, fated to be shot down in a political argument in 1879. He had been thinking of writing to Grady, he said, proposing that the two of them, associating themselves with the Creole Alex St. Claire-Abrams, buy the Atlanta *Herald* and run it in competition with the *Constitution*.

To say was to do, and that night before going to sleep Grady was part owner of the Atlanta *Herald*. The three partners were too much alike. They proposed to run a brilliant paper and they carried out their purpose. For all of its heady talk, Atlanta in 1873 was a relatively small town, but the *Herald* was as metropolitan in aim, at least, as the most expensively operated papers in New York. In order for it to quell its competitor, the *Constitution*, its editors chartered special trains to make its deliveries to Macon and other centers of population. They did not have to charter special trains long; the bankruptcy courts made that unnecessary. Grady's education was getting on.

Politics in Georgia during all of these years was obsessively engrossing. The sordid business of carpetbag rule, reflecting the ultimate abuses of the Government in Washington, the shifting back and forth of the Confederate veterans toward and away from the reconciliation proffered them by the national Congress, were fit to stimulate frenzy in a mind naturally more phlegmatic than Grady's. But Grady was a hero-worshipper, and he normally sided with Toombs and Stephens, the irreconcilables, rather than with Hill and Brown, who in general commended acquiescence. If by chance he was personally well acquainted with a prominent man in a group he normally mistrusted—and he came in time to know them all, intimately—his conviction on the fundamental issue was likely to be much shaken. And besides, the convictions of most people on the fundamental issues, even those of the great protagonists, were at times inconsistent. For Confederates though they had been, apostles of a sort of philosophic medievalism, they were nearly all of them in a way robustious American frontiersmen, and they were living in the latter half of a century when the very ether through which the world went spinning drunkened earthly creatures with grandiose expectation. The doctrine of the depravity of man had been adhered to quite boresomely long, and Rousseau's agreeable alternative had hardly had time to grow perceptbly threadbare before it was reinforced by the pronouncements of Darwin. Now, truly, it might be conceded, many of God's creatures, as you looked at them, might leave much to wish for; but who could believe that within the next few generations, all defects might be remedied? To doubt that was to doubt the Principle of Efficiency in the Universe—thought, somehow, to be clearly evident—and to doubt even the benignity of God.

What had a man in his twenties, everywhere popular and most blissfully married, rich, and careless of money and its ways, prominent enough to have been already the prospective partner in enterprise with the lion Robert Toombs—what on earth had such a man to do with any hint of cosmic despondency? Why, a world one needed to repine about was in no sense an appropriate residence for gentlemen, and it was palpable that gentlemen were residing in this one.

The *Herald* went down, and Grady tried again, this time with a paper of his own named the Atlanta *Capital,* in deference to the plans then afoot—to materialize in 1877—to change the capital from Milledgeville to Atlanta. But again his management was poor; the *Capital* collapsed and Grady was left financially impotent.

He was offered the editorship of a paper in Wilmington, North Carolina, at a salary of $1200 a year, and he made up his mind to go to Wilmington and look around. Wilmington—he knew the place by hearsay, and he did not much favor it. A sort of inferior Savannah it was, like Savannah, ridden with the fashion of hatred. In those coastal towns, much of every man's time was given day in, day out, to a vain denunciation of the Yankees, to a stultifying glorification of the Past, and to sunning oneself in the warm sun. Worse, there were people in those towns, a few people, who were not nobodies in any sense of the word, erudite but monomaniac gentlemen who offered what they believed a philosophic justification for Southern people's refusal to submit to the inevitable—and hence proper—New Order of life. General Toombs himself had a touch of that feeling but the General was old, and he was a good fellow, full of inimitable good stories.

So much for Wilmington; the railway-ticket that Grady bought went past it, and shortly he found himself registered at the Astor House in New York—with a round-trip passage in his pocket and little else. He had his shoes shined, paying, he explained later, twenty-five cents, a nickel for the shine, and the rest—*O Charles Dickens, late of London, and now of Heaven*—for the privilege of conversation with the shine-boy. Then he went to the office of the New York *Herald,* and obtained an interview. "Do you know anything about Georgia politics?" asked the editor. "If so, write me an editorial on that subject and leave it with me. I shall let you know later at the Astor House if it seems promising." And the *next* morning the *Herald* used the editorial, and Henry Grady, encouraged by the editor in a further interview, and walking on air, and with nought but air, incidentally, to sustain his vigorous body, took his train back to Atlanta.

That was a time of free-lancing for him. He did articles for whoever would accept them, often for the *Herald,* and about whatever he felt would prove interesting. It was not a very fine way of living for a young man of twenty-five, who had got off to such a dazzling start a year or two earlier. There was a possibility of his finding regular work in Augusta, Georgia. Augusta was like Wilmington, a little—enough like it to to serve complacently for many years as the forum of that Carlylean prophet, Charles Jones. No good word was Jones to speak for the New Order, and Augusta was to prove of a temper to tolerate him. It was as if Grady caught all of this by prefiguring. Those gloomy brethren extolled the Old Order, berated the newer one as clean deluded by the false gods Speed and Mass, berated it as bound to be fatal ultimately to the traditional concepts of the Family and of Religion. They were intolerant, those brethren; *both* orders were worshipful, the old along with its antithesis; those brethren should be broader. And as for the Family and Religion, how could those brethren that talked so much of God, believe that God would suffer the Family and Religion, both essentially dear to Him, to suffer any manner of decay? "O ye of little faith," saith Scripture. And there is no going behind *that.*

Nonetheless, Augusta was not unanimously so committed. There were happily in the town some happy spirits also. And there was always one's duty both to make a living for oneself and to convince the erring. And Grady was just about to leave for Augusta during the fall of 1876, when his friend, Evan Howell, offered him a position on his lately acquired, eight-year-old Atlanta *Constitution.*

Grady went to work there immediately, applying as many of the metropolitan notions he had acquired in his Alston-Abrams days as Howell felt compatible with the financial stability of the paper. Very soon, Joel Harris, who was at the Kimball House with his family—refugees from a yellow fever epidemic in Savannah—was persuaded also to join the *Constitution* staff.

Those were important transactions in the history of Southern thought. Howell and Grady and Harris, each of them in his way a person of extraordinary abilities, were all nicely complementary to one another. The paper that they together devised was always vigorous and, as newspapers go, which is a long way, it was unusually sincere and sensible. Its opinions came rapidly to be quoted with respect the country over, especially in New York; and it is said that the number of subscribers it had in Iowa, for instance, exceeded that of any other non-western journal.

All over Georgia, and in Atlanta especially, the *Constitution* became a sort of lay-Bible. Its news-service and its editorials, whether local or cosmopolitan, were both excellent. There are tales still current of Grady's mighty feats in getting the news—by methods that were primitive but which none the less achieved results—fully and promptly. As special features, the paper carried sketches by Grady and Harris, by Bill Arp and Betsy Hamilton the humorists, and, as time went on, by A. A. Lipscomb on "classic literature" and Bishop Atticus G. Haygood, a new-school, liberal Southerner, on religious matters.

Grady was utterly and ecstatically absorbed in his work and in his passage in general through this world. As it had been with him as a child, it was still—he loved everybody, and everybody, unable to think of anything more appropriate to do under the circumstances, ended by loving him in return. A bright western sky fascinated him, and he wrote a piece about it; a newsboy, dying at last from tuberculosis, fascinated him, and he wrote a piece about him; an old drunken pauper fascinated him, the Capitol at Washington fascinated him, a farm-house fascinated him, and the breezy new life of Atlanta, a second and more relevant Phoenix, fascinated him and fascinated him and fascinated him. He wrote pieces about everything. Oh! what a fine man nearly every man was; and oh, what a superb lady every lady was, whatever. Particularly was Joe Harris a fine man—with his delicious Uncle Remus waggery. And particularly was Evan Howell fine—how one could run on jocularly with Evan about the *expense* of the *Constitution,* Evan protesting about the operating cost, oneself protesting that, above all, the news simply must be had, that above all Atlanta and the *Constitution* simply *must* grow in wisdom and in stature whatever the expense—for, nothing risked, nothing gained, and that was a proverb, and there was no going behind a proverb.

All of this time, Grady was working not only with the *Constitution* but also as a special correspondent, with the New York *Herald*. For the *Herald*, he reported the South Carolina election-riots of 1876. A little later, reporting for the *Herald* the special investigation of the Hayes-Tilden election in Florida, he made a "scoop" which brought him recognition the country over as one of the most competent newsmen anywhere. At Tilden's request, former Governor Joe Brown of Georgia was in charge of this investigation. That fifty-five-year-old politician had only recently emerged from a cloud of dark popular displeasure in Georgia—he had been understood to be too complacent toward Yankee wishes, as too ready to spring into the debacle of after-war confusion, and salvage what he could for his personal profit. The twenty-seven-year-old journalist had suspected him as much as it was in his power to suspect anybody. After the time they spent together in Florida, Grady suspected him no more. The old Governor, he said, was a wonderful, wonderful man, embodying all the best qualities of the Puritan tradition, just as Robert Toombs, who was quite equally wonderful, embodied all of the best qualities of the Cavalier tradition. Both of those gentlemen were unquestionably able, and also, as fickle as the times had been, both of them were rich. And being rich—well, surely God rewards the virtuous; and you would hardly care to go behind that, would you, now?

By 1880 Georgia was on the way to a certain kind of recovery from the desolation of war and reconstruction; of the million and a half people in the state, 350,000 had not been there in 1870. Atlanta was growing rapidly. If a prominent doctor, say, or a prominent banker of the time had been asked about Henry Grady, he would probably have known him as, reputedly, an extremely competent newspaperman; as the writer of some rather touching sketches, suggesting Dickens himself, people said; as a good but not preeminent speaker, at banquets and so on; and, surely, as a most engaging and vital sort of acquaintance.

In 1880 Grady took a brief leave from the *Constitution*, and pleasured himself with a visit to New York. It was thought good that one of the actual staff of the *Constitution* should spend a while at the great center of events and learn what was what. There he did some work for the *Herald,* nosed about promiscuously, and wrote frequent articles for his home paper—comments ranging in subject from large politics to the slum-child who caught his fancy and whom, in recompense, he conducted to Coney Island.

Among the visitors who also came to New York at that time was General John B. Gordon. The picture of this hero which is given in the most considerable complete history of Georgia, is thus identified: "John B. Gordon, Lieutenant General in the Confederacy, Governor, Thrice United States Senator, and Capitalist." The special capacity in which the General was at the moment in New York does not greatly matter, but it is sure that his activities as a capitalist were not wholly neglected. He was, in fact, in personal contact with Cyrus W. Field, another capitalist of real proportions, and he brought about a meeting between his friend Field and his friend Grady. One of these friends of his shortly afterward lent the other $20,000—with which the recipient was to go home and buy a fourth interest in the influential newspaper he worked for there with such distinction.

The clergyman Dr. H. M. Field remembered years later, and took occasion to record his memory in *The New York Evangelist,* the association between his brother Cyrus and the young Southerner, who had, as it were, flitted into his brother's parlor. He remembered how the young Southerner looked, how Cyrus had turned over the money, and so on. But the Reverend Doctor did not tell what either Cyrus or Henry said at that momentous interview; nor has anybody else told.

Of course, one is at liberty to suppose anything. At the time, Field was upwards of sixty and Grady—barely thirty—looked scarcely more than twenty. It is possible to assume that the great promoter, who was interested in railways and who knew the economic potentialities of the South, did not feel it unbecoming of him under the circumstances to offer to his boyish impecunious debtor, along with his check, an extended fatherly discourse. It is possible, probable in fact, that that discourse, if made, was not without its pietistic interludes. And it is also possible that it touched upon the South, saying how good it would be for the South, and incidentally for all of America, its railways included, if the South would cease repining for its losses and, heedful of manifest destiny, fall into step promptly with the nation at large. It is also possible that the great promoter, captivated by Grady's manner, merely handed the young man his check and suggested that the two of them hurry away to the races. But all of this is *purest* conjecture.

There is another supposition, somewhat more abtruse, which may be interestingly inserted at this point. This supposition is that the Civil War, fought against John C. Calhoun or all he stood for, by Jay Gould and Emerson and Lincoln or all they stood for, resulted superficially in a victory for Emerson and Lincoln, but basically in a victory for the one of the three partners who was most silent and most cunning, namely Gould. By 1880, Calhounism, or the only phase of it repugnant to Gouldists, its potentialities as an economic rival, lay in wreckage. Emersonism, too nebulous for this world, was clean dissipated, existing only in the clerical Emersonian likeness formed of good stupefying factory smoke—quite harmless. Lincolnism was asleep, gorged on insubstantial sops like the Presidency of the United States; for if Wall Street consistently pulled the Presidential strings it was at least true that the Executive was usually one who had been born west of the Alleghenies and in a log cabin. In 1880, there the nation was, with the Gouldists masters of it, masters, but thwarted in a vast part of their realm by ghosts too unnebulous to give way in any decent fashion. There the South was, potentially rich, relatively undeveloped, ripe for exploitation, but the sullen and recalcitrant people there would not cease repining for their losses, and, heedless of manifest destiny, they would not fall into step with the nation at large. . . . But all of *this* is conjecture —maybe so; maybe not so.

The fact is that Grady, after his lucrative interview with that eminent Gouldist, Field, went home and spent his twenty thousand dollars for a quarter interest in the *Constitution,* and that, at his death nine years later, as his eulogists took care to note, that quarter interest was moving on toward a tenfold increase. Grady was so persistently vital, so ebullient, that it is difficult to think of him as part-owner of the paper he had worked for, feeling very much more spirited than he had felt formerly. And it is hardly possible to feel that he was, for all of his being a capitalist, the more warmly regarded by his friends Howell and Harris. But it is sure that in Atlanta in general he came quickly to be held a person of great substance, cherished appropriately by other people of substance.

In 1881 he fathered the great Cotton States Exposition in Atlanta, to the wonderment of the entire nation; and, in the way of writing, besides his regular journalistic work, he did two ambitious articles. One of these was for *Harper's Magazine* called "Cotton and Its Kingdom." The other, written for home consumption while he was on a visit to New York, was called "The Atheistic Tide Sweeping over the Continent, The Threatened Destruction of the Simple Faith of the Fathers by the Vain Deceits of Modern Philosophies—an Attack Christians Must Meet."

The *Harper's* article, whether cooled in the editing or pre-cooled by the author, self-conscious at the prospect of writing for a Northern audience, is a faithful, unemotionalized account of the Cotton situation in 1881. Ten years after the war, Grady says, the big plantation happily seemed to be doomed, and countless small farms dotted the entire South. That trend was soon reversed. The yeomen, dazzled by the ready-money aspect of the cotton crop, and refusing to devote any of their land to food crops, were from autumn to autumn forced to live on credit. And that credit, because of the slight resources at their command, they could obtain only at fatal rates of interest. The remedy is said to be in easier loans—fortunately at the moment banks from as far away as England were entering *that* field; and, above all, in the willingness of the farmers to diversify their crops. If those two things are accomplished, and the recent miraculous advances of science are requisitioned and cotton mills set to spinning at the source of their supply, then one may look to see a final disappearance of the ancient cotton oligarchs and the development of a truly prosperous South.

The article about Atheism is considerably warmer. It says that the struggle between Atheism and the Church is at last definitely upon us. The wicked have habitually aimed their darts at the Church, but between them and the object of their animosity, has always stood a great number of people who are in-the-main virtuous but not aggressively Christian. It is this group, in effect the rampart of the Church, whom the Atheists work upon most tellingly. This is a scientific era, and Atheism, one of the natural manifestations of science, is the penalty of progress. Atheism is quite inconceivably horrid in itself, and will surely be a million times worse than that in its effect on mankind. Yet the Church will win in the struggle because the Church is right . . .—But whether the promised annihilation of the foe will come soon or late, and whether or not it will involve also the annihilation of its inescapable corollaries, progress and science, are phases of the question which the author never gets round to.

His neglect was apparently not held very culpable. In 1882 Grady's reputation in Atlanta was so high that a great number of the most prominent citizens addressed him a formal petition, asking him to offer himself for the National Congress. The compliment was most gratifying and the prospect of Congressional prestige in no way unpleasing. But at length Grady decided that he would for the time being keep out of politics—at least personally. In thanking his petitioners he took occasion to sermonize with rotund eloquence on a number of things that interested him. He talked about his own devotion to journalism, about the disposition of too many Southerners to run for office, about the need for developing the farms and industries of Georgia, about his affection for his young son and for his friends and for his native land. And by his very refusal of the candidacy he rendered himself more highly desirable as a candidate than he had been before the petition took form. He was a favorite son, and nothing of importance could happen in Atlanta without his participation.

The death of Benjamin Harvey Hill in the summer of 1882, at the age of sixty, caused a great upstirring over the entire South. Long a public figure in the state, in the Confederacy, and in the nation, he had once alienated his compatriots by his complacency toward the North, but had later much endeared himself to them by his stubborn and effective opposition to a North that seemed to him obscenely negrophile. It was determined to erect a monument to him in Atlanta, immediately; and when time came for the monument to be dedicated, old Jefferson Davis, eagerly importuned, fared like some fabulous, royal, resurgent Arthur, clean across the land from Mississippi to Georgia, to get the dedication done adequately. Neither Julius Caesar nor Charlemagne nor George Washington nor, likely, St. Peter's self, appearing in Atlanta, could have wrung more hearts at once with awe and ecstasy. Jefferson Davis, King That Was! King That Will Be! (in a spiritual sense, we mean). It was Grady who introduced him to the crowd, Grady, herald-at-arms to the Victor-Victim on that Most Auspicious Day.

One of Senator Hill's actions which had displeased the South was his Congressional endorsement of the Philadelphia Exposition in 1876. The Southern attitude at the time was that Southerners had small business celebrating the centennial of a freedom which for them no longer existed. But much water went under the bridge during the late 'seventies and early 'eighties. Above everything else in importance was the fact that the mass of ordinary citizens, North and South, were still governed by the frontier traditions of America and by the still dominant romantic impulse of West-European civilization. It was not in their Code to go about nursing grudges eternally. There were terse proverbs ready to fit the situation, whether one reviewed the late unpleasantness from the standpoint of "Yankee" or "Rebel"; and however tenacious one might be of animosity, there were always those proverbs to counsel truce. The Georgia-born, Mississippi extremist Lamar, for example, found it in his heart in the early 'seventies to proclaim reconciliationist ideas from his place in the Federal Senate in connection with the death of the New England extremist Charles Sumner. The South-baiting poet Bayard Taylor was instrumental in thrusting into great prominence the Georgia poet Sidney Lanier in connection with the Philadelphia Exposition.

The average Northern citizen was as yet unaccustomed to the economic order of the new industrialism, with all the talk of corporations and rebellious labor. Disciple of Emerson or Lincoln as he was, he was disheartened by the growing complacency of his late allies, the Gouldists, at the steady reassertion of Calhounism in the South, and by indeed the assertion of Calhounism—or what he had taken for Calhounism—the country over. He was dismayed utterly and unsteadied in his convictions by the financial panic of 1873. He wondered, in fact, if after all he did not have more in common with a man in the South circumstanced like himself than he had with a plutocrat on Broadway. The plutocrat, on the other hand, was respectful of the South for two reasons: he might well already have investments there or be in process of making them; he knew increasingly well that there was a likelihood always of alliance between the South and whatever remained of Old-America in the North. He had the need to walk warily—and he had the craft to walk so. Plutocrat and common man alike were stirred by two other passions the nation over—one, the new sense of nationalism, or intersectional curiosity, resulting from the physical uprooting of many young American males during the late war; another, the universal human impulse to talk and even to think prettily about the dead-and-gone.

All of these things working together brought to pass a strange thing. Unyielding theorists might wail as they would—and did—but the fact stood, as early as 1880 that the South had become the unrivaled focus of national romantic yearnings. The tall columns gleaming in the moonlight, the mystical magnolias too opulent to withhold anything, the far stretching cotton fields crowded with happy Negroes, singing—all of these, so lately the symbol of Abomination, became suddenly the symbol of something utterly delectable. A foreign reader, looking over American magazines, someone complained, might well conclude that there was never a thing either good or interesting in America that did not happen south of the Potomac. The *really* interesting things going on with us, of course, were not of the order then thought proper for magazine-pieces.

However all of that was, a sincere and passionate patriot like Grady, overbrimming with universal good will, was bound to be pleased by what he saw. His dear friend, Joe Harris, was writing of Uncle Remus for an audience that overnight grew from local to national and then to international. And in New Orleans Mr. George Cable was writing of the Old Days in a manner that stirred everybody. Suddenly Mr. Cable began to proclaim something very distressing. He declared that whatever might be said about the Old South, its sweet lackadaisicalness, it wondrous loyalties and so on, it was true that the South of 1880 was in every way evading the essentials of its commitments on being re-admitted to the Union. The Negro, Mr. Cable said, for whom so much had been done by enactment, was by shameless malfeasance held, really, still in the status of a slave. That was the truth, he said, and he felt it his duty to let everybody know about it, par-ticularly people in the North, who were so virtuous that they too romantically supposed all other people to be virtuous also.

This announcement was altogether more than Grady could abide peacefully. It was not true, he thundered, not true, not true at all, what Mr. Cable said. And it was so wrongheaded, not to say so malicious, of Mr. Cable to talk in such a fashion. The South walked in bitter thralldom to poverty, Heaven knew and Mr. Cable knew. The South was about to be redeemed from that thralldom. The Sun of Progress stood tip-toe on the misty moun-tain tops, and the beneficent dew of Northern capital could be seen already, here and there, making certain pastures mighty lush—with here a coal mine, there a cotton mill. Would not those sustaining dews disappear, might not others fail to come, if the Northern attitude of suspicion toward the South should be reawakened? He would tell the North the Real Truth of these matters, quite frankly, recording what the Negroes had gained, what, so far as he could see, they would never gain, and of right *ought* never to gain. He would state just that, and he would risk the South's attitude's being endorsed overwhelmingly by people outside the South.

In his article "In Plain Black and White," which appeared in the *Century Magazine,* April, 1885, he made his statement and assumed his risk. The risk was justified. Until then, he said in that article, no really authentic voice from the South had been heard in the recent interminable discussion of the Negro. The North had undertaken to settle that question and the South had determined to keep quiet and see what happened. But the North had at last fumbled the solution badly. Then Mr. Cable had spoken, but, delightful romancer that he was, Mr. Cable, Northern in ancestry and Southern in birth only, had recently confessed himself spiritually an ingrained Northerner. "To be in New England," Mr. Cable had said, "would be enough for me." He, then, is hardly a competent witness for the South.

Grady was reasonably sure, the implication runs, that *he was* a competent witness. The emancipation of the Negro was accepted by the Southern whites with surprisingly little objection; his enfranchisement was also accepted, though less willingly; his exaltation to social equality with the white, the whites of the South resisted and will continue to resist; and even the Northern resolve on this matter had finally collapsed. The secret of this progress is that the Right will prevail. What was done righteously, stood; what was done wrongly, fell—that is what will happen always. And God has willed that the white race shall rule; the black shall be ruled. And that is all there is to that. Not to acquiesce in that is simply to waste one's energy. The two races of the South live apart because each of them so prefers to live. There is an instinct to that end, but if there were no such instinct it is as well to say, incidentally, that the South would be compelled to make one. The South—by this term, Grady, though he never took the trouble to explain himself, meant always the White South—the South is going to deal with the Negroes honestly.

As late as 1870 the Negroes were not dealt with justly as to schooling. But the right will prevail, give it ten years; and by 1880 that injustice was corrected. Some Northern missionary teachers say that injustice still obtains, but these people are mostly sorry sisters, like one who recently felt herself thrilled almost past bearing over being taken for a Negress—as "one in blood with the truest, tenderest, and noblest race that dwells on earth." In the churches as in the schools, the separation is com-

plete. The two races work together, but do not eat together, and
at night they go to their homes in separate localities. On the railway cars, separate though equally comfortable accommodations
are provided. In the courts, respectable Negroes serve on the
juries. In the theaters they sit in opposite sections of the same
gallery. But even if by some miracle the Negroes should overnight
be rendered into whites, thus setting at nought the racial aspects
of the question, it would still be disastrous, so long as they
remain ignorant and irresponsible, to give them any appreciable
share in government. For the control of society must be in the
hands of the best people, let the numerical majority be what it
will.

Altogether, Grady's sentiments so far as they might work in
practice were of an order that John Calhoun, living in Grady's
time, might have perceived unruffled. They would have seemed to
him too confident in their implications about the prevalence of
Right, too optimistic about the schools in general, which, ill
adapted to the whites, were open now at last to the Negro, to
whom they were worse adapted, perhaps now at last a double
menace. To the mordant-minded Calhoun some of the statements
would likely have seemed down-right unjustified, for it was only
by an interpretation too romantic for him that the educational
opportunities of the two races could be held at all equal. Doubtful also would have seemed the statement about the theaters, for
while whites and blacks might sit in different sections of the
same galleries, it was true that, with money, a gallery-sitting white
man could, but a black man could not, buy a seat in some portion
of the theater besides the gallery. To the suppositious Calhoun
and also to all Gouldists—who were the people who really
mattered at the moment—the observation about the necessity of
government by the best people seemed equally sound.

To the dominant majority Grady's entire pronouncement was
satisfying. He unfailingly exhibited toward both God and the
Negro an attitude that was in the South completely orthodox.
His attitude on both of those subjects understood, it was possible
for him to deviate somewhat freely from the standard judgment
in other matters which were conceived of as less important and
on the whole more difficult to understand. Grady must have been
aware of this, for almost invariably when he declared himself, no
matter what the announced topic, he took care to proclaim his
conviction—a quite sincere conviction—that God should be assiduously exalted and the Negro assiduously delimited. Such a prac-

tice was sure to commend him to any audience in the South, and, he discovered, not by any means sure to discount him elsewhere.

This was a day that paid allegiance to Sweetness and Light, or to the semblance of them. Grady was abundantly endowed with both these qualities, and he had been stimulated in his adherence to them by the esteem in which they were held by his friend, wise Joe Harris. He came to be acknowledged North and South as being an authentic spokesman for the Southern point-of-view. His prestige even with people who had never seen him was most high; with people who *had* seen him, who had come under the spell which his presence exercised, he had already long since acquired seraphic haloes. There is nothing to do about persons of that sort. They are born and not made and they swing in their orbits, uttering wisdom or folly. If they speak well, that is fortunate; and if they speak badly, that is unfortunate. For no matter how they speak, lesser men will hearken to them. That is the sort of man Grady was. Born rich and beautiful and charming, born too gaily improvident to retain his riches, born lucky in having riches a second time thrust upon him, born warm-hearted and boisterous enough, though not too boisterous, to enchant a time sated with decorum—there was nothing to say to such a man, once he showed himself in the majesty of his attributes.

Salaams were reserved for him when on December 21, 1886, he addressed the New England Club of New York on the subject of The New South. Who proposed his name as guest of honor for that occasion is not known. He had many friends in the North by that time in addition to Cyrus Field, his friend of years' standing; and proposals of people as guest-speakers are frequently communicated by grapevine. Whoever it was who suggested that Grady be invited, had early cause to congratulate himself, and whether or not it was Field who suggested him, Field, surely, was pleased over the content and manner of the speech, and over the reflection that Grady was after all in a certain fashion his protegé.

The gathering that night was distinguished. General Sherman was present, and the famous ecclesiastic DeWitt Talmadge made an oration filled with huzzas and so forth to recall the splendor of the victorious Northern armies as in 1865 they marched through Washington.

It came Grady's time to speak. A little stocky, boyish in face, a little treble in voice, he stood up. The words flowed. He was a provincial, he said, and vastly pleased, if dismayed, to be speaking in such exalted quarters. He would remind the gathering that there had been Cavaliers in early America as well as Puritans; he was persuaded that these two groups had long since fused and that the ideal American, Abraham Lincoln, had been the result. Extemporaneously, he referred to the speech of Dr. Talmadge, pictured to his audience (symphonic oratory here) the return of the Southern soldier from the war, not in triumph but in defeat, broken in everything but his spirit and his determination to keep the faith as an American. He extolled a yeoman society and all of the yeoman virtues (*pace* frontier democracy); he declared Slavery inherently evil (*pace* New England Transcendentalism). The South, he said, (symphonic oratory again) had nothing to retract. It fought the war in full sincerity, but mistakenly, and providentially, to no purpose. The South was ready to forget old grievances and begin anew. Would the North join in such a pact? If not, the South would have to get along as best she could; if so, then would the vision of Daniel Webster when he cried "united, all united, now and forever" be at last justified. The words ceased —they had beaten for about twenty minutes. The orator, swinging in his orbit, swung to rest. The audience was astounded; it was wild with enthusiasm. The papers next morning everywhere were equally wild. And Henry Grady was one of the recognized major prophets of America.

It is all a little sad, even in retrospect, and at the time Grady was himself both sad and joyous, chastened—weighted and inspired with a sense of what he had done, and what he ought to do. He remembered the Bible, thought upon his widowed mother, contemplated loving-kindness which is divine and the reverse of loving-kindness which is of Hell. He thought of himself as, no Prince surely, but as a poor Servant of Holy Peace, Peace which is not merely the cessation of violence but which is a state of mind, and, oh! more important still, a state of heart. "He knew then," wrote his friend Harris, "that his real mission was that of Pacificator. There was a change in him from that time forth, though it was a change visible only to friendly and watchful eyes. He put away something of his boyishness, and became, as it seemed, a trifle more thoughtful. His purpose developed into a mission, and grew in his mind, and shone in his eyes, and remained with him day and night. He made many speeches after that, frequently in little out-of-the-way country places, but all of them had a national significance and national bearing. He was preaching the sentiments of harmony, fraternity and good will to the South as well as to the North."

Mission or no mission thus cosmic, Grady had the *Constitution* to work on daily, and he was perpetually busy to do something for the betterment of the South. There were great possibilities in oranges, he thought; and since his visit to Florida in 1877 he had exhorted about oranges. There were possibilities in watermelons —let the people around Albany in southern Georgia plant more and more of them. There were possibilities in peaches—a man in Marshallville, in middle Georgia, had in one summer made $64,000 on peaches alone—let us plant more of them. And so on, for the home folks.

But we must let the world know of our advantages, and to do that there is hardly anything better than an "Exposition." In 1887, then, and again in 1889, he instigated successful Expositions in Atlanta. And in the interval he inaugurated a shortlived and never very prosperous "Chautauqua"—situated some twenty or so miles from the city. He was constantly entreated to go everywhere to make speeches, and he went often, once to Joe Harris's boyhood home, little Eatonton. Joe wanted him to go and he went; there was mighty little he could refuse anybody, especially Joe Harris. And whenever Grady spoke, the magic *worked,* almost without exception.

In the avalanche of invitations that poured upon him was one to make an address at the Texas State Fair in Dallas, October 26, 1887. This invitation he accepted. He prepared his speech with great care, a new procedure with him, and with a party of friends in a private railway car set out for Dallas. His journey was a triumphal progress—homage to the New South, as it were, suggestive of that other journey which Jefferson Davis had only a few years before made from Mississippi to Atlanta. Eager crowds met the train along the route, and, in Dallas—"West," still, in those days, with a heart that was glad and free—the welcome broke up into a general and thoroughly well-disposed riot, greatly enjoyed by everybody but most notably the pilgrim Lion. As time for the oration came on, the Lion gained one conviction very surely; that he could not for the life of him roar that day according to the prompt-sheets he had made out in Atlanta. So he made up his mind to extemporize, to dip into those prompt-sheets only when he chose; and then he felt vastly more at ease.

The speech, which ran for about an hour and a quarter, said essentially, with much interesting corroborative material, that the South must for the present remain "solid" in politics, that it must diversify its farm crops, and that it must establish mills and

factories. It said that if the South would do all of this it would be
unprecedentedly well off; and that, in fact, the orator, visioning
the accomplishment of so much, could vision this nation's having
within his life-time a hundred and fifty million people; and more
than that, that he could vision the glory of Almighty God stream-
ing through the Everlasting as, well-pleased, "He looks down on
His people who have given themselves unto Him and leads them
from one triumph to another. . . ."

This speech was acclaimed universally, and, during the month
following, on Thanksgiving Day, Grady spoke again, in Augusta,
Georgia. There, because of trouble with his voice, he was forced
unwillingly to stop in something less than an hour. One of the
themes of his speech also was that the South must remain politically "solid." This is dangerous, because it is inevitable that a
solid South will encourage a solid North; but for all of that danger, the reverse danger is vastly more appalling—that of a divided
white ballot in the South yielding the balance of power to the
Negro ballot.

Northern people cannot realize that in spite of racial difference
Southern white people and Negroes are really personally fond
of one another. In the South, when one says "The Negro," one
means in a general sense "Labor." Remembering that, it is possible to say that the relations between "capital" and "labor" in
the South are vastly more amicable than they are elsewhere. This
is because in the South capitalists and laborers, man for man,
know one another personally, regard one another as human
entities rather than as units in the human abstraction. (O Joe
Harris, it is *your* talk Grady is talking here, you talk, nostalgic
for little Eatonton!) Yet we must have cities, and a vastly greater
population (in which, Joe Harris, people can continue to know
one another personally if they are the right *sort* of people, now
can't they?).

We must induce Northerners to settle here, but let them be
the right sort of Northerners. Not every immigrant will do, be
sure of that. Strange doctrines are raising their heads in the
North, blasphemous in their questioning of God. "It may be that
the last hope of saving the old-fashioned on this continent will be
lodged in the South. . . . Let us . . . highly resolve that we will
give ourselves to the saving of the old-fashioned. . . ." To do this
we Southern whites must keep united, must not be broken into
factions of Old-Southists and New-Southists. "Somebody has said
that 'certain upstarts and speculators were seeking to create a new

South to the derision and disparagement of the old.' These are cruel and unjust words. . . . One of the 'upstarts' said in a speech in New York: 'In answering to the toast of the New South, I accept the name in no disaparagement to the Old South. Nobody more than I gives reverence to our fathers'. . . . Let them sit, therefore in the dismantled porches of their homes . . . and gaze out to the sea . . . beyond the horizon to which their armada has drifted forever. . . . Let them rest . . . until God shall call them hence. . . ."

From an objective point of view the New York speech of 1886 was, of course, the most notable event of Grady's life, but from the standpoint of subjective biography the Augusta pronouncement far transcends it. During the time between the Civil and Spanish-American wars Southern thinking divided itself loosely into the creeds adhered to by five different groups—the People, who were naturally in the majority and who perceived little except their daily wants and the satisfaction of them; the Patriots, who were unusually gifted in vindictiveness or surliness; the Prophets, who were really Platonists, somewhat after the pattern of Thomas Carlyle; the Populists, whose thinking was already in Grady's time making itself manifest; and the Promoters, whose performances have persisted actively enough for them not to need identification. Grady was inherently a Promoter. His spirit was too good for him to be a "Patriot." Nor could he be a Populist. He understood this doctrine and was in a measure in sympathy with it; but his basic conservatism, his personal friendships, and, above all, his convictions about the solid South held him on this score a traditional Democrat.

It is doubtful whether he ever understood fully what the Prophets were talking about. To him, an American of his day, dizzy with frontier optimism, they were likely to seem, as he implied in his speech in Augusta, no better than this: a group of people wrapping themselves in the sacred memories of the Old South merely to hide their own weakness or to strengthen their own failing fortunes. Now that, possibly, is what the Patriots were; but the Prophets were something else. They perceived the issues that, long before, dismayed John Calhoun, that dismayed Edmund Burke and Thomas Jefferson, issues that Carlyle had long been thundering about in England. They thought with Grady that a mechanistic philosophy was one of the inescapable corollaries of Progress, but, unlike him, they felt that (bound then that day to choose which god they would serve) they must in whole conscience for-swear Progress or be damned utterly. Less trusting than Grady, they did not believe that God could be depended upon to reserve His cake indefinitely for a people who persistently devoured it.

However great may be the suggestion that he was wise, it is not set down anywhere that Jeremiah was vastly popular. And Grady was popular beyond measuring; nearly everything that he touched prospered. His Chautauqua activities were unavailing and his mighty "prohibition" campaign in the fall of 1887— waged in high good humor against his *Constitution* colleague Evan Howell—hardly brought about the Dry Millenium that he advocated. But on nearly every other front he was, or seemed to be, victor. He loved the unofficial exercise of political power, and he had become a master at acquiring it. *A*, pining to be senator, learns that certain gentlemen in Atlanta think *B* more fitted for the job, and straightway *A* finds his health too precarious for much exertion. *C*, engrossed in his private pursuits, is told that by announcing as a candidate he may be Governor—certain gentlemen in Atlanta, noting his ability and integrity, have determined so.

It was getting around to the point that all that Grady had to do to get a thing done was to tell his wish. There was a hard winter, and there were prospects of a Christmas Day on which many Atlantans would go hungry; Grady spoke, and there was superabundant manna. Many Confederate veterans in Georgia were impoverished and unhoused; Grady spoke, and there was succor for them. And, as there had come to ancient Greece before young Paris for judgment, three goddesses, there came to Atlanta in 1888 to receive her just obeisance, one goddess. *Young Paris, ease your mind, here is the lady for your golden apple, and no doubts. Never ponder, on, but that I might divide my apple. Why divide it? Here is Juno, here Minerva, here Venus, all in one, Frances Folsom Cleveland.* And through the golden air did Frances, she of ambrosial locks, come gliding, and she alighted at the Christian Home of Henry Grady, and stood for a reception there before a mantelpiece banked lavishly with the costliest florists'- blossoms.

From triumph to triumph Henry Grady mounted, humorous and friendly and unspoiled. Joe Harris had observed him as inspired by a new seriousness, but to ordinary men his familiar gusto seemed undampened. He was likely still to leap shouting from *any* nabob's carriage to give hot chase to rabbits that came within his notice. He was likely still to shout and romp and tussle, when he came to visit his mother in Athens, with the wondering sophomores whom his mother had in her house as boarders. But, though he let the ash-cakes burn, King Alfred was not any less a King. And so Henry was not Henry less, for all his rollicking. It was understood that he was a "genius." He was made a trustees of his *Alma Mater*. Another accolade came to him in the form of an invitation to speak at the University of Virginia in June, 1889. He accepted it, and he accepted as readily an invitation to speak during the same month in Elberton, forty miles or so east of his boybood home in Athens.

Virginians have traditionally thought and spoken highly of themselves, and the legend of their superiority was long ago well established. Grady was nurtured on that legend, and it was a part of his creed to esteem Thomas Jefferson inordinately. He particularly wished to justify himself in his speech at Charlottesville, and he prepared his remarks in advance, carefully. But once he began talking, he found himself talking without great reference to what he had written.

This speech, "Against Centralization," and the Elberton speech, "The Farmer and the Cities," testify that some new things had lately come into Grady's consciousness and that he was reckoning with those things admirably. Made scarcely six months before his death, they are bound to stir, in the mind of anybody reading them, speculation as to what turn Grady might have taken had he lived to be seventy. Would he, for example, have maintained unbroken his relations with the growing brood of Southern capitalists whom he had fostered? Would he, adopting Populism, have so transfigured it as to make it broadly acceptable to all America? Or would he, disheartened at last about his American Dream, and quite ineffectual, have turned mildly nostalgic, piping till the end about how thoroughgoing an optimist he was?

It is sure that the pronouncements in Charlottesville and Elberton, closely related to each other though not identical, exhibit in common on the part of their author a weakened confidence in mankind. The factors he had isolated as disruptive of Southern prosperity were undoubtedly tottering, but as they collapsed new foes appeared to bind and stultify. The old disciples of Lincoln and Emerson were at last somewhat placated in their antagonism to the South; but the Gouldists, who had seemed to him not concerned with antagonism, now quite palpably, to him as well as to the Southern "Prophets," had somehow taken into bondage not merely the South but the Lincoln country also. He spoke with sternness and even with violence of this chance. We must break down the present tendency toward centralization of government—America is too big for a highly centralized administration—no one man nor group of men can comprehend a phenomenon so vast and so complex. Similiarly we can no longer tolerate the present tendency toward consolidation of capital. There were highwaymen and robber barons in the old days; we have them still, and now they are protected by the laws governing corporations. The Federal government has exalted the city at the expense of the village and the farm. That is disastrous. We must change it; for there are remedies. The little man, everywhere, has suffered; and especially has he suffered in the South. One-fourth of the farm lands in Georgia are mortgaged to Northern bankers. Since 1865 Georgia has paid an annual average of over two million dollars for Federal war pensions, and the rates increase so rapidly that this year Georgia is contributing to that behemoth three millions and a half. "The South has played a patient and a waiting game for twenty years, fearing to protest . . . in the fear that she would be misunderstood. I fear that she has gained little by this course save the contempt of her enemies. The time has come when she should . . . declare her mind and stand by her convictions."

Yet . . . perhaps education will save us. The wars of the future will be fought bloodlessly, in men's minds and on ledger-pages—other wars are wasteful. The South must be educated. Something *must* save us. . . . I am no pessimist. . . . I always bet on fair weather in America. The situation is grave, but God will not permit to be too grave because we in America are surely his very special favorites. "The struggle for human rights never goes backward among English-speaking peoples. . . . The world moves steadily from gloom to brightness. And, kneeling in prayer, I vision this United Nation, virtuous and happy and loving, inducting into virtue and happiness and peace all other nations, everywhere."

Back in Atlanta there was much to do in that summer and fall of 1889. The Exposition was afoot, and that at last came off satisfactorily, with a pyrotechnic likeness of Grady—along with Governor Gordon's—blazoned upon the skies one night in recognition of his eminence and of his services to every useful thing. The heavy work of the Exposition behind him, he turned himself to the series of articles on "The New South" that he began publishing about then in the New York *Ledger* and to the speech on

The Race Problem that he had promised to deliver during December in Boston.

The articles, published in six installments of about 2500 words each, are historical, descriptive, and hortatory. Made up largely of sections of his previous declarations strung together with some new transitions and a few quite fresh and delicious anecdotes, they exhibit the breadth and thoroughness of information about Southern affairs that Grady uniformly commanded, and, of course, the contagious passion about Southern affairs that uniformly commanded Grady. The series was concluded in the *Ledger* December 21, 1889, only two days before Grady's death; and, published in book form in the endemic emotionalism that followed that sad event, they remain—a posthumous issue—the only considerable volume ever set forth over Grady's name and primarily devoted to his writings.

Grady thought that the active preparation of a speech was rather mercilessly onerous. But he was driven at that time to submit himself to that ordeal because of his impending address before the Merchants Association of Boston. He worked at that speech hard. When time came for him to go, he was so ill that his doctor advised him to cancel his engagement and go to bed. But he felt bound to do as he had promised. And in Boston he made his speech. Grover Cleveland and Andrew Carnegie were guests, but Grady's appearance was, as the saying goes, the feature of the evening. His speech offered in substance about what he had said in his *Century* article on the race problem years earlier—a statement of the situation as it appeared to a fundamentally conservative Southern white man who was also benign and intelligent. Thoroughly candid, but ingratiating, embellished with the most exemplary talk about God and about the Union—sail on, oh, strong and great—his remarks were received in Boston if not with enthusiasm, certainly with sympathy. And over most of the rest of the country, especially in the South, the speech was pronounced a masterpiece.

He had gone to Boston with a party of friends, and people there were anxious to exhibit to the visitors various items of interest about the city. Among other wonders exhibited to them the morning following, was Plymouth Rock; and Grady, racked with bronchitis as he was, enjoyed that sight ardently.

That afternoon, the floods of historic patriotism stemmed at last, Grady appeared at a meeting of a Democratic Club in Boston. His cold was worse, but he managed to talk for about twenty

minutes. He condemned centralization as he had done in Charlottesville; he exalted the little man; he told how the South had
developed within his memory toward a self-sufficing economy; he
lyricized the Union; he said good-bye—"I want . . . to thank you
. . . for all you have done for us . . . and to say that whenever any
of you come South just speak your name . . . and we will meet
you at the gates . . . Forget thee will I ne'er, Glencairn, and all
that thou hast done for me."

And then the train home. He was poorly and tired—tired out.
A physician who saw him in New York was reassuring; he thought
the patient in no danger at all. In Richmond a great crowd met
him at the station and he went out to speak with them, and a
wreath of flowers was put upon his head. *Oh, Pericles!* In Atlanta
the world and his brother too met the train to receive home the
conqueror, to convey him on his appointed rounds in a carriage
with six white horses. But he knew beforehand that he was too
sick for all of this and an hour or so before reaching the city he
telegraphed his doctor to meet him, please, and to take charge
of him, and to do what he could for his distress. The doctor came
and took him, driving through the mute multitude, driving on
till he got him home.

I'm afraid I'm going to be mighty sick, said Grady. He had
said this for several days, and he said it still—going to be mighty
sick. Alas, not *going to be,* but *was.* He was about to die. The
famous physicians came hurrying. The notable and the unnotable
friends came trooping. And telegrams from worthies the country
over came zipping in to make a paper Pyramid. And little white
prayers and great gaudy prayers jostled one another as they sped
on high. But none of these things mattered. "Tell Mother," he
said—so they told his mother, later, her badgered boy in Atlanta
had sent word to her—"Tell Mother that Father died fighting for
the South and that I died talking for it!" That was the end; and
really there was nothing more to say.

But more *was* said; and that is one of the facts least open to
question anywhere. Jefferson Davis had died only two weeks previously—the Old South and the New, ten thousand times alas;
and Christmas—Christmas that Grady had so exulted in, Christmas that Tiny Tim had spoken of so beauteously—holy Christmas
lay but two days ahead. Oh, the young warrior cut down! Oh, the
newspaper editorials; Oh, the monsoon of condolence from the
four quarters of America. Oh, the sweet poetic elegies, ever and
anon drifting. Oh, the Sermons—henceforth, adjured the Protes-

tant Pope of the time, the Reverend Talmadge speaking in New York, henceforth let all men know it possible to be both great and Christian; Gladstone has said it, Grady has proved it. Oh, the memorial meetings held here and there—at the one in Atlanta a full panoplied chemistry-professor collapsed from his emotion. Oh, the sumptuous double-page cartoon devoted to him in a famous national magazine—a sculptor, dead, with hammer still in hand—"Literally," the caption read, "Loving a Nation into Peace." Oh, the memorial tome put forward soon in Atlanta with its mention on the title page of the great journal which Grady had worked with and which was still open for business. And oh, above all, the little Southern lads who were to declaim through the successive years the dead herald's winged words interminably— "Let me picture to you the footsore Confederate soldier as . . . he turned Southward from Appomattox . . . his social system swept away . . . What does he do, this hero in gray with a heart of gold? . . . In my native town of Athens is a monument that crowns its central hill. . . ."

And oh! that monument, become at length as all things must, a traffic hazard, and demoted to a site less coveted than its habitual hill—the entrance to Grady's Athens *Alma Mater*. That monument! become a resting-place for alien students, who sprawl casually and refresh themselves with coca-colas, and, in rosy trance or with indifference or gibe or leer, appraise the surging co-eds! O, that monument, functional at last!

⊰§⊱

Old Wine in a New Bottle

AN OLD LADY I know had a house party recently for three ancient cousins of hers. There was much merriment among those girls. Not since childhood had the four of them been together in their grandfather's house. "Cousin," said one of them, one day, "when in the name of conscience was it that we were last all together here?" "Cousin," said the other, inscrutably, so that I could not tell for all my effort whether she was in earnest or not in earnest. "Cousin," said she, "surely not since the spring of Appomattox."

All of that was scarcely more than yesterday, and whether those ladies had actually not foregathered in that house since 1865 does not greatly matter. What does matter is that a living being in 1934, wishing to say that something in her experience happened long ago, ran naturally into the idea of Appomattox. That idea marked something very definite in her mind; it was like saying *before I was born* or *before my marriage,* or *before Columbus.* Before Appomattox, there was one world; since then, another— or certainly, in many ways, another.

It is sure that that war's end brought relief and happiness to many people in the South. The vain and bitter struggle was over, they thought; and, though possibly there would be no more slavery, they would take up as well as might be where they left off, and live on much as they had done previously. Young Jack's bones, truly, lay at Gettysburg, and young Tom's, rescued, lay securely in the burial plot at home; but life was not just now coming to be partners with death. Those two were indeed twins inseparable, and it was no secret that whoever trafficked with one must needs traffic with the other. And besides, there was God, to heal wounds, to sustain and strengthen, and to give good com-

From *The Virginia Quarterly Review*, XI (April, 1935) , 239-252.

fort. Surely there was God, and there was the need of sanity in the world. And there was General Lee, saying—living, rather—*act well thy part, act well thy part*—the rest, one knew.

But occasionally there was someone who could not believe that all was ended—could not believe it. Were not young Jack, young Tom (such a person wished to know) treacherously dealt with by this eventuality? Had they given over their bright lives for quite nothing? Such a person had believed, those boys had believed, that there was a thing at stake which is not possible to compromise about—namely, principle.

Now, was there a principle at stake? There had been many to say so as long as it had seemed possible to enforce one. When it seemed no longer possible to enforce anything, many people, aware that principle does not offer itself to compromise, reversed much of their accustomed declaration and concluded that whatever else had been the issue of the war, it had hardly been principle—certainly not the kind that is spelled with a large letter. Or, fantastically, other people told themselves that there had been no compromise. Among the survivors of that war, there were some who could find no spell-word till they died, to persuade them that what had happened had happened well.

One of these people was Robert Lewis Dabney, who had been born in Virginia in 1820 and had always lived there. After studying at Hampden-Sydney College, the University of Virginia, and the Virginia Union Theological Seminary, and after serving for seven years as a Presbyterian minister—among other places, at the Twinkling Springs Church—he became in 1853 a teacher in the Union Theological Seminary. He was a learned and profound man, and his fame in that regard had by 1860 become national. He had opposed secession, but once war was inaugurated he entered the Confederate Army as a chaplain; and, in 1862, as a major, he was on the staff of his dear friend, Stonewall Jackson.

During the war, already a kind of prophet in Virginia, he repeatedly gave his word that a Southern victory was essential. He meant that, as it stood. He could not, with the war over (say, the day *after* Appomattox), indicate that a Southern victory had not after all been of great importance. He was impelled to say that defeat was, simply, not to be endured. The geographic South, the physical South, was undeniably conquered, but what of the South which was not geographic, not physical? What of that South which he felt had somehow, by God's grace, in knightly

fashion, set itself to save the world? The quick demons of dis-
integration and chaos—active throughout western civilization, and,
in the northern United States, in fair way of becoming dominant
—were fiercely menacing; there had been a South to defy them.
What of that South? He had one solution: let true Southerners
migrate to some other land, to Australia, to Brazil—a *colony* of
Southerners, numerous enough to gain concessions for itself. He
talked of all this, wrote of it, consulted Lee about it—all, vainly.
People would not heed him. As a minister, in his pulpit, he was
hearkened to. Outside his pulpit, though he showed never so
plainly that the forces he denounced were deadly hostile to his
pulpit and sought in the end to destroy it and all pulpits, he
could gain no hearing.

Albert Taylor Bledsoe felt almost as sharply. Dabney's contemporary, he had grown up in a Virginia family living in Ohio,
and before the war had taught mathematics at the University of
Mississippi and at the University of Virginia. During the war,
Jefferson Davis kept him for a long while in England, collecting,
among the American Colonial archives, material that might
sustain the constitutional right of secession. Soon after the war,
he inaugurated in Baltimore a magazine which was dedicated to
the interpretation and defense of the Southern cause. He was
alert, learned, indefatigable, and valiant, a fit comrade for Dabney, with whom he saw eye to eye in most matters.

Charles Colcock Jones had grown up on the Georgia seaboard,
derived (several generations down) from the almost nomadic
New England group that had lived some fifty years in South
Carolina before coming in the mid-seventeen-hundreds to settle
finally at Midway, below Savannah, in Georgia, where they became the most Southern of Southern people. He was a Princeton-
schooled lawyer, somewhat younger than Dabney and Bledsoe.
During the war, he was a cavalry officer, and afterwards for a
few years he practiced his profession in New York. But nostalgic
impulses early moved his mind, and soon the rest of him, back
to his home. Much of his time in New York went into the preparation of his monumental *History of Georgia* (from earliest times
through the Revolution) and of his authoritative monographs on
Southern historical subjects. Later, as a lawyer in Augusta, he
proclaimed till his death, in a series of countless speeches delivered on public occasions, the doctrines already published by his
seniors from Virginia. He was intelligent and passionate, and

his own contribution to the creed of Dabney and Bledsoe was highly pertinent.

There was developed, then, a sort of Dogma. Among the saints it spoke of—or might have spoken of—reverently, were St. Thomas Aquinas, Erasmus, Edmund Burke, and Thomas Carlyle, and, in America, Thomas Jefferson, John Taylor, Beverly Tucker, William Grayson, John Calhoun, and Edmund Ruffin. It abhorred Alexander Hamilton and Daniel Webster, and foreshadowed in dark and nameless abstraction the whole glut of predatory lords who had led the entire western world to something that (since the cataclysm of 1914-18, and, in America, specifically, since a day in the fall of 1929) has come to look appallingly like dissolution. These predatory lords, true to the implication of Dogma, were the inevitable emissaries of the gods our world had given itself over to—the jealous, jealous gods of Speed and Mass, who will brook nothing that does not favor them.

The conflict was as wide as Christendom—this conflict between the true Lord and the dual Anti-Christs, Speed and Mass. Its American phase was of particular interest because it was specially our own, and because here the antagonists found their partisans more clearly than anywhere else (though never absolutely so) arrayed against each other along geographic lines. The contest was also more critical here. We were as a people singularly loosened from code and tradition; those supports, lost in the passage hither, lay for all one could tell on the Atlantic's bottom. We possessed as a people no physical memorials of a great humanistic past—no cathedrals, for instance—to serve as a bulwark against the swift flood. (All of this was to be the case later in Russia, where great tradition had been an exclusive snob; great memorials, relatively few and most often flashy.) In America, society had been gravely unbalanced, in a fashion, since the withdrawal at the time of the Revolution of forty thousand Loyalists—who were on the whole traditionalists; and at the conclusion of the Civil War it was further unbalanced by the political annihilation of the Southerners—the only substantial and organized group, who, in spite of pioneer handicaps, were determined to keep constantly in mind the values of a proven immemorial culture. As a crowning ill-fate in America, the sporadic natural-allies of the Southerners in their distrust of Speed and Mass were diverted by the comparatively minor and irrelevant (because it was surely doomed) issue of slavery. That issue was palpable and spectacular, readily visualized by a naive people such as most of us were without regard to section.

The South too, then, had it not been identified with slavery, had it not been driven by self-interest to sharpen its wits, might possibly, like the North, have been diverted into slavery as an issue more nearly paramount than the other issue of economic rivalry, that, in later times, has been revealed to everybody as the actual one. Whatever the source of the South's superior discernment, it seems now indisputable that for clarity of comprehension in those days one must look to Calhoun rather than to Emerson or to Lincoln. For those latter two, prophets of romantic individualism—allies, for all of Emerson's complacency at Lincoln's death—were, surely, vastly more affiliated in spirit with what Calhoun stood for than for what came to be represented by Mr. Midas Got-rox. Confused by the institution of slavery, the sage Emerson and the hero Lincoln combined, in spite of their own natures and in spite of Calhoun's warnings, to pull from the fire the baneful chestnuts of Mr. Got-rox.

The remarkable fact is that Dabney, Bledsoe, and Jones, through all the wild frenzy of war and reconstruction, managed to see most of this clearly and to talk about it pointedly. The idea became the zealous, urgent passion of their lives—ultimately religious; and the Dogma they erected became as imperious as it was sacred. If this Dogma seems now weakened rather than strengthened by the febrile intensity of its phrasing, the rhetorical fashion of the time may be offered in explanation—and the panic-lashed recognition of its sponsors that their vision was about to be repudiated.

The Dogma held that the impostor gods, Speed and Mass, were really demons. But the western world would not believe them so. "They will none the less," said Dogma, "one day lead whoever follows them to a Pit he will to his sorrow learn the name of. Once dominant, they will cry, 'Go far and go swiftly, make much and make it quickly'; over and over, goad-handed, they will cry this cry till there is no peace. To the objection that in such a process quality will surely suffer, cheapness pervade everything, everybody, they will answer only with the same cry. They will demand in efficiency's name an unremitting uniformity and mechanization of men and things, and will compel a rationalistic materialism capable in a trice of justifying itself to the dullest.

"Imbecile, they will rage for surfeit, reckless of fated dearth.

They will cry 'make more and make more' till the warehouses of all nations that follow them will be filled to bursting. Within those nations, millions may be perishing for actual bread, but Speed and Mass are insensate; they will not care. Those millions will not have money to exchange for bread, and there can be no slowing down to provide them money. Speed and Mass are tyrannous, they are stentorian. 'Money,' they will cry, 'must be had, and on the instant. Without money there can be no purchase of the implements-of-creation, and without purchase of the implements-of-creation there can be no purchase of the creations of implements-of-creation.

" 'Vent your stores, our nations,' they will cry, 'on alien nations heretic to us, on nations who, disregardful of our harnessed lightnings, are less rich than you, but who, thanks to long time, still, in their laborious, ox-cart way, have laid by some share of money. Enforce these nations, your victims, to purchase, while their money lasts, the creations of your implements-of-creation and to purchase even the implements-of-creation so that they too may create to be purchased creations that will justify the purchase of further implements-of-creation.' [And this is the house that Jack built.] Speed and Mass are treacherous. To one of their nations, they will whisper, 'Seize now for your very own, resolutely, with all our sanction, the nation known as *Backward People X.* It offers a rich and unexploited market.' And concerning the same people, they will whisper to another of their votary nations the same counsel. . . . And Speed and Mass will revel in the ensuing carnage, demanding only that it be always vaster, always swifter."

The Dogma went on: "In America, that treachery has indeed only now been finally executed—and with a unique barbarity. For here, the victim to be exploited, rendered alien now in all but windy pronouncement, has been most integrally part of America. Safe, now, for a time, Speed and Mass can range as they will across this continent, assured that they may exploit alike the South which of late defied them, the West which of late fought for them. Safe here, they may applaud the denunciation of Oraory against the quite horrid imperialism of Europe.

"Speed and Mass spare nothing. The flower of religion, the flower of honor, the flower of chivalry, they will ride down under their wheels, their followers banging madly after them, all fiendlike, joy-riding quite joylessly round and round the shrunken world—looking for sensations. There will be a flower of simple

faith in one's fellow to be ridden down. And there will be a
flower at long last, growing indeed far, scarcely this side of ruin's
brink—the flower of one's caring, really, what happens, at all.
This flower too, these fiends will ride down till it is dust." . . .
These were the tocsins of Dogma.

But Dabney was old, Bledsoe was old, Jones was aging. They
were dignified, a little stodgy perhaps; they were top-hatted and
bewhiskered, somehow all of them ecclesiastical—and, indubitably,
all of them wholeheartedly given to rolling and splendiferous
rhetoric. The mode for all that they were, was passing; whatever
such men stood for was in a sense automatically rendered unsym-
pathetic. Soon the three prophets would be dead—and there was
no mode in *that* outlandish direction at all. The *ton* was very
different from that.

Yet the resistance of many Southerners to a cultural and industrial uniformity with Great America persisted in formidable
manner till well into the 1900's—and in one manner or another
it persists still. The aggressive resistance came chiefly from two
unrelated sources: from the Populist Party and from patriotic
organizations like the Confederate Veterans and the Daughters of
the Confederacy. The negative resistance has come chiefly from
the ample, native bogs of human inertia, and from valid tradition,
often, erroneously, not distinguished from inertia. As strong as all
of these forces have been, they have usually carried within themselves elements repugnant to some common human mood; and
the result has been that the very assertion of these forces has often
seemed to recommend whatever might be in opposition to them.

The Populists, for instance, offered the most substantial challenge to the ways of Great America heard since the surrender of
Joseph E. Johnston. But to Johnston's successor (whose remote
but crucial battle they were fighting—the enemy being a common
one) the Populists seemed deplorably identified with a near-at-
hand, unschooled rusticity, and worse, with what Johnston's
group had been accustomed to call the mudsill of society—namely,
proletarian labor. The Confederate Veterans were old and the
Daughters of the Confederacy were feminine—and those considerations hardly recommended unreservedly the doings of either
to the great mass of dominant, hale masculinity. Further, those
patriots were sentimental—or were suspected of being so—in a
day becoming leery of sentiment, and were dedicated to Reminiscence in a day dazzled by Darwin. As for the inertia which
thwarted the South's participation in the great national scheme,

that, though perilously discredited by its very name, has remained (for one to bless or curse according to his light) the most obstructionary barrier that Speed and Mass have been obliged to reckon with.

In the Reconstruction South the common citizen grew restive, at last, under his persistent divergence from the world surrounding him, and he was very weary of his persistent, quite wretched poverty. For all of his being a Southerner, he was a frontier Protestant and a frontier American. His religion taught him that God gives money to those who please Him, and his observation and experience in this new land had by and large (up till 1861) confirmed his religion. For all of his being a Southerner, he was also human—unable to probe the future impressively farther than his own nose. He was in fact too tired to probe anything very earnestly, tired clean out, and inexpressibly disheartened. Was he not, perhaps, vaguely suspicious that the South in its wilful avoidance of the common course had erred in God's sight, and had justly merited God's chastening?

What could he do, then? Many had abandoned the South—left it, utterly robbed, as it was, of the verve and strengh of its best men, burdened as it was with the unparalleled burden of a shiftless race that could not be driven but that surely must be fed. He could not abandon the South; he loved it; he owned it; it owned him. Perhaps if *he* would change, *much* would change. Perhaps he should help the South to be like the Great America it was part of. There were many to say so, some good men, some bad —aggressive people, he heard them called admiringly; up-and-coming people; sooners, God save the word; protagonists of a new order—some in rags, some in tags, some in velvet gowns.

He could cut down, then, his cape-jasmines in the garden, too suggestive of funerals; cut down the sombre, lawn-littering magnolias, root out the musky boxwood; he could have a lawn, in short, unbroken save for the presence of an iron deer, plumb in its geometric center; and he could take down the white picket fence, secure that the deer would not range, but not enough secure that it would be unavoidably observed, like its fellow deer at Saratoga. He could borrow his friends' diamonds to wear when being photographed. He could lay by the old ideal of form that had governed him in building (that he *would* strive for, though often in performance he had had it shoddy) and aim at the sturdy, the snug, the—if truth must be told—mediocre,—a descending series, leading at bottom to the chastely cute. He could shift his diversion from inexhaustible conversation to inexhaustible whist. He could move to cities, he could pump and prime his cities into beatific bigness—"Yes sir-ree, it's a regular little old metropolis— New York of the South we call it, 89,000 people last census—and *Progress? Gen-tle-men, Progress? I'll say Progress."* He could form stock-companies, he could water stock—not very well, alas, but he could try. He could build factories—not very big ones, but he could do his best. And he could advertise; he could turn his whole mind, his whole energy, to money. Thus, muttering to himself a foolish jingle from out the depths of memory, he contemplated a day when he might at length be rich indeed. Hand on stomach, lest the organ turn, he muttered, adapting, typifying to himself all his people:

> When I'm a man
> I'll be a Croesus if I can
> And I can
> When I'm a man
> Bye and bye.

Among the protagonists of the new order, there came at length a transcendent troubadour from a tonic city, Atlanta. His name was Henry Grady and his banner bore a strange device that is not to this day generally understood. The large meaning of this device said one thing, but its reservations often said quite another. This troubadour loved everybody; he was magnanimously polite, and politeness (whatever it may cost) buys everything. He talked to a North that was sated with vindictiveness, and to a South that was sated with being sullen. "My countrymen," he said to them, echoing another patriot, "know one another, and you will love one another." That was noble sentiment.

Clean-shaven, youthful, a brisk journalist, dressed as a bona fide man of business, Grady reflected fully in his person and manner the pervading generosity and sincerity of his nature. He was genial, easy, and informal; he had a bright story to point up any idea he adopted; and he had always a genuine tear for the Lost Cause, for the virtue of Southern womanhood, and for the old darkies. He was irresistible. He was completely earnest in his patriotism; and he was a superb orator. He loved the South in more ways than he could count—as people often do. He saw the South broken and impoverished; he passionately wanted it to be strong and happy—stronger and happier, one suspects, even than the North,—not that he was guilty of envy—that sin, his mother had soundly enjoined him against. He felt toward the South as a lover feels for his lady—he wished her so extremely well that he wished she would abandon being herself and try to be another lady, more robust, more practical. It was *his* lady, never doubt it, whom he wanted, but he felt it so palpably to her interest to . . . Why could she not, for instance, without, of course, abandoning her leisurely manner, which he loved, leave off her fruitless brush-and-easel work and operate a chromo-press, advertising and selling her produce, giving employment incidentally to perhaps hundreds, perhaps thousands?

There was an answer: already it was too late for her to install her implements-of-creation to any long-range advantage: the chromo market (every market, in fact, unless the economic structure was to be fundamentally altered) was already pushing toward saturation. The crafty gods Speed and Mass had seen to it that the manufacturers of the South would be obliged to lay down a pretty penny indeed—and a most discriminatory one as compared with the manufacturers of the North—to get their chromos shipped anywhere. This answer Grady could not read. He was an optimist.

When Grady died, tragically short of his time, he was a hero all the way from Boston to Galveston. Under the spell of his beautiful voice, that entire massive territory had almost tumbled over itself in its speed to endorse his doctrines.

He had somehow marshalled the Christian soldiers ("We are not divided, all one body we, One in hope and doctrine . . ."). It was fitting that his successor, who could hardly expect to equal him in personal charm, proved in an age with little turn for lyrics to be in the main prosaic, closer to the ideal of an era which remembered very well that time was money. The new marshal was Walter Page, an able and aspiring man who was resolved not to live obscurely. He had grown up in North Carolina, a state that was often, if wrongly, disprized by its neighbors; and his family had been more remarkable for sturdiness than for either social or intellectual brilliance. After a time at a Southern Methodist college he carried on his work in classics at the newly organized Johns Hopkins University. Then he was a journalist, in the Middle West and at home in North Carolina; but very early he went to New York, where he remained most of his life (except for a few years in Boston) until he became Ambassador to England.

As surely as Grady, he was an optimist, a true-to-type, frontier-governed American optimist; and all the Greek in Baltimore could not greatly change him. Less lovable than Grady, he was equally sincere in his devotion to the South, and if he was not more profound, he was definitely more subtle, more learned. To him, the South was a highly esteemed sister whose claims upon his concern he fully recognized. It seemed to him that this lady very wilfully stood in her own best light and that she distressingly rationalized (this was what maddened and exasperated him) her misfeasance and even made a virtue of it. When she resented his childing, asking him to mind his own business, he moved away, to straighten her out by voluminous correspondence, and by tempting her, with really princely gifts, to do many things which she hated but which he was wholly sure were good for her.

Now it may be repeated, because it is important (whether or not it is or is not gratifying), that Southern people have remained through the years American and even human. When the compulsion of being peculiar, and of justifying their peculiarity, was lifted from them by the abolition of the peculiar institution of slavery, they were—many of them—as willing as the next people to fall in with dominant ways of their age. The ways habitual to them were obviously not flawless, and a new set of ways, followed by all the world, might well prove delectable; not only were they modish, they were from the South's standpoint unfamiliar enough to seem perfect, new enough to be fascinating.

Old Charles Colcock Jones lingered into Grady's time to challenge him; but it was clear who had the victory. Grady was thought the better of for the encounter, for his chivalric handling of a venerable and perhaps doting assailant. The Daughters of the Confederacy, no eye unwet, shook their fans menacingly on his secure Olympus. The Populists, convinced at last that the nation was unaffectably complacent in its treatment of the farmer, burrowed into the earth they had arisen from. Only inertia was left, that great bog, spreading through the whole South—to be deprecated by all right-thinking men. Grady had said drain it; Page had said drain it. It, only, prevented the South from looking like the rest of America; it only, said the liberals (always amiable and sometimes sensible), remained to hold us from the course followed by the rest of our countrymen with such conspicuous success.

Old Jones lay mouldering in his grave. But Grady and Page went marching on, endorsed and even far out-distanced by the more sophisticated of their disciples. For these disciples, hard and modern, could not be diverted even by a memorial sigh. They were hard and modern and organized, and by the fall of 1929 they had so ordered their environment that a young Charleston-ian, say, (as he established his virility by smoking a cigarette) might, undisputed, set up as a penetrating wit on the bare capital of declaring Charleston not at all so much to his taste as, say, Detroit. That is how they had ordered things by the fall of 1929.

Lorenzo Dow

LORENZO DOW (Oct. 16, 1777-Feb. 2, 1834), evangelist, was born in Coventry, Conn., fifth of the six children of Humphrey Dean and Tabitha (Parker) Dow. His parents, natives of Coventry, brought up their children frugally, educating them, as Lorenzo said, "both in religion and common learning" (*Journal,* p. 1). In 1794, he began preaching, making his evangelistic excursions on horseback, and in 1796 he was accepted into a tentative connection with the Methodist ministry—only to be suspended after three months. Then he preached again independently, desperately poor and generally ill, but frequently within one week traveling as much as 150 miles and preaching as often as twenty times. In 1798, readmitted to his former status with the Methodists, he soon afterward, though opposed by his ecclesiastical superiors, set out to carry his gospel into Ireland. After about eighteen turbulent months there, he returned to New York in May 1801, and almost immediately left by sea for Georgia. He preached there for a few months, returned to New York, and in November, 1802 again turned southward, this time overland, proclaiming everywhere his threats of hell, and hopes of paradise, bringing in many converts. He visited the Indians, delivered the first Protestant sermon ever listened to in Alabama, talked in Charleston freely enough to be, at a later time, convicted for libel, and turning northward, preached through the Carolinas, Tennessee, and Virginia. Remembering that in Ireland he had seen "the first pair that I thought were happy in marriage" (*Eccentric Preacher,* p. 77), he decided to take a wife and accordingly on Sept. 3, 1804, in Westernville, N. Y., he was married. The bride, Peggy Holcomb, born in 1780 in Granville, Mass., entered into the union upon the express understanding that she would never

From *The Dictionary of American Biography,* Vol. V, 410.

hinder him in his roamings. Leaving her the day after the wedding, he began a swing to Mississippi and return, preaching constantly, and jotting down in his dairy notes of dreams and of actual occurrences. By April 1805 he was home again; in July he started for the Carolinas; in November, taking Peggy with him, he embarked for England. There Peggy bore a daughter, Letitia, who soon died. They returned to America in June 1807, and together, from Boston to Natchez and Natchez to Boston, they toured the country, he, long-haired and braced in a little leather jacket, calling himself "Cosmopolite," reputedly rich both in money and in the gift of prophecy, and she everywhere and always abetting him. In 1818 he again went to England, but soon after his return in 1820, Peggy died. Three months later he was married to Lucy Dolbeare of Montville, Conn. From then on, he wrote more and preached less, issuing, after his habit instituted in 1804, a chaotic torrent of egoistic pamphlets, and constantly revising his journals. Living on his farm in Connecticut, he accummulated affidavits about his own good character, compounded medicines recommended for biliousness, quarreled acrimoniously, litigated, to his sorrow, with his neighbors about a mill race, and stormed incessantly against Whigs, anti-Masons, Catholics, and finally against Methodists, who, he said, were badly tainted with popery. Death came to him suddenly in Georgetown, Md.

PART III

Selected Reviews

Georgia Scenes

By A. B. Longstreet

THERE USED TO BE a story about an old gentleman who went
to a young ear-specialist to complain of his bad hearing. When
the doctor asked him how old he was and he replied eighty, the
doctor gasped, "My Lord, man, haven't you heard *enough* by
now?"

In view of all that, I suppose it dangerous to talk of having read
a book in 1920 and again in 1960, both times with scrupulous
attention. Except as to the Bible or Shakespeare, perhaps, anybody
carrying on in such a way these days might shock a listener by
being still vocal, or even sentient.

The grown people whom I knew in my childhood had doubtless all of them read Judge Longstreet's *Georgia Scenes* fondly,
but they were not intent for the next generation to read it too.
They doubtless felt that religion and education had won too
recent and unsteady a victory for hobbledehoy reminiscence to
be permitted to walk up and down at all. The little boys of
Thomas Nelson Page, Joel Chandler Harris, and Frances Hodgson Burnett were good examples for the young, and there was
no use for the young to know about rough persons or acts, especially right here in Georgia, or anywhere like Georgia. It was true
that Judge Longstreet had in the 1830's prophesied that religion
and education would probably extirpate ill men and deeds in his
life-time, but those redeemers were running far enough behind
schedule seventy-five years later for people to be a little nervous
in that matter.

But in Boston, religion and education had had time to work
longer than in Georgia—to what ultimate effect let him judge

From *The Georgia Review*, XIV (Winter, 1960), 444-447. This appeared in the
department of the *Review* occasionally devoted to "Old Books."

who can—and there, by the time of little Lord Fauntleroy, it seemed venturesome and delightful, and also safe, to ponder the picaresque. So in Boston one could consider Huck Finn, who was so extremely remote that contamination *via* him was hardly to be thought of—unless, incidentally, you were Mr. Howells, who had Ohio haunting him and still knew a thing or two.

So, Old Remus and Br'er Rabbit were by race or by species remote enough from the Georgia of the early 1900's to be judged harmless. Not so Huck Finn. What with Missouri's being so extremely near, Huck was a potential plague-carrier and the less said of him the better. He was too likely to raid your scuppernong arbor or your melon-patch for you to find him captivating. Better far to let the mind rest upon Sir Galahad!

For all that, Professor Trent in New York itself kept talking about *Georgia Scenes.* I had been at Harvard and I had told Barrett Wendell that I was interested in "Southern Literature." Poe, perhaps? Lanier? Who knew? Not I. Wendell thought, then, he said, that I had better go down to New York and work with Professor Trent, who knew more about Southern Literature than *he* knew. That was an excellent thing about Barrett Wendell as a teacher: he would say openly that there were people who were in certain lines more informed than he was. So there I was at Columbia University working with Professor Trent, and the year was, in a way of speaking, 1492.

I was from Georgia, said Professor Trent, and there was a subject cut out for me: Judge Longstreet, the author of *Georgia Scenes,* one of the really first "American books" in the Whitmanian sense of the phrase, the forerunner of many other notable books, even at last, most likely, of *Tom Sawyer* and *Huckleberry Finn.* The date, as I have remarked, was early, and the speaker was in consequence still able to name all of these names standing rather than on his knees.

I doubt whether either Professor Trent or I knew for several years thereafter how fully he had involved me in something that was getting to be a "Mystique" in a hurry, in something that was sort of pre-Homeric—or pre-Twainian, which is saying the same thing. All that I knew for a long while was that Judge Longstreet seemed to me a better-than-most good Georgian and that I found his book entertaining and him more entertaining still. I did not know much about Americans' constituting a new Order in the world, or about *ibid* or *op. cit.* but I read away interminably, just the same, at many libraries and wrote inquiries and procured interviews over this broad land and tried to shake down into a book every particle of the fascinating stuff that I found. I even had the hardihood to show some of my composition to a friend of mine, who thought so well of it that he had the hardihood to show it to a friend of *his* whose critical faculties he much esteemed.

Alas, that friend said No. The style, he declared, was not at all like Lord Acton's style and that was a pity. Better to throttle the effort right off. But at last the book was published and *The New York Times Book Review* mentioned it somewhat favorably. That was interpreted to mean that the *Times* was poorly off for reviewers of Southern books that post-date Dr. Gildersleeve's.

However deficient that biography was, it ran on at vast length and, with a previous biography, it considerably increased the bulk of Longstreet books that had been accumulating since 1835—eleven editions of *Georgia Scenes* alone by 1897. It is now conceded everywhere that Longstreet was the first and for several decades the best of the distinctively American humorists; and the literary historians, Parrington and De Voto, for example, in apotheosizing the "West," have certainly spread his fame. He is now securely enshrined. Yet one may wonder whether some, at least, of his seeming to out-rank so far the others of his group does not trace back to his being relatively easy to find out about.

Longstreet was born in Augusta, Georgia, in 1790 of parents who had recently migrated from New Jersey. He early came under the influence of John C. Calhoun, whom he followed through Yale and a New England law school before inaugurating a law-practice and marrying a young woman of prominent family in a Georgia village. Now came the blithe and robustious years to him, when out of the superabundance of his energy and zest for living he wrote *Georgia Scenes*. Nothing else of his voluminous writings during nearly fifty years is still remembered. But these 10-12 page, salty, realistic sketches, first published anonymously in newspapers, written now in measured prose, now crude dialect, dealing with people in high position and low, white and black, in town and in the backwoods, can still breathe a substantial show of mist upon anybody's looking-glass who will take the trouble to hold it right.

As a forerunner of One who gave his mind to frogs' jumpings lest cosmic grief fordo him, Judge Longstreet might appropriately, while seeming to jest, have scowled inwardly at the universal world, pell-mell, helter-skelter, ding-dong, *et cetera*. But in face he seems to have accepted happily the "better thought" of his time and place—particularly as to white-and-black race-relations as he knew them. He would have been completely at a loss, for example, to understand a present-day journalist of my acquaintance who thinks that no moral excellence can exist in company with a consciousness of racial differences. In the first place, the Judge would have believed such a consciousness "natural" and therefore right. But even if he had believed it wrong he would still not have despised a generally good man who erred only in the one matter that he himself at a given moment most deprecated. Life is neither Pegasus nor Magic Carpet, but it is given us to ride and we must not look into its mouth or its twill too closely. Also— and a fig for proverbs to the contrary!—better a good chain with a weak link than another chain that is from end to end plumb sorry.

The death of one of Longstreet's children turned him from law and politics to the Church and the ministry, and it was in that connection that he spent most of the latter half of his life, as the effective and somewhat circumstantial president of various colleges, among them, Emory in Georgia and the Universities of Mississippi and South Carolina. All of his days, he was never able to go gentle into anything, and least of all did he go gentle into War of the Sixties, during all of which he raged against what he felt sure was the slow dying of all proper Light.

But he had ebulliency, and before his end in 1870, he had come to believe at times that most of the Great Values might not only survive but prosper. And it is possible that his nephew, General James Longstreet, his son-in-law, Justice L. Q. C. Lamar, and his grandson-in-law, Chancellor Edward Mayes, reflected, all of them, in their somewhat "progressive" point of view, some of great Nestor's faint yielding to the spirit of Things-as-they-Were. Or certainly, As-they-Seemed.

This little essay is set off by the appearance in 1957 of still another edition of *Georgia Scenes*. It is a paper-bound volume in the American Century Series, published in New York, and it runs to 198 pages plus ten pages of admirable "Introduction" by B. R. McElderry, Jr. of the University of Southern California.

Prodigal

MR. SINCLAIR LEWIS has pronounced Thomas Wolfe's writing so deep and spacious that it deals with the whole of life. Undeniably it is very deep and spacious; but it hardly deals with everything. Religion, for example, however vestigial it may seem to be in the contemporary world, was, as late as 1884, in Asheville, North Carolina, a force that moved weightily and in general in worthy directions. It is highly probable that in 1935 it may still be found here or there performing nobly. It is even possible that in 1984 it may in one form or another be among the dominant forces of the world. Yet, for all of Mr. Wolfe's testimony, religion might never have existed to any good purpose. Like the waiter he tells about in the café at Nice, he apparently thinks of himself (and of everybody else, in fact) as not susceptible to religious sentiment—certainly not to ecclesiastical sentiment. Now, this is all very well for a way of thinking, but it does not fit in cleanly with gusty paeans about catholicity, and about the splendor of a young man's wanting to experience everything—oh, *everything*.

The insatiate young man who is the hero of both of Mr. Wolfe's novels, *Look Homeward, Angel* (1929) and *Of Time and the River* (1935), is named Eugene Gant, and he is referred to in the third person except at rare times when the disguise somehow lapses and the hero becomes quite frankly Thomas Wolfe—"I," the text has it,, "did this or that"; "reaching through the darkness she touched *me*," and so on. Both of the books relate primarily, then, to the author himself. Substitute his name for his hero's, and substitute Asheville, North Carolina, for Altamount, Catawba; and the identification is pretty thoroughly accomplished.

Eugene Gant was born in Altamont, Catawba, in 1900. He was the last of a large number of children born to a dissipated and

From *The Southern Review*, I (July, 1935) , 192-198.

impetuous but lovable and generous father—a Pennsylvania-born, Baltimore-trained stone cutter, and to a penurious, industrious mother, member of the prolific, sturdy family of Pentlands, native to Western Catawba for several generations. The first novel makes clear the origins of the boy's parents, but news of his gestation is given on the twentieth of the 626 pages in the book, and from that time till the end—here he graduates from the State University at Pulpit Hill—Eugene dominates the story. He and his observations and experiences and sentiments are, indeed, all that is offered. Characters drift in, manage to assert themselves for fifty pages or more, and drift out again; except by lucky chance, Eugene only endures. And he endures with the utmost intensity and turbulence, unable, unwilling—even unaware of the obligation—to believe that he is not the absolute pioneer in living. Neither he nor anybody else is ever for an instant merely so-so. Nothing is merely so-so. Life is a flame that BURNS.

The same flame BURNS in the second novel, for five years, though 912 pages. Eugene leaves Altamont for Harvard; remains there for three years; returns home; teaches English, to young Jews, mostly, at a college in New York City; week-ends, once, (nearly one-sixth of the book) with some Hudson River plutocrats; spends a long time in England and France; gets on the boat to come home. People drift into his life and drift out again. There is much, much talk of them; and they are no more. Until the last page of the second book, only the very dull are not bitterly and hopelessly lost—then, on that last page occurs a miracle—an incredible, unprecedented miracle; Eugene and a young woman who is not named, see each other and fall in love—and then two young people who are quite acutely not dull, oh, not *that,* are acutely not *lost* any more, either—forever.

The two huge novels, covering the time from 1884 till 1925, are enheartening proof of a man's ability, in our time in America, to write in the grand manner with sustained strength. When Mr. Wolfe's publishers announce that in the last five years he has written two million words, they do not mean to imply that he has necessarily written by some wholly mechanical routine; they mean on the contrary—and they are thoroughly right—that he is a very remarkable person. The two novels already published are part of a series of six, which completed (two of the others are now ready), will range in time from 1791 to 1933. The whole great collection—and this does not guarantee that it will pass into the popular consciousness immemorably—will undoubtedly constitute one of the monumental performances in the history of American literature. For whatever are the faults of this writer, he has the virtues of stupendous gusto and energy, and quite remarkable omnivorousness. So far, his work has been the record of his own passage through the world. Whether he can transfer his peculiar virtues to books in which he is not himself protagonist, is something that the performance only can indicate.

Whoever writes so much so hurriedly is bound to write something badly. The two novels now published are not impeccable. They are occasionally repetitious and verbose merely. There are rare instances of downright bad rhetoric and there is a considerable amount of trite phraseology. In spite of his ado with *umlauts,* the author lets his American prepossession with spelling lead him into some bad dialect-recording, particularly in the sections of the book that deal with Englishmen. The hero is permitted at times to describe minutely events which in the nature of the case he had observed only fleetingly and cursorily; he uses similes out of experiences which are as yet ahead of him. Sometimes he divulges a too facile knowledge of matters that are highly technical, like medical prescriptions; and sometimes, aggressively cosmopolitan, he is provincially homespun enough to say "reasonable" when he means cheap. But these strictures are against occasional lapses only. In the main, the story is conveyed with subtlety as well as vigor, with a sure implication of the author's really welling power, and a sure and welcome implication of his acquaintance with the great humane tradition of the world.

There is the memory of Greece and Rome and of the Renaissance arts floating across great sections of the writing, and the author's wide knowledge of English literature is forever there, a sore of sounding-board for all he says. There is a sweeping command of language and vocabulary, and a majesty of style. There is a large and beautiful mysticism, attained apparently by no road yet followed, and toward which no road is marked in these books —a mysticism, then, that is in a sense regrettably selfish. The memory of medieval culture is seldom if ever present; there are no sounding-boards for any except a bigoted and sterile piety. But the richness and depth of the past are more than usually well implied; and for what is offered in that line there must be grateful acknowledgment.

Many old and good tricks and a number of new ones are requisitioned for the reader's benefit; Dickens's method is plain in the scenes relating to the stout lady who set herself up as patroness of the arts at Harvard; Sir Walter Scott's in some of those involving comic relief; Sinclair Lewis's in all of those involving the dictaphone technique; and even James Joyce and Gertrude Stein are from time to time suggested—faintly but with unmistakable Wolfeian accent.

The adroitness of the Lewis-like episodes is a commentary on the ease with which that artifice may be acquired—and abused. To devote nearly a sixth of a book that supposedly covers five years of time to the conversations of a railway journey from Asheville to Baltimore evinces an evil intoxication with one's command of mimicry. But the space given to the superbly reported conversations of the "arty" (and leprous) intellectuals around Harvard University is more to the point; the subject is fresher, and the matter treated has bearing on the central issue of Eugene Gant's development—in its stupid mincingness, its inane irrelevancy, its dead and rotten bawdiness. It has as the author hints, sad bearing upon the development and damnation of us all, and of this nation. This waspish sophistication is worse than the vulgarity of Altamont, the jaunty unconcern of Pulpit Hill, or the surly unconcern of the City College; it is more menacing, because it is more comprehensible, than the gibberish of the intellectual expatriates in France. All of this Mr. Wolfe makes clear. However much space he takes to do so, he is heartily welcome to.

The author is a young man, born thirty-five years ago, and if on many scores he behaves himself still in the fashion of one born considerably later, he is in some ways fortunate, and may be forgiven a good deal. Too often, the folly of youth is supplanted only by the drabness of age; that should mitigate some of the doubts that might arise concerning Mr. Wolfe's literary manners. But in his particular case, it might not be too sanguine to risk wishing that time, which surely rolls, would roll a shade the faster; he is hardly likely ever to prove drab! and it is not a painful thing to imagine the day when he will no longer utter persistently, with defiant relish, many of the words that still delight him. He may not much longer find the word "guts," for instance, irresistibly fascinating, may not say "whore" as often as he now finds it good to do; may, though continuing to regard himself as basically non-Christian, come to feel that the ejaculations "Jesus Christ" and "By God" are less pertinent than he once thought them in the business of demonstrating one's self safely independent. He may conclude, even, that (mature, at last) he should try the feat of mastering his audience without resort to the hard and raw brass knucks of sex scenes. For about sex scenes there is this: in fairness to his audience, a desperately—oh, desperately—frank and earnest and fearless writer is bound to offer either more detail than Mr. Wolfe offers or quite definitely less. It is not admirable to insist upon the individual whim with volcanic eruptiveness, and to keep all of the exciting lava meanwhile safely, meticulously, within permitted channels.

Mr. Wolfe is very unhappy over the fact that nobody really knows anybody else, and he does not derive comfort from the idea that this was true formerly and will be subsequently, world without end. He says that at twenty-two he was a madman and a fool— and that everybody else at twenty-two is also. He says that to be a great writer a man must be something of an ass. He says that he wants to experience everything, to escape nothing. All of this is very romantic sounding. Yet he long ago ceased to think of Shelley as pre-eminent among the poets; he was properly exasperated, early in his book, to have his family think of him, because he wished to write, as different from the rest of them. Yet, again, he exhibits something indistinguishable from the conventional grade of moral indignation in his attitude toward the drunkenness and perversity of Starwick, and something very close to the aphorisms of Benjamin Franklin (which Babbitt loved) in his attitude toward the importance of getting his work done.

It is surely true, as Eugene Gant declares, that no form of political government will offer surcease from the invisible worm that works unremittingly on man's heart. It is conventional to say that romantic love is sovereign in this regard, and Eugene accedes to the convention; at least he seems to value romantic love as an agency of temporary relief. It is also conventional to say that priggishness is a good remedy; and there Eugene accedes too. It is also conventional to say that religion, sweetness and humility of spirit, a sense of obligation, a regard for the happiness of one's fellows, mental as well as physical—that all of these things, while not curative in this world, are none the less palliative of man's lasting wretchedness. But talk of that order, Mr. Wolfe cannot endure, and, Holy Christ, by the blood-and-bones-of-God, he will not put up with any such s. o. b. twaddling cant, be good-and-God-damned if he will, so help him Jesus! And soon . . . It is not going too far to feel that this is very distressing.

Another remedy for man's pain, older far than sulphur and

molasses or than sassafras tea, is the sense of being identified with one's people, of being actually a part, as an oak is, or a cabbage, of the earth from which one derives. It is a remedy highly spoken of, and Mr. Wolfe has evidently had word of it. He discusses it at length in connection with Eugene's disquiet in Europe—his fixed impression that neither he nor any other American could be at ease there—and his belief, which may or may not have materialized, that at home, in America, he would be less tortured.

It is a safe bet that America alone did not solve Eugene's problem effectively. For that large equation is very vague, and the problem involved demanded something definite and pointed. Away from the United States, Eugene might idealize it readily, rhapsodizing over its magnitude and the big, swift trains that go roaring across it. That idealization could not have been ultimately deep. He says in fact that for getting one's work done (that is, one's very best, artistic work, the sort of work that demands the whole functioning of the artist's nature) one place is as good as another. So much for those who feel it necessary to think of home only in terms of a continent. It would be as practical to think of the continent in terms of a cottage, which, for all the fables that science has abolished distance, the continent still very positively is not.

Eugene's friend Starwick was a Middle-Western American, and although he wished himself something else, it was true, as Eugene rightly and unanswerably explained to him, that he could never be a Frenchman, nor anything indeed except what he was. Well, Eugene is a Southerner, and though the South may not be so culturally alien from America at large as America at large is from England or France, there remains surely, for one of Eugene's sensitivity to recognize (indeed he talks much about it) a disparity between Northern ways and Southern ways. Altamont is assuredly not Mobile, nor is Eugene to be confused with, say, Lucius Rhett—fancy young Lucius, aged nineteen, shrieking to his mother "Now, for God's sake, I don't want to hear what you are saying. God-damn it, can we have no peace?" Fancy that. Oh, Eugene is not Lucius (whether he is better or worse, does not matter here); Eugene for his part forswears the South belligerently—it had jolly well never given *him* anything; he exults in his determination never again to live there. None the less, Eugene is a Catawba, mama-and-papa-saying, Presbyterian Southerner; or he is nothing. And he is very emphatically not nothing.

"Oh, lost, lost!" is the refrain, constantly echoed, that this man from Old Catawba, immured now in Brooklyn, N. Y., cries piteously through most that he has written. It would be an interesting thing, and worthy of much wonder, if in his case this should prove inexorable: that to live validly and with satisfying peace he should be driven to a reconciliation with his origins; should be obliged, in the vast area of his sympathies, to make room for the people who bred him.

✄§⸙❧

Sweet are the Uses of Degeneracy

MR. ERSKINE CALDWELL was born in rural Georgia in 1903. His father is a Presbyterian minister, an intellectual, solicitous about the well-being of the poor; and his mother is a school teacher. During his youth, his parents roved over most of the Southeast, and the boy went to the public schools at whatever place his father happened at the time to be preaching. There are tales of his having early, like Shelley, become convinced of the perfidy and dishonesty of school-masters. By the time he was twenty, he had ended a brief matriculation at the University of Virginia, and was ready for the great world.

According to the jacket of his first published book, he has been a farm hand, a cottonseed oil mill and lumber mill worker in Georgia; a cotton picker and hack driver in Tennessee; a book reviewer in Charlotte, North Carolina, and also in Houston, Texas; a stage hand in a burlesque theatre and a soft-drink dispenser in Philadelphia; a lecture-bureau manager in Scranton; night cook and waiter in the Union Station at Wilkes-Barre; and a professional football player in Allentown, Pennsylvania. He worked for a year as a reporter on the Atlanta *Journal*, and then, auctioning off the contents of three suitcases, he went to Maine, to live in Portland and the town of Mt. Vernon.

While all of this was going on, he found time to marry, and, once he was nineteen (1922), to write and rewrite stories and send them away to magazines and receive them back, and send them off to other magazines repeatedly, till 1929. In that memorable year, his first published story appeared in *The New Caravan*, and the hero came into his own. He has continued to live in Maine, but he breaks his residence there by long winter-visits to

The Southern Review, I (Winter, 1936), 449-466.

his parents in the small Georgia town of Wrens, close to Augusta. And he continues to write, with no promise of abatement. All of this busy rushing from place to place and from one occupation to another with what seems a keen and proud enjoyment of the process is typical of this era—a new Renaissance.

Time, in old Florence, stretched suddenly farther backward than people had believed it could, or could have need to; and Space, after Magellan, stretched round to meet itself at the antipodes. With those great bonds gone saggy, it was hardly possible to believe any bonds any longer resilient. Only the very wise, and those who were so happily dull as not to bother themselves about Time or Space, further than to know the dinner hour and the distance to the spring, could hold consistently to their accustomed courses. Witness Cellini, contemptuous of bonds till it came to his work, to the thing he wholly cared for. Witness ourselves, reeling with the new knowledge that Time too, like Space, stretches round to meet itself. Who will keep his course in our hour? The wise will keep it as fully as Cellini did, and more fully to be sure; and the dull will keep it too, well, as they did formerly—and that is a thing to be grateful for.

But the wise are few and the semi-wise are numerous. And it is easy to conclude, since Time, which passed for stable, has proved suddenly to be less logical than quicksilver, that men too are under obligation to stand unobligated, to be meeting themselves philosophically all day, and physically as often as possible, face to face, at a point undesignated, somewhere between whence and whither. So goes our hour, as Cellini's did, and it is candor and not pride that makes it necessary to say so. If personally we are chained, we must needs dote upon those who are free, and Mr. Caldwell has proved among the most industrious dashers-about known to us.

His literary pieces have appeared regularly in the smaller "intellectual" magazines and at times in the more widely circulated ones; and he does book reviews from time to time for the massive book-review sections of the New York newspapers. He has published seven books:

American Earth	(stories)	1930
Tobacco Road	(novel)	1932
God's Little Acre	(novel)	1933
We Are the Living	(stories)	1933

Journeyman	(novel)	1935
Kneel to the Rising Sun	(stories)	1935
Some American People	(sketches)	1935

In so far as he belongs to a "school"—*pretty far,* that is—he follows the styles of brevity, simplicity and sharpness of expression, and violence of action. His world is the one standard to modern intellectualism, in which the reign of sordidness or weakness in the world is broken only by persons indifferent to all of the traditional assumptions of whatever it is that has passed for civilization. Look not to rich-man, doctor, lawyer, merchant, chief (or pastor or master, for that matter) he seems to say, for any solace; *that* can be gained only from poormen, beggar-men, thieves, rogues, vagabonds, common liars, and so on. The formula is well known, and its reason for being, in the arts as well as in ordinary human thinking, is plain to anybody who has observed the principle of action and reaction in the universe. But comprehension does not of necessity involve a blind endorsement, and misgivings as to the over-simplification of Sir Walter Scott are not to be allayed in any real and helpful sense by reading *Ivanhoe* word for word backward.

The parts of Caldwell's writing that are most dependent upon this formula are probably doomed. The formula is faddish and topical; it is school-boyish in its preoccupation with easily shocked Miss Nancys; and, to cap all, there is little evidence, except that of current popularity, for its being basically sensible. A great artist often transcends the limitations of the artistic convention that governs him. If his acceptance of that convention is interpreted as having been on the whole sincere—and only time seems able to determine satisfactorily on this score—the artist's acceptance is rated as perhaps charmingly naive and quaint; but it is, after all, tolerated for the sake of qualities it is bound up with and is not admired independently.

It is interesting to assess the Caldwell virtues and to wonder whether they are virtues good enough and numerous enough to sustain for very long the impression that he is important. He is, of course, important in a certain sense—it would be impolite and even silly to suggest the contrary. In a sense we are *all* of us important—the writer of these words, and the Idiot Boy and any Unknown Soldier, and William Shakespeare, and Mr. Sinclair Lewis. The question is, and it would seem to be a pertinent one from Mr. Caldwell's standpoint, to know whether 1945 will maintain the 1935 rating for him any more faithfully than 1935 has maintained the 1925 rating of Mr. Sinclair Lewis. If it will, why, indeed, will it?

He is, as one of his advocates in New York has pointed out, "an original American humorist with a gift for selecting his material from indigenous sources, and he has an instinct for converting a casual episode into a symbol." That is fine indeed. And he develops his situations through characters (created with a tenderness unknown to Mr. Lewis) that are more likely to prove constant than either Carol Kennicott or Babbitt or Arrowsmith. His humor and his sympathy, then, are the attributes that he must look to for permanence. Whether those attributes will be worth searching for after ten years under the welter of fashionable but transitory trappings he ties onto them, nobody can say surely. A good American should know that a good vein is worth mining thoroughly, and, since journalists of the sort we know are a glut in America, it is worth remembering, in Mr. Caldwell's connection, that a man who can be both humorous and sympathetic, and who can write, would do well to get the newspapers once and for all well out of mind.

American Earth is made up almost entirely of stories, many about the South and many about New England; the remainder of it, called "The Sacrilege of Alan Kent," is a prose production, some thirty to forty pages long, divided and subdivided formidably into Roman-numeraled sections running about three or four to the page. This composition, it seems, is impressionistic autobiography. It talks first and last about most things, including God and Sex; and so many of its divisions are so very simple that the entire production may well be listed as poetry. As for instance:

Section xxxvii in Section II, " A man walked in a restaurant through the front door and ate all he wanted to eat"

Section xlii in Section III, "When the daily temperature was nearly 100 degrees in the shade, and often more than that, the heat of the midday sun was maddening."

As there is no further poetry in the seven books published, it must be concluded that the author's judgment forbade him for the time at least to work farther in that medium. It was a prohibition nobody will quarrel with.

The stories deal with country and village people, among whom, as the publisher's blurb makes clear, "love is direct and immedate; hate the same." They deal, in short, with just the sort of people that sophisticated New Yorkers and would-be New Yorkers —the major part of the book-buying population of America—can at once most envy and marvel over and deplore, with the sort of people best calculated to satisfy at once the current vogue for primitivism and the constant vogue of metropolitan complacency. Here is God's plenty to prove that country people are, when not amusingly simple, quite horribly brutal; it is all a very sad commentary on the unhappy folks who have not had the wit to move to some of the nation's many Fifth Avenues or Greenwich Villages, or perhaps even Boweries. And it is all very authentic-sounding, written by one who clearly knows the regions he describes. There is no end of direct and immediate sex; there is a *bona fide* lynching with coca-cola served during the intermissions; there is an idyl of two utterly brutal white men monkey-wrenching five gold teeth from the mouth of a dead Negro; there is another idyl (admirably handled, be it said) of a fine and innocent girl who, to avoid starving, is said to have been obliged to become a prostitute. The New England countrymen are in their essentials much like the Southerners, as stupid, if less violent, and more frustrated and niggling.

Tobacco Road, piously dedicated to the author's Father and Mother, has remained by all odds his most widely known work. Here he offered all that he had offered previously—and vastly more. It became evident that the effective simplicity of his style could be maintained over a long stretch of material. The broadly human commentary that his readers had become accustomed to was supplemented by a fierce and pointed accusal against the always sensitive South. And that accusal carried an implied accusal of New York itself as largely responsible for the conditions the books tells about. The book has been read by metropolitan people, particularly, it seems, by the intellectuals, with all of the credulous earnestness that certain classes of people even till today consider the appropriate mood in which to attack a sociological survey.

The well adapted and superbly acted play based on the book has for several years kept New Yorkers and their visitors interested in a matter they might otherwise have forgotten. As ordinary human beings they have been exhilarated by the special quality of the book that the liberal courts of our time are always busying themselves to declare within the bounds of decency. They have learned a great deal about an alien and *primitive* people. And they have had their vanity flattered (never was a New Yorker so depraved) and their consciences set easy (if the people whom the Civil War disrupted were of *this* stamp, then disruption was what was the best for them). The implication concerning New York's own responsibility for the sad event depicted, few have stressed. The Communists have perhaps been aware of it, but with them it has been more comfortable to rage against the tangible South, with "respectable" human company, than to rage without such company against the intangible Order of the World.

Tobacco Road is an entertaining story of a Georgia white share-cropper of this time, named Jeeter Lester, and of his family and associates. Jeeter's farm, once owned by his grandfather, had long ago passed into the titular possession of a local *grand bourgeois*. Under this landlord and under his successor in ownership, a city bank, Jeeter continued upon the land, uninfluenced by the increasing number of his kind who flooded past him to become mill-workers in the cities. The difference was that before his local patron (tangible, and an acquaintance of his) was forced by the economic set-up of the nation into ignominious bankruptcy, it was possible for Jeeter to procure money advances from time to time for his living and the production of his crops; and after the bank (intangible, and "foreign" to him) had assumed owner-ship, he could get no advances whatever. When the book opens, Jeeter is in wretched poverty, sustained only by the gusto of his own nature and by wistful reminiscences of the happy days when, already hopelessly in debt, he could none the less wheedle money from his quite impoverished feudal master.

The characters of the book are consistently morons whose be-tattered clothing and whose religion (of a type so low as to be perhaps the chief agency of their degradation) are the sole relics of the humane tradition left to them. But clothing and religion are not the sole relics of the *human* tradition left to them. Liars and thieves, they are filthy, lazy, blasphemous and cruel, and as lecherous as monkeys. They are everything, in short, that the human creature is when he abandons all of his restraints and inhibitions. On that account, being somehow what we all might be under conditions other than the ones we know and prize, they are in a way vastly comic. And this, in turn, is testimony to their unreality, to the basic subhumanness of all they stand for.

A recognition of these characters' sub-humanness might miti-gate the wounded feelings of Southern patriots who are outraged by the book for its depiction of their country. It *might*—with reference to the book. Whether it might with reference to the book's author is another matter; for Mr. Caldwell has apparently persuaded himself and many others, among them the editors of the intellectual weeklies in New York, that Jeeter Lester and his kind are fairly typical of twenty million Southern countrymen. It is his privilege perhaps to be so persuaded—after all, it is his mind that they are the creatures of; but the intellectual weeklies are theoretically under an obligation of skepticism at least as stringent as that governing the ordinary private citizen. And the ordinary private citizen of sound mind could never, it is to be presumed, rate *Tobacco Road* from a social standpoint as anything more than an individual case-study, a "particular," not in any sense a "universal." Shakespeare, it is said, made his Caliban, but *The Tempest* is not *filled* with Calibans, and the back-drop for the monster's appearances was not London with the double towers of old Saint Paul's, nor any other place to be pointed out on any map.

God's Little Acre is the story of Ty Ty Walden, compatriot of Jeeter Lester, and in many ways Jeeter's counterpart, including gusto and primitive comicalness. The Micawber blood in both of them stirs more vigorously in Ty Ty, and the author, in creating Ty Ty, was more pointedly conscious of Sigmund Freud, and of his own disposition to consider the Land—the Good Mother Earth—as the mystical Restorer and Savior. Ty Ty is probably more orthodoxically evangelical than Jeeter, but in the course of the book concerning him, Love, which was direct and immediate and insistent in the previous books, becomes all of these things so extremely as to appear in the guise of something usually thought of as abnormal and perverse—not the Oedipus or Pluto or Narcissus grade to topsy-turviness, but rather that Frank Harris grade, or more mildly, the grade of D. H. Lawrence. "Oh God," Mr. Caldwell writes somewhere, "give us a city where men stalk the streets day and night in search of a woman's scent. A city, Oh God, where women scream when a man looks at them and run to their husbands for protection."

Ty Ty is convinced that there are great deposits of gold hidden beneath the sandy fields of his farm, and he is perpetually forcing himself and his grown sons to dig for it. The chief result of the digging so far has been the necessity of shifting from place to place over the farm, as the mine-holes gradually spread, the particular acre which is dedicated to God, and from which all the produce (in reality none of the farm is cultivated) is to be sold for churchly purposes. Two of Ty Ty's children live away from him. One, long resident in Augusta, is the prosperous husband of a "first-family" but, unhappily, venereal wife. The other, a daughter, is married to a mill-worker in South Carolina, named Will Thompson. One of the residents of Ty Ty's house is his daughter-in-law, Griselda; and there is something about love, known to her and Will Thompson and Ty Ty (and to dogs, Ty Ty says) that most people do not know about at all. This is said to be a very wonderful thing indeed, and there is considerable implication that the knowledge and practice of this thing might well save the world, or something of that kind. We are on the grounds of religious mysticism here, apparently; and we are requested to rise above low talk of evidence, and mount the higher plane labeled Act of Faith.

For all of the book's implication about saving the world, its plan for achieving this desideratum by way of an increased versatility in love-practices was so novel that *God's Little Acre* was shortly after its publication hailed in court for obscenity. The court decided that the accusation was false, but this was not determined upon before it was set forth in the defense testimony— mostly judgments from critics and book reviewers—that the book was as pure as anything, and that the author was the resplendent Saint of a New Order.

There has been a full chorus to this effect. Mr. Jonathan Daniels, among Southern critics, has pronounced the book a fine study of the Southern poor white, and the author "a poet, occasionally almost lyric, whose sensitiveness to life is strong and whole, and who does not once cease to be the artist." It is hard to know how Mr. Daniels could have expressed himself more enthusiastically about Phoebus Apollo. Mr. Alexander Woolcott has vouched for the book's ability to "enlarge the listening heart," and Mr. Marc Connelly has called it weirdly authentic. And London has taken up the echo of New York's wondrous praise and set it flying. *The Times* is circumspect: "thoughtful comedy," it says, "with an intensely serious moral impulse." *The Daily Mail* is enigmatical: "equally masterful in comedy or tragedy." But Mr. John Cooper Powys is, as Mr. Daniels would say, almost lyric: he finds the book picturesque, original, vivid and striking, the characters *in* the book—there is something so naive and frank and sweet and childlike about all of them, that a wonderfully pleasant and wholesome and fresh taste is left in the reader's mouth—even with all their shameless sayings and doings.

Mr. Powys' commentary leads back to the idea of mysticism, and it is agreeable to testify in this connection that the mystical point of view about the Land in *God's Little Acre* is more substantiated than the necromancy about sex. In this book and in most of Mr. Caldwell's writing, that point of view is hinted at, and it may well in his mind occupy a position equal with his sex-ideas as the central theme of his writing. His reviewers have not taken just cognizance of this phase of his work. They have recognized his insistence on sex with the discernment of a Sahara-dweller in recognizing the sun, and they have talked frantically of the bad, low, cruel, insensate people in the South who crush out the lives of poor whites and Negroes. They have paid little attention to the fact that *that* baby, the protracted economic depression of the Southern farmer, is in each of the Caldwell books set morally somewhere distressingly close to Wall Street's own front doorstep.

For the reviewers' neglect, Mr. Caldwell has himself partly to thank. It is surely evident to him that they cannot be expected to recognize any theme other than that of sex unless it is stated with ultimate vigor. He has not so stated this theme, and he is in truth doubtless himself somewhat muddled about it. The son of a roving minister, growing up in the South but not really identified with its basic life, he may easily have magnified in his sensitive memory some boyhood unhappiness he suffered as a kind of "outlander." He may easily minimize the perplexities, exaggerate the opulence—Lord save us all!—of the Southern *grand bourgeois* farmer trying very hard to be a country squire on a yearly income not sufficient to meet land-taxes. He knows the condition and he knows that the blame (if blame it is, in a savage world) rests in large part somewhere hardly south of the Potomac, hardly west of Pittsburgh.

Conceive of Gulliver, weakened after extended battle with several men of his own sort, cast into Lilliput; and conceive of Lilliput, blockaded and strangled by Gulliver's enemies. If there was one pone to be had, Gulliver would eat; if there was one cloak, he would go clad; if there was one horse, he would ride—while Lilliputians, if necessary, king and commoners, went hungry, naked, and afoot. In a better universe, perhaps, Gulliver's great concern through the pervading dearth would be his little hosts rather than himself; but in this universe, where we must live if we are to live anywhere, it seems less in order to rail at Gulliver than to rail at his assailants and oppressors.

Yet Mr. Caldwell's persistent railing is aimed at Gulliver. And it is bitter, bitter, bitter; vigorously, passionately, fiercely bitter, bitter, bitter; obsessively, orgiastically, whirling-dervishly bitter. It is sincerely bitter, too convincingly bitter to be laid, as many have suggested, in any great degree to Mr. Caldwell's desire to ingratiate himself with Gulliver's oppressors—it may achieve that end, truly; but that, so far as he is concerned, is mainly incidental. Why, then, is his incrimination against Gulliver so flaming? What seer knows that answer? What was the forgotten thing—or was there anything—that happened one day long ago that all of this should stand momentous as it does today?

We Are the Living holds to the Caldwell story-book formula established in *American Earth*. It is predominantly concerned with rural people in the South and in New England, but the characters are in general of a fairly satisfactory socio-economic order. From an artistic standpoint it is the bravest of the author's publications; he here frequently runs the risk of impressing his audience without an eternal clanging of the gongs of wonderment and stupefaction—and he succeeds beautifully. Two or three of the Southern stories and all of the four New England stories are examples of the robustious, gusty humor that is among the best of their author's qualities. Only about half of these few stories turn definitely upon the idea of sex and even these treat the subject with gratifying circumspection.

One of the humorous stories, "The People's Choice," is in the long tradition of anti-democratic political satire that Americans from Brackenridge to Mark Twain have at times written in exuberantly. Proud of his election as Baptist deacon, Gus Streetman goes to a village carnival on the night before his induction into his new office. As the evening flies on, he becomes so thoroughly drunk that it is impossible the next morning to sober him up thoroughly before it is time for him to go to church. He goes none the less, to mistake the soprano soloist for one of the carnival artists whose performances he had much enjoyed only a few hours since. He exhorts the lady so ardently to enliven her performance, as he had with success exhorted the other lady a little earlier, that he is arrested; and the meeting is utterly broken up. The crowd follows him to jail by way of seeing the episode through, and there in front of the jail resolves, in response to his eloquence, to elect him sheriff of the county, come the next election. "Country Full of Swedes" is an uproarious account of the bewildered stupidity of native Down-Easters—the characters excellently presented—before the stupidity and recklessness of some transient foreigners. In most of the remaining stories the reader is asked to marvel over the mental attitudes rather than over the physical actions of the characters. The writer is apparently a Sherwood Anderson who has profited by the experiences of Winesburg; the discerning tenderness of his sympathies is largely evident.

Very seldom in *We are the Living* does the writer attain his standard degree of pure sexiness; but if a disappointed Caldwellian inferred upon the publication of the book that his favorite author had undergone a change of heart, there was encouragement waiting for him around the next corner. And if he inferred, to his confusion, from the complacency of the good Baptists in "The People's Choice" that Southern country folks are not, after all, dominated by reprehensible evangelicalism, there was encouragement on that score too, quickly to be made manifest.

The novel *Journeyman* presents as its hero Semon Dye, a self-constituted preacher who is compact, among other vices, of lechery, treachery, gluttony, and grand and petty scoundrelism. Yet he is hardly conspicuous for these traits among the other characters in this book—the inhabitants of a Georgia rural community so definitely localized that the knowing in those parts should be able to penetrate the swamps and tell the name of it.

There is a Georgia village, which Mr. Caldwell has somehow missed, to which was brought back, one clear, bright autumn day in January, the dead body of a long-absent native son. He had made money and an exalted marriage and a high reputation in his wandering, and he had quit the Methodists and gone over to the Episcopalians. But he was dead and he was at home and his kin who had not wandered went that day to the cemetery to see him buried. There was a priest crying the solemn ritual. He was in white and he had assistants; there was fine pageantry. But one of these home-keeping kin, himself as sensitive to grandiloquence as dogs are to the moon, was brought to wonder if even that high ritual, which he adored, booming reminiscence of medieval splendor, were not a sort of defilement in the clean and luminous air of that autumn afternoon, sweet with the fragrance of tea-olive. It was not *that* Georgia village that Semon Dye converted, whatever other village it may have been, anywhere.

Let the newspapers and reviews, busy to substantiate Mr. Caldwell's fame as a sociologist, spare themselves the trouble of conducting an investigation in that village, ever. There are phases of life there relevant to much of the Caldwell implication, but there is little relative to his fame as a factual social scientist. And since that is the main aspect of his work ready for the purposes of sensationalism, it is hardly likely that the newspapers and reviews would be interested.

The publishers of *Journeymen* say that the book is for all of those who admire the other Caldwell novels, and who recognize him as a new, authentic American voice. They speak broadly; it is possible to recognize him as fresh and interesting and to have admiration of a sort for both *Tobacco Road* and *God's Little Acre* without being able to summon up for *Journeyman* any admiration to speak of. The sentences are grammatical and the writing has due regard for the principles of unity, coherence, and emphasis. But one must persevere, and not admit, whatever the temptation at times, that that much achievement alone is enough to constitute a masterpiece.

Semon Dye, unannounced and unknown, puts up at the house of Clay Horey. Clay, already, as he says, "four or five times" married, has an establishment made up of his fifteen-year-old wife Dene and a mulatto woman cook (whom Semon promptly seduces) and the cook's mulatto husband (whom Dene seduces). There are other Negroes living on the Horey farm, among them an old woman who has charge of the syphilitic small boy Vearl, the son of one of Clay's former wives. These people and a hard-drinking neighbor, Tom Rhodes, and Vearl's mother, Lorene, who (vacationing from her professional activities in Jacksonville) comes on a visit to her former husband, Clay, are the main characters in the book.

Among them there is unremitting violence and drunkenness, and much gambling, at which Semon at last strips Clay even of his wife; and there is a protracted revival service during which Priest Semon and all of the huge congregation, yes, every one, fall into orgiastic goings-on as mathematically complete as ever satyr and nymph transacted, the better to glorify their deities. During the reaction that follows the excitement of the revival, Semon and Lorene escape in Clay's automobile and in the direction of Jacksonville, meaning to live off the intervening country by means of further revivals. And behind them they leave only regret among those Georgia countrymen for the going of one who had so vividly broken the *monotony of village life*—a literary convention that originated in the Middle West, and thrives chiefly in New York.

The more direct and harsh manifestations of sex are a diminishing factor in *Kneel to the Rising Sun*. And as time goes on, Mr.

Caldwell tends to become less emphatically engrossed in Southern matters. Of the seventeen stories in *Kneel to the Rising Sun,* six only are based upon essentially Southern themes. It seems that the first grade of the author's violence and recklessness is still available mainly when he is looking South, but the second grade is good and bloody, and at times even the non-Southern stories are all that the most despondent could ask of them.

Three of the Southern stories treat of poor whites; in one of them the hero is victimized by his own stupidity and mildness, in the other two, by economic want. One man, in crazed frustration, shoots his dog, named Fiddler, and beats it to death with an axe; another shoots his eight-year-old daughter because he cannot bear to hear her say she is hungry. Of the stories involving Negroes, one exemplifies the vulgar pleasure with which a group of "respectable" white people at a New Year's dinner witness the antics of an adolescent, imbecile Negro boy, kept by their host as a sort of court-fool. Another tells of a magnificent and perfectly innocent Negro wantonly shot to death. The third, the story from which the title of the book is taken, offers, by way of establishing "atmosphere," a harrowing description of a foul and brutish landlord's obscenity cutting off the tail of a dog belonging to one of his white tenants named Lonnie, and also, a hardly more harrowing description of Lonnie's starving old father, eaten up bodily by fat hogs. Finally, Lonnie's fellow share-tenant, a Negro named Clem, is lynched—as innocent as he was at birth—despicably betrayed by his friend Lonnie, who had let his racial affiliations take precedence over his occupational affiliations. That is the sort of story this is, and it is told with gruesome effectiveness—and Clem's bullet-torn body lies on the earth for the red, round rising sun to make of it what it can.

Three of the stories in this volume have to do with the troubles that assail city dwellers. Two of the characters are fine young girls (one, aged nine) who are forced by hunger into prostitution; another is a man, through no fault of his own unemployed, who is run down and killed by a callous and very rich young fellow in—of all places—Augusta, Georgia, that well-known haunt of the Crocuses.

Some American People, the last of Mr. Caldwell's publications, is made up of a wise introduction and three purportedly non-fictional reports on the state of the nation, skillfully written on the basis of observation and casual conversation. The first of these reports begins with Oregon and comes eastward via St. Louis and

Chicago to Portland, Maine. The next deals with Detroit; and the last, by far the briefest but still the fiercest, deals with the South. Nearly everywhere, the reports say, there is desolation and despair; and masses of people, long since crazed with hunger, are now starving—except in New York, perhaps, which is not discussed, and in Maine, where they serve you putrid meat in the restaurants, and in Iowa, where times are good, but where people would do better to starve than to persist in their attitude of jaunty irresponsibility. The government efforts for relief have been worse than useless. Foreigners here recognize the malign capitalism which is the source of all our ills and would die in bloody strikes rather than submit to it, but native Americans, ignominious, can be bought off with thirty pieces of copper.

According to the Detroit report, Detroit and other cities of its type are beyond doubt the most iniquitous and wretched places in the world. Here the writer's arraignments are direct, and actual names are named freely. All of the automobile plants, he submits, are controlled by men whose exclusive desire, so far as the plant is concerned, is to make more and more money. In one plant this aim is most evident in the multiplication of personnel devices contrived to render human beings into mechanisms. There are restrictions against smoking, chewing, talking, sneezing, nose-blowing, and toilet-visiting. The spy system makes it indiscreet, if a worker values his job, for him to complain of heat or cold or boredom or fatigue; and in the realm of praise (which is alone permitted) one had better not lay one's self open to the suspicion of satire. In other plants, machines are speeded up without warning to the operatives—and capable fingers, snipped off, go their untrammeled way to Tophet. Then the worker must be wary; for if he loses another finger he is useless to the plant and will be dropped. In other plants the remorseless turning of the sacrosanct machines cannot be stopped though a worker is being crushed and mangled. In all the plants, there are slow chemical burns; there are injuries not seriously regarded by the plant doctors which none the less require amputations; there is unmeasured filth—one wash-bowl to the thousand workers.

There is wholesale prostitution brought on either by the threat of starvation or by the girl worker's knowledge that she retains her job only by compliance with the wishes of her boss. Worst of all, perhaps, there is madness, not acute but alarmingly progressive. One worker after another surrenders, hopeless, interns himself in the putrid and verminous refuges for his kind provided by the

Plant, and there, in those virtual prisons (fair from without and as high up as the ceiling of the first floor) gradually slumps downward to his end—partly rusted out, more largely rotted out.

It is interesting to know what Redeemer Mr. Caldwell, as prophet, looks to right these heavy wrongs; and it is disheartening to find that the suggested deity is not after all tremendously impressive. If, the prophet implies, the workers could substitute for the government-sanctioned company-unions a rank-and-file union of their own, all would be well. *Rank-and-file Union*, then, *Hominum Savior*. Two things would this Redeemer do: he would reduce the speed-up and he would install and operate safety devices that could not be disconnected by the foreman. For his children's benefit he would flout the Essential Progressiveness of the machine, at one time itself named Savior; he would turn back the clock (*reduce* the speedup), not hold it still merely; and while he was doing all of this he would install a machine (in the form of a safety device; but a machine just the same) so inexorable that not even a foreman could bring it to any sort of terms whatever. What this Redeemer would do to the minds of foremen and of super-foremen and of directors and board-chairmen, if anything, is not disclosed. If those minds are unaffectable, there is good argument for any self-respecting Redeemer's withdrawing from the human scene to Mars, or elsewhere, with what shreds of dignity he can salvage. But if he or any of his entourage are persistent creatures, and earnest, it is perhaps written in their natures for them to remain, always, nagging a Humanity they are basically hopeless of, and to pursue their victim from time to time with such nostrums as occur to them. There is nothing left for it but to judge the prescriber, somewhat, by his nostrums, and it is grave, therefore, as regards Redeemers or their prophets, when their best nostrums are at best trivial.

To reduce the speed-up is at least half of what is counseled. In the farming South, that much, at any rate, is concededly accomplished, and it would seem that there perhaps the state of affairs would be less noxious. But that is not Mr. Caldwell's conclusion, for in the particular section of his latest book called "Southern Tenant Farmers," he permits himself a clean superlative: "In parts of the South," he says, "human existence has reached its lowest depth . . . men are so hungry that many of them eat snakes, cow-dung, and clay." He tells of a man and his wife and eleven children who live on a dollar a month, and of another family whose children subsisted on a diet of bitch-milk. Formerly such oppressed people could solace themselves with an occasional rabbit to eat—but there is hardly a rabbit left now; or, all else failing, they could drink water—but there is hardly any water left any more, either, the land was semi-arid to begin with, and everything will be magnificently bad surely, just as soon as ever the rapidly failing wells can dry up thoroughly. Then the primordial deserts will repossess it; and that would make a flashy headline, truly. In the meantime, the unhappy tenants of the doomed land, white and black, are said to be the most sterling of people, desperately eager to work and to pay their own ways always, faithfully; and they are said also to be like slum-dwellers, "the backwash of America." But the cruel and predatory owners of all of this desolation are said to wring from it regularly a rich living. This is the case with about half the area of the state. The other half of Georgia—the section with Macon as a center—is incredibly well-to-do; "if one were able to buy a farm in that section, even a few acres, he should be comfortable for life." But Georgia on the whole is terrible; the state government is insensate and the relief efforts of the Federal Government in the state have been so bungling and foolish as to do harm rather than good, and the best thing to do with Georgia is to federalize it instantly.

The paragraph in which Mr. Caldwell offers his solution for the difficulties of all the cotton country testifies incidentally to his assumption that America will remain capitalistic. Then, after reckoning with and discarding as impracticable the unionization of farm labor, it advocates the abolition of private land-ownership, and the operation of farms on a large collective basis—like (does he mean?) the large collective basis of the automotive industry in Detroit. If that will not do, another choice is offered: perhaps the big land units could be broken up into small acreages to be intensively cultivated by one or two people. But whether these one or two people are to own the land or to keep it on government sufferance, is not disclosed.

The vexing question is to know what a common American citizen is to think about the spectacle of his country's heaping its awards upon a young man who talks so very loosely and so very much. The young man may be so personally attractive and so remarkable in mind and character and literary skill that nobody in his right senses could fail to value him; but there are certain other qualities he ought to manifest before a calm and judicious nation, or an individual, for the matter, acclaims him very notably. A harsh conclusion for the common citizen would be that the nation is neither calm nor judicious and that Mr. Caldwell (who can count shrewdness among his virtues) recognizes as much and means to give his patrons what they ask for. A more restful conclusion would be this: that New York is not America by any means, and that the responsible portions of the nation, however few current books they may buy, are far from being much exercised by Mr. Caldwell—are not indeed aware of him.

In a sense, that is a loss to everybody. Truly, it is a damaging thing to say of an author that the more one may know of a circumstance the author describes, the less, very often, one is disposed to credit his report. Much that Mr. Caldwell has written is unquestionably misleading. One of his most widely publicized pronouncements, concerning the terrorizing by arson of Negroes in Georgia, went unsustained despite grand jury investigations. And many of his reports which are offered as typical are bound to be very narrowly specific. The story about bitch-milk, for example, brought about an investigation by one of the Georgia newspapers; and the result of the investigation was to sustain the drift of the story in its bearing upon individual cases of want and gross stupidity. Proportionately there was about as much of both along Tobacco Road, the investigation said, as there is normally in New York or Gopher Prairie. And the New York weeklies trumpet the acknowledgement to Heaven, garbling it to suit their own ends. And all of this is very nettling. Yet the rapid and sensible introduction to *Some American People,* (a little sermon in Travel, it is) gives evidence—as there is plenty of evidence through all his books—that the writer is a man of considerable power. And it is likely that his entire literary output would be more impressive if—a good Southerner still—he were not as plaintively anxious as he is to please the kind and class of people that he has come to be affiliated with—the detached, nervous, thrill-goaded metrocosmopolitans of his own day.

PART IV

The Fabric of a Vision

The Dugonne Bust

MY NAME is Dugonne Truman V, and I was born in 1926 in South Carolina. After getting my bachelor's degree at Harvard and at Oxford, where I was a Rhodes Scholar, I have taught History for some years at Denominational College in one of the southeastern states. My grandfather, Dugonne Truman III, felt strongly that Southerners should devote themselves to the South, and it was he who influenced me to choose this position among the several teaching positions that were offered me when I "came upon the world."

If the old gentleman was not wholly enthusiastic about the scene of my efforts, he was better pleased for me to teach here than he would have been for me to teach at any college in, say, Connecticut or California. I learned that the Denomination that directs my Institution is intent not to be called Protestant, but my grandfather classed it so just the same. It used to please him to think at the beginning of my present tenure that I could be comfortable here, in spite of any loose-construction ideas regarding dogma that I might have picked up in my travels, or earlier, indeed, from him. "For we Protestants," he would declare with a kind of wry satisfaction, "seem to me sometimes to be at great trouble and expense to maintain, in devotion to something called academic freedom, entire faculties to negate our prime reasons for being."

Nearly anything would set my grandfather off, particularly as he and I sat in the cool of the evening on our front veranda with our feet on the banisters. "Not that that worries me," he would resume, "we're all of us in certain moods like lemmings, and it may well be—to use our parson's word—'God's plan' for us to yearn periodically for immolation. That does seem strange."

From *The Georgia Review*, XVI (Spring, 1962), 3-16.

"But a lot of things seem strange. Nay, *are*. For example, consider, my boy, how we have come in our time to pride ourselves on trusting in our minds wholly. Our whole minds? Or the great or small part of our minds that we in great or in small part realize? So we hear worthy people going about fulminating against superstition and prejudice—when much of their worthiness is in response to assumption merely. *They* are governed, they insist, only by what can be proved. Yet, they are stout ones for God and for the idea, in general, that their own lives are surely worth holding to."

The implied duplicity of my being here as a teacher often confronts me, and yet my grandfather's constant reflection about wisdom and judgment as weighed against mere fact confronts me too. I hope I am a good historian—and in the light of that hope I often wonder if in advocating my coming to this place my grandfather, who wished me to be near him, was not as the saying goes, merely "rationalizing." But it is a bad assignment for anybody to go remorselessly into what mere rationalizing is or isn't.

The truth is that I suppose I am what would be called a "mixed-up young man." No wonder. I was brought up an only child by my grandfather, my grandmother having died in 1910, and by his widowed, childless daughter, my aunt, Cordelia Dobbs; and behind *that, my* grandfather had been brought up by *his* grandfather.

My Aunt Delia died in 1950, and my grandfather, of whom I shall write more, later on, died shortly afterward. So I was left without immediate connections, and my work at this college, which began about then, occupied me in a way that was most helpful to me.

My life at this place has been pleasant. Whatever my being here implies as to overbrooding orthodoxy and so on, I can truly say that I have never been conscious of the spying and the coercion of opinion that the highbrow weeklies in New York would indicate lurk in every corridor of places like this. This college is in a sizeable old town with a social life that I often think is all too active. After teaching here for three years, I was given an extended leave of absence to obtain my Doctor's degree from Columbia University in New York.

This brings me to 1957, when I returned to my position here with a gratifying raise in rank. That Christmas I was married at thirty-one to a girl from this city whom I first knew well in New York when she spent a winter with an aunt of hers who lives there. Of this girl I need only say that she offers all that I have ever hoped for in a wife, in every way. It has distressed us not, so far, to have presented the world with a Dugonne Truman VI, to keep the line going, but we have at the moment active hopes in that regard.

But I set out to write a note upon the Past. My father, Dugonne Truman IV, perished in Florida, where he had gone on a fishing trip, in the Hurricane in 1926. I was born several months after his death. And my mother, born Saradosia Powell, was drowned the next summer in the surf before the Powell summer-place on Sullivan's Island. All of my Powell relatives had numerous children of their own, and at the Family Conclave which sat immediately after the calamity of my mother's death I was delivered over to my father's father and my Aunt Delia.

My earliest memories, then, have to do with those two and with the ancient house where they lived on the Dugonne Plantation. I am sure that the economic awards of the farms had by that time become scant indeed, but my grandfather had other sources of income, and Aunt Delia was well-to-do through her late husband. People used to say that Mr. Truman was among the few who could still make his land pay off and that hardly anybody else could afford to live still in the fashion of the spacious days that had gone.

I think that I was related to a high percentage of the people around us. Countless uncles, aunts, and cousins were forever coming to visit us, and we were forever returning their courtesy. Looking back upon these people as objectively as I can, I feel sure that most of them were definitely better, as human beings, than most run-of-the-mill citizens. Not that we saw much of *some* of the Family. There were too many. And besides, it was generally understood that any of the relatives who might be thought of as lowering the clan-quality were morally treacherous—anathema, to be shunned and avoided.

My grandfather used to say that he thought it implied arrogance and presumption for a man to consort with his relatives who made no effort to uphold the Family—that for him, he needed to be elevated, not debased any further than he was already! So with us a fifth-cousin who strove to be excellent was closer than a first-cousin who was content to be mediocre. There was a point there.

And my grandfather had another point regarding the large Bust of John Dugonne I, our ancestor, that in our front hall faced all comers to our frame-built castle. When the ladies in the Family would descant, as they were commonly doing, about the Founder's superlative distinctions, my grandfather would always interpose a chilling modification. It was not enough, he would say, to be descended from a Hero—one must *justify* the Hero; people descended from a Hero are more strictly obligated to be virtuous than people are who are descended from nonentities only.

I believe I can say in all conscience that that sermon fell upon young ears to good purpose, specifically as to the Bust, an icon that had immemorially occupied that pedestal casting its spell upon all of us. I know that in spite of our snickering at the time, my young cousins and I, gazing upon the Bust, burned each of us with secret resolution to give our Founder cause at last to be proud of us: I can testify that eight or ten of these young relatives whom I used to play with have already become exceptionally notable for their time-of-life, and we have in late years often confessed to one another that we are all of us the Founder's children as much by way of Bust as by way of blood.

My boyhood, then, was spent in such a welter of kinspeople and stories about my kinspeople in the past—most of whom were reported to have been fine indeed—that I hardly knew the difference between the quick and the dead in that company. And I heard so often the Legend of our Founder, who in antiphony and in plaster, shared our house with us, that I was placed further back in time than I should have been naturally by the already retrospective phases of my rearing. By the time of my twelfth birthday I was in effect in many ways a hundred years older than I was by any proper calendar.

There is no question that John Dugonne I was a genuine Revolutionary big-sachem with much solid achievement behind the glitter by which he is generally remembered among his descendants. He was eight generations ahead of me, and where he and his brother Lewis came from I do not know for a certainty. But on their first journey to America, around 1750, they were captured by pirates, from whom they soon escaped to achieve these shores at last when John was twenty and Lewis, eighteen.

The legend goes that the two brothers were splendid to look upon, tall, blond, cavalier, and perhaps a little swash-buckling in manner, but withal faithful communicants of the English Church. They wished, one of them wrote, "to store up, before all is over for us, a treasure in both worlds."

Hardly more than a year after his arrival, John, in the City of

Charleston, abducted from her fiancé and from her father, Mein-
heer the Reverend Van Schmitt, the Reverend gentleman's daughter, Bertha, and promptly married her. Bertha is said to have been
blond too, looking enough like her husband to have been his
sister. Evidently both of these two were "Nordic"; for John,
whether he was of Norman or later immigration to Britain, is
said, in spite of his French name, to have known only the English
language.

By 1776, the two brothers, John and Lewis, who had perser-
vered in their intimate relationship with each other, were both
of them men of considerable substance in their common neighborhood. John's interests had turned mostly to planting and
Lewis's to shipping, and both of them had held responsible office
under the King. During the summer of 1776, Lewis with his wife
and children quit Carolina for Newfoundland, but the two
brothers of their descendants continued to correspond among
themselves for nearly a century before the relationship at last
became too tenuous to persist.

John remained in Carolina. After the Battle of Lexington, he
organized a regiment of patriots, proceeded from Colonel to
General, and engaged in hostilities constantly till 1782. On Christmas day of that year he was surrounded at his home and overcome
by an irresponsible band of professedly loyalist guerillas, all of
them disguised, and by some suborned Indian associates. Those
"brutal men"—I tell it here as it was told to me—hated him not
so much as an enemy in war as a representative of a class of beings
that they could not comprehend.

Fetching the captive's wife and daughters to the scene, the
guerillas bound the General to a tree, with the threat of flogging
him with a cat-o-nine-tails before taking him away with them.
Bertha Dugonne was frantic, and in her appeals for mercy she
disclosed the gold wedding-band upon her finger. The hostile
leader demanded the ring. The lady said that since it was difficult
to remove she would have to work it loose with her teeth. Then
quickly she swallowed it, and flying upon her persecutor, bit him
savagely upon the hand before she could be subdued.

The man was naturally beside himself in anger. He drew his
sabre and rushing upon the bound Dugonne began slashing at
him savagely. So then did the other guerillas, and in a little while
the victim had sure occasion to be grateful for the treasure that
he had laid up in World II. A little later, the legend continues,

the vile perpetrators of this crime eluded a band of American soldiers that rode up, clattering, and fled out of danger into the forest.

This is substantially the account of the massacre that Bertha Dugonne and her daughters, who were the only witnesses, gave ten thousand times thereafter, the more frequently as the years passed, a kind of liturgy that they chanted into the great age of all of them. So among their descendants the tale went down, an echoing fable that tolled long to celebrate the saint and the Martyr-for-Liberty, an *ultimate* in looks, manners and probity, in clear solvency and in largess, and in any other virtue that one might think of.

There is no measuring how real our Hero was to us. Once, when I was a lad, my grandfather promised to take me into Charleston with him for a day if I would learn and declaim for him Anthony's oration about Caesar. That seemed to me a good proposal, and shortly afterward I was sawing away at the great lines before him and my great-aunt Felicia, who was making her customary winter visit to us. Suddenly Aunt Felicia declared that the oration reminded her too poignantly of the Founder for her to bear listening to it any longer. That was a pretty pass. But my grandfather bore up calmly. Ceremoniously excusing himself, he called me quietly into another room and told me to take up again where I had been interrupted. "And you will not blame your Aunt Felicia," he warned me, "for as long as I can remember, her health has always been most delicate."

The Founder had a number of children. The two daughters married and had children of their own who eventually, not Dugonne in name any longer, inaugurated "lines" that tended to drift out of the Family's knowledge. The youngest child, Hamilton, and his descendants were also lost and apart. At a precocious age, Hamilton was involved in a shooting affair over the good name of a prominent lady. He fled the state for the West and soon abandoned all communication with his more responsible kin. For this he brought upon himself their long denunciation— but so far as anyone knows he only repeated the neglect that his father, the irreproachable Founder, had executed earlier toward those whom he had himself abandoned in Europe.

There is a story that John Dugonne IV, in Texas at the time of the Mexican War, encountered a numerous and able but uncouth tribe of Duggans. This tribe was headed by an incredibly senile and decrepit Nestor, called Pa Ham. The old man was

always mouthing nonsense, but once when he was talking to the
young Easterner, he said quite clearly that *his* name was really
Dugonne too—and then he drooled off again into vapidness.
Nobody paid attention to that declaration at the time except the
alien visitor, who immediately began thinking odd thoughts,
thoughts that he kept to himself till he was at home again. Too
bad! For the Duggan clan in Texas, at last cattled, oiled, colleged,
married, and mansioned, is known, now, and deferred to all over
this country and in much of Europe.

The sons of the martyred General who settled at home, and
their descendants for several generations, were for the most part
prosperous, stable, and unspectacular. Among the descendants,
John Dugonne V and my ancestor, Dugonne Truman I, fifth
cousins who were brought up in the same household, behaved
themselves in ways that must be told about. John married a lady
of great wealth in Philadelphia and soon came to preside over
her father's vast business and notable art-collection. Dugonne
Truman I, specifically my great-great-grandfather, a farmer in
Carolina, married Elvira Wortham, who was fifth cousin to him
and to John Dugonne in Philadelphia and who like both of them
was four generations removed from the great Immigrant.

The Philadelphian, John Dugonne V, had one child, John
Dugonne VI; and the Carolinian, Dugonne Truman I, had two
children, Dugonne Truman II, and a daughter, Amanda. And to
cap all, Amanda became engaged to her double-seventh cousin,
John VI, in Philadelphia.

But war is a poor Man-Friday for any good soul to look to. The
young Northern man was killed in battle fighting for the Union,
in the early 1860's, and the young Southern man, loyal to Carolina, perished of exposure in a war prison in Ohio, leaving a
widow and an infant child, Dugonne Truman III, who became in
time my grandfather. The young widow was at the time of her
husband's death well into her second pregnancy, and shortly afterward she died in giving birth to a still-born daughter.

In 1870, the bereft young Amanda Truman married the distinguished diplomat, Biddle Beckett, whom she had first known
when visiting her former almost-father-in-law, our Cousin John.
She thereafter spent most of her life in London.

After his daughter's marriage and removal to Europe and his
wife's death a little later, in 1874, Dugonne Truman I was left,
except for a stream of transient guests, very much alone. There
was only his grandson, the war-orphan, Dugonne III, to live in

the house with him; there was only his Cousin John in Philadelphia as an available dear friend and consultant. The little orphan was in a sense "mothered" by these two gentlemen, and it was this orphan who, as *my* grandfather, many years later mothered *me* through *my* childhood. It is from his long remembrance that I know most of what I know about our Family.

My grandfather said that his grandfather and Cousin John were very dear to each other, often exchanging visits and always exchanging letters, becoming in spite of their common war-afflictions—perhaps because of them—more and more intimate with each other as they grew older. Once the two gentlemen went to Europe, where they spent a month in Rome and another in Paris and visited at length with the Beckett relatives in London, who arranged for them to be presented to Queen Victoria. For the most part, Cousin John was nervous at his home, and, less concerned with his business, he devoted ever more and more time to his Art Collection, making constant expeditions to Boston and New York to seek out objects of art.

During the year or so before the great Centennial Exposition of 1876, he was as a *bona fide* Philadelphia magnate eagerly concerned for the success of that enterprise. He regarded it passionately as a kind of great "tocsin," he wrote, that would re-unite spiritually as well as politically the nation that was still within itself to grievously torn. His letters of that period, many of which are now in my possession, are full of pride in the Georgia poet, Sidney Lanier, whom he had helped influence to write the Centennial Hymn for the Exposition's opening. And they are fuller still of his pride in presenting to one of the historical exhibits of the Exposition the heroic marble bust of his ancestor, John Dugonne I, that he had come upon recently and almost by accident, he said, in the course of one of his regular expeditions among the art-dealers.

Unhappily, Cousin John, on the day of the Presentation, just as he concluded his carefully devised speech, suffered a fatal stroke. That was a dolorous thing for good Pythias from the South who had been sitting beside him on the platform, and who, it developed under Damon's Will, had been left a considerable fortune in securities. Naturally the endowment was most welcome in those slack days around Charleston, but the *manner* of the bestowal was welcome too. For in the Will itself the fund was described graciously: "not so much a gift as a mark of gratitude to the beneficiary for his having so long against such odds main-

tained the Dugonne Tradition and Lands in our common country,"—something like that.

My grandfather, as he grew older, used to talk to me frequently
about the Bust. The original work that Cousin John discovered
had mysteriously disappeared from its Gallery, and the copy in
our hall was of plaster only, one of several copies that had been
made for the discoverer to give out to the various heads-of-families
in our connection. That distribution covered a wide field, all the
way from Baltimore to Galveston, with Nashville thrown in for
good measure.

About Nashville I did not know till I was an undergraduate at
Harvard, when a young Tennessean whom I had met, Maxwell
Maison, on learning my first name proclaimed himself my relative. It transpired that he as well as I had grown up—he and his
two brothers—under the steady gaze of a plaster Bust, the subject,
their famous ancestor, John Dugonne. So the two of us, strangers
till that day, were, by blood, we calculated, perhaps thirteenth
cousins (a relationship that we shared with doubtless ten thousand others), and by way of Bust, in a certain sense, practically
twins. In any case, we became dear friends, and it has often
amused me to hear Maxwell discourse in his sour fashion about
the Bust and about the pious sermons that *his* father used to make
to *his* children—how like the sermons I had heard!—every time
that Bust came specially to his mind. Good! For today, still in
their thirties, the three Maison brothers, in their various en-
deavors, are probably unexcelled for real eminence by any other
three brothers in this country.

My grandfather said that *his* grandfather was always talking to
him about that Bust, particularly when, as an old man, at the
time of the Spanish-American War, he fell in with the martial and
patriotic impulse that was then aflame. His grandfather had, indeed, delivered a kind of Roman oration upon that subject to
the young man as he set off with his regiment for Cuba. Yet,
shortly after the Victory and the home-coming, his grandfather
had clearly indicated to him his insecurity about that bit of
plaster that had proved to be so important to so many for such
a long time.

In my own boyhood around 1940, my grandfather remembered
clearly what *his* grandfather had thought about the Bust around
1880. The older man had never believed fully that there had
been an authentic image of the Founder prior to Cousin John's
almost stumbling upon the Bust in Boston. So my grandfather

would explain to me, and, translated at times by some witchcraft or other—with me presumably translated into *him* at the age of twelve, he would run on, quoting a voice that was by then long ghostly.

"The only likeness of the Founder that I ever heard of before the middle seventies, say five years ago," he would exclaim, "was Dugonne Wortham! This Wortham was the Founder's grandson through his daughter, Elizabeth, and the father, in turn, of Elvira Wortham, my lamented wife." Dugonne Wortham, he continued, "is indeed said, with perhaps some romantic embellishment, to have been a living replica of his grandfather, but the only likeness of Dugonne Wortham I ever saw was the gruesome daguerreotype made of him when he was very aged and already disfigured by the facial cancer that ultimately destroyed him. . . ." So much, then, as to all that, from *my* grandfather to me, concerning what *his* grandfather had said to him perhaps sixty years earlier. All of that was a Chinese puzzle, to be sure.

The Bust plainly suggested the Houdon Washington in pose and costume, but it had about it what one could fancy was a Dugonne "look," and the name, "John Dugonne," was cut upon its base, and Cousin John had written that "all" had declared it to be an excellent likeness. All? But that had been in 1876, almost a century after the Massacre. Who could then testify?

The present date is 1961, My revered grandfather died ten years ago, well into his eighties. I am sure that he was the most admirable human being I have ever known, and the Bust of *him* that stands in my mind is that of Marcus Aurelius—and no less. Yet he came to little that is tangibly impressive. Why? I tell myself that the obvious "defects" of character that retarded him practically are perhaps the stuff that they make wings of light from elsewhere, and that he is by now very likely among the Most High's most trusted Counsellors.

People who knew him used always to cherish him, telling him that he should be Governor or Senator or a great Justice in Washington. Yet he would never consent to run for public office. The electorate, it seemed to him, had become too gullible and erratic for its choices to have any meaning. I remember his saying that the world, which was always being declared small, was in fact too big for any one man or group of men to understand it—much less, to run it to any good purpose.

As a private citizen, he had the money that had come down to him from Philadelphia, he had the control of Aunt Delia's prop-

erty that she had inherited from her husband, he had the plantation, he had his law practice, among the best anywhere around,
and he had his incessant reading and authorship—mostly of articles on local history.

Perhaps one might say that it was his independent financial
status that to some degree permitted him to indulge his misgivings
about Society—if rarely about men. But for all of his wary examination of himself on that score, and for all of his humorous outlook, he pretty well despised—and could give you reasons for
despising too—most large, public intangibles and all heroic
declarations. He flatly did not believe that most politicians,
captains-of industry, labor-leaders, clergymen, economists, and
newspeople—above all, newspeople—command, even when one
can posit their integrity, the basic advantage of knowing at all
what they are talking about.

He knew in his own county of Yeamans many people instructed
by both church and school for generations, who were yet far
from heroic. And he could not, then, bring himself to assume that
the hoards of ordinary, crab-grass beings everywhere could be
counted upon, above their self-seeking, to conduct themselves
with nobility or even fairness.

For his part, his beneficences, which were numerous in personal
interest and in money, he would accordingly dole out, as anonymously as possible, to people and to institutions that he could
trust to make proper use of them. As for the State, the old phrase,
"God Save It" seemed to him still a good one. Who else *could*
save it? Could Mr. Harry Truman save it, or Governor Long of
Louisiana? Could Mr. John L. Lewis save it, or could the Pope?
Or could Mrs. Roosevelt save it? And besides, who would wish
to save a state at the risk of annulling the people who live in it?

But enough of all this. When I went back to the old house upon
being notified of my grandfather's sudden death, I found among
his effects an envelope addressed to me, "Personal." The letter
was dated only a few weeks before his death. He had hoped to
talk with me, he said, about what he was writing, but believing
that something might happen to him, he thought it wise to use
pen and ink immediately. He had of late in rummaging through
some old papers came upon a document that he thought would
be of interest to me, and he would trust me, in my "wisdom and
judgment" to conduct myself in the matter as I might think best.
"But I suggest that you wait a year or five, or even *ten*," he wrote,
"before you disturb the *status quo*." To my wisdom and judg-

ment! Lord, how could he bring himself to talk so about the infinitesimal?

"At this point," the letter directed, "before reading further, kindly examine the inclosed folder, without as well as within, and when you have done that, you may come back to my letter." The folder was an ancient parchment-like thing with two silhouette pictures, the right and left profiles facing each other, silhouettes of a young man in the costume of the early 19th century, apparently in middle age. And on the back of the folder were some notes. The first line of these notes said in bold and masculine writing: "Dugonne Wortham, Savannah, Geo., October 9, 1804." And beneath that, in a faint and delicate handwriting *this* appeared:

Augusta, Ga.,
Nov. 23, 1874

For my dear daughter, Elvira Truman:

These are shadow pictures of my father, Dugonne Wortham. Keep them carefully. It is said that he closely resembled his grandfather, the "Founder of our Family in America," and I believe that these silhouettes offer the best indication available of the physiognomy of the martyred General. Upon the insistent request of Cousin John Dugonne, I some while ago lent these pictures to him. They have just now belatedly come back to me. I am too old and sick to be responsible for them any longer and I hasten to post them to you this day.

Your devoted mother,
Maria Wortham

"This note from my Cousin Maria to her daughter," my grandfather resumed, "was by seemingly incredible circumstance never so much as opened until I chanced upon it recently. But I remember that the *date* of the letter was only two days prior to the death of the recipient. The confusion in the house of my grandfather incident upon his wife's fatal sickness accounted for the letter's being placed, it was thought temporarily, into a small cabinet of the deceased lady's belongings, and for its afterward being 'lost' there because of the relict's emotional unwillingness to probe into his sorrow.

"For myself," my grandfather's letter continued, "I consider the mystery of the Bust finally solved. Aware of the stories that one of the Founder's grandsons, Dugonne Wortham, closely resembled him, interested in the arts, enthusiastic over the reconciliatory aspect of the Exposition as to North and South, brooding always upon his son, the Union Soldier, our good Cousin John ran upon these silhouettes. I believe that his discovery of them almost unbalanced his reason, and that he caused the Busts to be made around 1874-75, with the accompanying shadow-pictures as his sole starting point. So, one might say, the grandson was father to the grandfather.

"I have in fact, since discovering this folder, called in confidence, for expert consultation upon this affair, our friend and neighbor, the famous portraitist, Miss Katherine Nedds. Miss Katherine confirms my opinion that the profile of the shadow-pictures and that of our Bust are, except for collar-arrangements, etc., practically the same; in fact, that the Bust might serve as an in-the-round representation of the countenance suggested in black and white only.

"Knowing me, my dear boy, you can know that I esteem all of this an exciting boon to be vouch-safed to one of my years. I feel again like stout Cortez (only somebody else) when he first stared at the Pacific.

"As for the opinions herein conveyed, do with them whatever you think best. You know that you have all of my love."

That letter, as my grandfather had known it would, left me definitely stunned, and it results, now that ten years have passed, in this writing—not history purely, perhaps, nor yet fiction, purely—a commentary, I hope, upon the comparative value of what-is and what-one-thinks-is, in this world.

Nor wise much, nor judicious much, I hope that I am too sensible to be any man's iconoclast. The names, accordingly, and many of the details in this narrative I have disguised, for I know better than to challenge half of the world to do battle with me! And in truth I conclude that I am not so much a breaker of images as I am one who calls attention to how plainly useful images can be, and how simple it is for anyone who craves a set of household gods, to have one, if he can ever get Tweedledum and Tweedledee together on the same story.

On Jordan's April Banks

HOUSTON COUNTY, originally much larger than it is now, began to be somewhat fully settled in the 1820's. The western part of it, extending to the Flint River—a section that later became Macon County—was the focus of an impressive migration from the Orangeburg section of South Carolina. This notable migration, strongest during the 1830's, was composed of people who were in good part Methodists. It was these people who cut short the brief years of this section as a fully authentic frontier. Already somewhat sedate—though their ecclesiastical tastes might seem "primitive" to their descendants—they looked with cold favor upon some of the harsher extremes of frontier evangelism.

An entry in a diary kept in 1847 by a daughter of one of the immigrants—Clara, she was, a young lady much given to reading the poetry of Mr. Pope—records some of her impressions of a church service she had attended recently:

Preaching at Asbury, to which place we went and returned home to dinner. The ride is long and unpleasant. We ought to be well paid for it. Mr. Kelsey preached. His text was from the Romans, first chapter and sixteenth verse. He preached more with the Spirit today than usual. Poor little fellow has gone through a fiery ordeal a few weeks since. Some of the Church find objections to his wearing gold spectacles, and brought him up before the Conference. The presiding elder thought he does no wrong in wearing them; I find today he still has them on. It is so absurd, I am almost ashamed of it.

Nearly all of the 1830, Carolina, Houston County pilgrims were of pre-Revolutionary stock which had obviously been either Episcopalian, Lutheran, or Presbyterian. Earlier, most of their ancestors had manifestly been Catholic, inheritors of the tradi-

From *The Georgia Review*, VII (Winter, 1953), 373-389. Excerpted from *The Marshallville Methodist Church from Its Beginnings to 1950*. Marshallville, Georgia, 1952. Bound mimeograph.

tional European culture—people who "crossed" the water before
they dashed it from the basin, people who "crossed" their knives
and forks on finishing a meal, people who taught these refinements not only to their slaves but to their descendants—some of
whom, for all their being "moderns," scientific on outlook, college
graduates, and so forth, were still practicing these refinements far
into the twentieth century.

The taboo against blasphemy and oaths, for example, that of
course by many centuries ante-dated John Wesley, was one of the
great concerns of his followers—a taboo that one came to terms
with as best one could. . . . A widely respected man who was outside the Church, indicated a desire to come in. "Will you," he
was asked, "give over cursing and swearing from now on?" He
would he said, unless, walking in darkness, he should strike his
shin on a piece of furniture; in that case he dared say he would
curse in spite of himself. He was taken into the Church, grieved
over for his weakness, admired for his candor.

Another man whose many years of zealous Methodism had not
quelled his native irascibility, was obliged to set an onerous watch
upon his lips against his own too vigorous denunciations of lazi-
ness, dullness, and inattentiveness on the part of his employees.
Cut off by his piety from all access to the conventional denunciations of the natural man, he indulged himself in denunciations
that he thought safely expurgated. "Oh, you low, low, vile and
miserable creature," he would exclaim to his black man, Friday,
or "you graceless, faithless, dull, mendacious worm, how can you
presume to show your revolting face in the sweet light of day? Oh,
you wretch, you . . .," and so on.

But the denouncer was not himself faithless, ever. He did his
best always. In spite of the saying that ignorance of the law is no
excuse, perhaps as to spiritual law, it *is* excuse. For Divinity can
afford for it to be so. And as for a man's exclaiming "By the
eternal Jupiter!"—what was that? How could he know that his
"Zounds" and *"Od's Bodykins"* were oaths by, respectively, *God's
Wounds upon the Cross* and *The Body of the Little Jesus?* How
could he know that the counting-out jingle that he taught his
children was most likely a Puritan taunt against Catholics, dating
perhaps earlier than 1600:

> One sort, two sort, Six sort, zal,
> Bob Tail dominecker, Deal, Dawl, Dal,
> Harum, Scarum, Virgin Mary,
> Sinctum, Sanctum, Buck!

Generally-extended customs and practices and outlooks rarely arise one day and subside on another, crisply. They reach over many years, originating and perishing along irregular fronts. Some of the matters suggested herewith were venerable when only the Indians knew this particular region—and some of the others have persisted till now.

In the early days of the Republic, few ecclesiastics from the older churches ventured far westward from the coastal towns. The torpor as to traditional church affiliations that naturally ensued among the laity was not relieved during the post-Revolutionary years by the memory that the Episcopal Church was undoubtedly, in a certain way, the Church of England, that is, the Church of their late enemy. After a while, into the silent void of the frontier came suddenly with stupendous vigor, the far from voiceless evangelicals.

By 1880, the evangelicals' children had become fully aggressive. . . . "*Bishop* Pierce, *Bishop* Pierce, did you say?" inquired an insolvent *grande dame* of Virginia origin, in Macon, conversing with her new and solvent son-in-law, who was a product of Emory College. "Do the Methodists actually call them *Bishops?*" Oh, that was not discreet of her! "Yes, *Bishop,* I said," was the reply. "Bishop, Bishop, Bishop, just why not Bishop?"

By 1900, with Imperialism riding the air generally, the evangelicals were ready for *anything.* One of the surprising legends of the Marshallville Church tells how the Reverend J. M. Austin, sermonizing one day as an old man, in the absence of the regular minister, suddenly galvanized a listless congregation. "Oh," he cried out, weeping copiously, "oh, if I but had a million dollars!" The congregation was aghast—and Mr. Austin the least mercenary of men! "Oh, if I had a million dollars, how generously would I endow Bishop Candler's College in Havana, to redeem Cuba from the Catholics!"

Denominational rivalries were intense. One spoke of peoples' being "admirable, though Baptists." One demanded that fellow churchmen patronize one another in business, support one another in politics. One was likely—baptising by immersion, with loud proclamation that only such baptism was valid—to be harshly challenged from the wooded banks, by guests, with loud inquiry about the jailer and his household. Years later, in rosy reminiscence, one could actually record, in proof of the *boundless* tolerance of the slave owners, that they *consistently* refrained from making a demand that they might have made very naturally—

namely, that the Negro convert join his master's church or no church.

For all this, the old rivalries seem, like the wars of chivalry, to have existed on a special plane that bore little relation, at times, to other planes. On occasion, Baptists and Methodists even married one another!

The diarist Clara, mentioned above, eventually developed a cousin who insisted upon being immersed. That was ahead of her —in both date and comprehension!

In the meantime, avid for sermons—she *was* young and Church *did* imply a crowd—Clara added her presence regularly to that of the zealous at various camp meetings, and at church services where available within a 12-15 mile radius.

In March, 1845, she tells how she entertained herself on a Sunday afternoon reading the history of "that distinguished lady, Esther." "My minister," she explains, "has requested me to give or collect every passage in Scripture respecting to her, which I hope I may do satisfactory."

During the next month, she with all of her family rose early on Sunday so that the Negroes might attend church at ten o'clock in advance of the white service at eleven. A little later, her diary bewails the spiritually cold and unfruitful season of the camp meeting just concluded.

As for the long excursions that Clara made to church services at one place or another, not all of them were dull mechanic exercise. Once, surely, she and her sisters, in silks—tailored *plain* in testimony of their Methodism, woven *heavy* in testimony of something not Methodism—once in their carriage, they proceeded to Asbury not boresomely. For beside them cantered some young gentlemen, snugly trousered, on horseback. The heat was excessive, and as the equipage passed a cool spring of water, one of the young ladies signed audibly for refreshment, audibly enough for Beau X to hear plainly. To hear was to act, for him, and he discounted quickly and stooped to the water. But he stooped not to conquer, for at that moment his snug trousers ripped disastrously —not always was a church pilgrimage bound to be wholly pietistic, Methodist though you might be.

*   *   *   *   *

In the early days of Christian church-going, a center aisle separated men and women worshippers. The two groups remained quite apart from each other, and they were on the church rolls listed separately. As late as 1910, surely, it was still customary in Marshallville to speak of the men's and women's "sides" of the Church. Negroes, also apart, kept to the rear or to a balcony till they were called up for communion after the whites. The tall columns that supported the ceiling served as props for the tilted chairs of the privileged "saints."

It is said that one notable Churchman used to refresh himself with soda crackers from time to time, and that even as John Randolph went with his dogs into the Halls of Congress, so went this apostle to his devotions. It is sure that "Miss Elvira X used, at church, to refresh her grandchildren with tea-cakes and apples and herself with crystallized ginger—and that once, bemused by the sermon, she disastrously proffered crystallized ginger to her infant attendant, her granddaughter, Edna. . . ." "Just go right up into the pulpit," whispered Elvira to Edna, by now practically incandescent, "and pour yourself a goblet of cool water and you'll feel better."

The talk of apples, ginger, and cool water suggests a phenomenon that ought to be noted. This is that the ideal of austerity, often associated with Methodism, was apparently not operative here so long as it might relate to—among other matters—food, drink, and interminable conversation. Possibly the great youth and exuberance of the frontier made youth and exuberance suspect, somehow rendered benign any dissipations of the aged. Dancing, for example, and all "frivolity" were frowned upon. The families of even the most prominent churchmen could find themselves in deep water on that score—and did. The young men could find themselves officially reprimanded, when circuses began to frequent Macon, for being seen at circuses.

At Church, when the benediction was at last over, there was a flood of secular conversation. "How are you, sister, how is your rheumatism, I hope better. Mine is not nor my Cousin Liza's either. And won't you come home to dinner with us, you, your sister's family too, for they are visiting you, and all of us at our house do dearly love her. No, they will not be too many, for there are only two carriages full of you after all. . . ."

Of course, nobody was so captious as to condemn a Methodist for consuming too freely of the fruits of God's garden—chicken, chitterlings, persimmon beer, figs, peaches, apples, leeks, cushaws, and on and on. God's garden—with you, in a sense, as His gardener. . . . God's good loamy soil, with you as His trustee—and His warm sun, and His rain. And your own sweet potatoes, for example, souffled with a generous amount of your own sweet butter—suppose they were "flavored" a little unorthodoxly—could hardly be held bad for anybody. Even incipient bishops could feast on these with something less than mortal sin. "Sister," one of these bishops inquired, "what is the *variety* of these potatoes; I resolve to grow some myself—I trust you will supply me with the slips." *Preacher Potatoes* this dish was named thereafter. . . .

Or suppose that your own scuppernongs, from your own back yard, should by natural processes turn into wine. One most faithful Methodist, a steward, held such liquid almost wholly innocent. "I had not dreamed," said he, "that anybody could believe it would be harmful." Persimmon beer was all right; apple cider was. Whiskey bought in bottles was to be watched carefully.

And nobody was so captious as to blame a man, after a Gargantuan Sunday dinner, with all of the guests one could gather-in at Church, and after an appropriate cat-nap, for interspersing an afternoon of pious prayer and song with a vast deal of aimless, light chatter, and with a vast deal of most practical talk about the rainfall and the cotton-prospect. Ideally, many of the guests were preachers, regular or "local," but friends living at a distance from the Church were also in special demand—all with their wives, children, and visiting relatives. Food and talk, and talk and food, over and over—it was a rich regimen, not easily bettered—and hard to get enough of.

As though Sundays did not come with sufficient frequency, the Stewards, meeting on first Monday evenings, often entertained among themselves with elaborate dinners. Sometimes they served oysters, which, along with rice and coffee, in memory of its Carolina coastal origin, Marshallville did not include among the store-bought grocery items that were likely to be blamed as "extravagant." All beef, pork, poultry and dairy products, and all breads were apparently regarded as almost free.

At nearly all of these great feasts, the children were obliged to "wait" for their food till the older people had eaten. Pious or not, they could on a Sunday afternoon amuse themselves officially with no light music, no rowdy play. Many of them, at an obvious loss for something to do, were assigned hymns to commit to memory—an activity which they lived to be grateful for.

Above all, swimming on Sundays was discountenanced. There is a story of how one staunch Methodist, around 1875—one prone to demand *several* grains of salt with most proscriptions—refused to his pastor's face to concern himself gravely with his son's sin in this regard. To the reminder of how many Sunday swimmers had met a sad end, he exclaimed that he hardly expected to raise *all* of his boys anyhow. . . . And there is another story of another staunch Methodist of the same type who, around 1900, forbade his son's swimming of a Sunday in Marshallville but permitted him to swim on a Sunday at St. Simon's Island. Still another story tells of an indignant father whose boys had been very noisy in his front yard while the minister was making a Sunday call. "You might," he exclaimed, "you *might* have had the decency to spare me embarrassment by going into the *back* yard."

But when the individual was himself an adequate learner, the teachings of the Church often worked out in a manner to suggest the Great Miracles. For by those teachings many simple souls, with little experience of the world, but endowed with the experience of God, believing in His presence, intent to justify His virtue and His gracious love, became at times themselves most of the things that anybody could ask of anybody, tranquil and beautiful and wise, with at once all companionableness and all high dignity.

* * * *

The deaths of two prominent early Marshallville Methodists occurred in 1869. Most likely, immediately following each death, a formally worded notice of the funeral was sent from house to house throughout the community. Certainly this custom, probably brought here from Carolina, was already thoroughly established in the earliest memory of the oldest Marshallville people in 1950—when it was still operative. Topped by a bunch of small, beribboned flowers, inscribed in Gothic-seeming characters, imbedded in a shallow box, the notices were solemnly presented by a Negro servant, at times riding a black horse.

Another custom, as ancient but sooner neglected, was that of slowly tolling the church bell immediately preceding funerals, one peal for each year of the deceased person's life.

* * * *

For around fifty years, one of the prime festivals in Marshallville was the grand-scale, inter-denominational, annual May Picnic of the Methodist and Baptist Sunday Schools—"Celebration" often called, perhaps in unconscious racial-memory of Spring ceremonials that were enacted for milleniums gone by. The grown people, burdened with their rich burdens of food, with their lemonade-ingredients, for lemonade must flow that day like Jordan rolling, gathered early in the grove east of the schoolhouse, equipped for the occasion with rough-tables. And the young "scholars," boys armed with silvered-over sticks for swords, girls armed with the primmest posies, deployed upon the railway station, Baptists from the east, Methodists from the west. Thence, headed by an authentic Confederate Major, his sword held high, mounted upon a white horse, they proceeded in solemn march to join their elders.

And then the food, dispensed from trunks by sedate great ladies, seated for their labors! And then the sonorous invocation, and then food, again the food, the intent proving of every pudding.

And after that, the seemly withdrawal of the gentlemen, given to the tobacco that was so revolting to ladies. And then, the dishes cleared and packed away, the servants ministered to, our ladies can themselves relax. And how do they now, within a secure cordon of sweet girls, observe Miss Jo, a valued guest and friend from Fort Valley, as seated within her safe circle, she lets down her remarkable hair, down . . . and down, till it sweeps the earth about her, too massive even to be lifted up by the rapt spectators' thousand sighs of admiration.

*   *   *   *

If dancing and card playing were eschewed, or supposed to be, music was certainly not eschewed. The controversy that developed over the propriety of using instrumental music in connection with Church services was fated from the beginning to eventuate in favor of the "progressives." But for a while around 1880, that controversy waxed, and waxed bitter before it was wholly forgotten. One staunch Churchman who had ardently opposed the idea of an organ, could never till his last day, it is said, look complacently at the organ that was finally installed. Another, while not inimical to an organ *per se*, could not bring himself to favor having one. He had for many years, he said, attempted to the best of his ability to raise the tunes with his tuning fork, and he was sad to think that he had not done the work to people's satisfaction.

In one special regard, the 1880's were notable years in Marshallville, tending to produce a distinguished generation of people. The physical trauma of the late war was beginning to be over with, and the old, wise lessons of privation and disappointment and grief were fruitfully mastered. For after all it was evident that one was alive and well, and that many people one loved were also. Others one loved were with God, surely. People whose youth had been shadowed by Appomattox and by the decade thereafter had known enough of bleakness for them to be ready to cherish *any* light—enough of bleakness for them, all their lives, to greet sunshine, when sunshine offered, with an almost holy exultation.

They knew that thin repining was a foolish impudence. They knew that mere sentiency untouched by pain is itself a bright blessing, the mere being able to look at sky and trees and sweet-sixteen, then being able to take part in laughter and light talk and lovely singing—oh, Alice, Ben Bolt! They knew that all these, coming at far more than any dozen for one's dime, were after all the best of things, beyond the buying of nabobs. They knew that all these, with fat fields and storehouses—"no want *this* winter, sir!"—were fair tokens of heavenly grace and favor to them specifically extended, to them, unworthy, though most truly striving! And they were at ease in their assurance that with God *for* them, few could be against them to great purpose.

Best of all, it was evident by the 1880's that the second generation of the ancient families here—truly ancient families here—truly "ancient," somehow, by American standards, though only fifty years were involved—would for all of its time maintain the distinction of its origins. For this generation exhibited in a surprisingly high number of individuals a physical resiliency, an elevation of mind and character, and a practical effectiveness that was remarkable in view of the economic and political restrictions then riveted upon the entire South.

Later, as these restrictions began to be somewhat loosened, they were loosened first in the cities. But for a long time the odds of city life were not clearly superior to those elsewhere, and Marshallville's second generation was irrevocably committed to the home of its birth. Another twenty-five years would display the situation more clearly and many of the more vigorous members of the *third* generation would go away. But that future was hidden, and as long as the second generation lasted—many of its members survived far into their eighties—the general personal level of this community was almost incredibly worthy.

A diary kept by a recent graduate of Wesleyan College, a niece of the diarist Clara of the 1840's, is poignantly indicative of its time. The entry for Christmas Day, 1883, records that the weather is heavenly and that, wondrously, the front yard is full of roses. Her family has had a fine dinner, her father and mother are napping, her sister and brother, both of them in their late teens, have gone off to parties. The diarist is alone.

She is alone with her gifts—several beautiful cards, several handkerchiefs, and a promise of voice lessons for the coming spring. She declares that with so many blessings she should be very happy—what girl so placed would not be happy? And yet somehow she isn't happy—immured somehow, she concludes, cabined, cramped—and there the great world is, somewhere clean past her reach.

She would devoutly dote upon seeing it, its wonders and riches, Vanity Fair, and all the rest. And yet she would hardly be so bold; for the seeing of that world is heavy with danger, the seeing of it has turned many a heart to stone and substances far harder. The seeing of it has made many forget their God. . . . Yet she will take the risk—and she by her written word then and there offers this pact to the Power that is and was and will be; that if she may see these glories, she will in token of her vow not to forget her God, read daily those words there written, read them over and over for a year of days. . . . This diarist traveled notably much and far before she died at well past eighty, a steward in the Marshallville Church.

* * * *

Until the shelling of Fort Sumter, the Fourth of July was celebrated here annually, with a vast patriotic and religious picnic. After Sumter, people were slow to make much of an anniversary that had somehow turned bitter to them.

Enough Marshallville people were involved in the war of the 1860's for that epochal tragedy to resound continuously as a distinch and tangible thing, for fifty years and more, in the minds of everybody in the community. Baptist and Methodist combined to make the Confederate Memorial Day—the *only* Memorial Day one knew about till 1918—a very high and genuine ritual. From spring to spring, there were on that day orations and prayers and solemn and stirring music; and there was the roll-call of all the youngsters who had gone from here to the armies there to die— their names responded to by one bereft—by father, mother, or otherwise.

* * * *

As the nineteenth century drew toward its end, there was perhaps less of social change discernible in Marshallville than in most other places. But, fortunate or otherwise because of this stability, even Marshallville was of course naturally shifting.

People were still regarded badly for dancing and for playing card games with regulation-type cards. A few conservative churchmen still refrained from reading mail or newspapers on Sundays.

One outstanding church worthy, on a transcontinental trip in 1903, could not bring himself, by riding trains on Sunday, to give a reason for anybody to work on that day. He managed, instead, to spend his Sundays at hotels. And as late as the mid-teens of the nineteen hundreds, a notable cleric here, unwilling to ride the Sunday mid-day train 14 miles from Marshallville to Montezuma, was often carried there in a buggy by a young member of his flock.

The taboos that 1950 reveres, perhaps as basically porous as those of 1900, are certainly less numerous—so emphatically less numerous that 1950 may be thought of as skirting narrowly upon the grave-danger-line of No-Taboos whatever. In case that the old proscriptions and ways-out may be needed again, some day, in an emergency, it is well to record a few of them lest they be lost record of.

There was a house that burned in the 1870's, a great house with twelve great white columns. The fire and the smoke billowed to heaven. Alas, what else could those people have looked for?—their house was full, *full* of French novels. . . . There was another house that burned about the same time, a big house with a big room that youngsters had often danced in. And as it burned, out from one of the broad rock chimney-bases writhed countless loathsome serpents. About that, the least one could do was to preserve an awful silence—for it would not do to neglect a token utterly. . . . Around 1900, in another house that later burned, some youngsters were having an obviously merry time in the "parlor" across the hall from their elders. "I declare," remarked the mistress of the house—lax, she was—"I do believe those young people are dancing, or maybe just playing twistification. . . ." "Not *my* Susie," cried Cousin Susie, Sr., visiting. "No, ma'am, she'd suffer her right arm to be taken off at the shoulder, before she would break her *church* vows!"

And in the roster of sins, there was of course the Theater. Shakespeare was permissible, sterile-pure as he was understood to be, and Ben-Hur and Rip Van Winkle were, but beyond those, there was a risk, beyond those, one would do well to think that the entertainment one had seen in Macon had been a concert, or a pageant, perhaps. . . . Nothing is more indicative of the loosening disciplines than the fact that movies and automobiles, that came late to the Feast, were never cried out against as the Theater was, or as Sunday horse-and-buggy-riding was.

And there were naturally other sins, some of them apparently specialized for gentlemen—secret poker-playing at night in the back of store-buildings—and well enough "secret," because of its *enormity,* whatever one might say about some of our very best gentlemen's indulging in it. . . . And there was horse racing. One could risk the preliminaries, risk the milling crowds, risk admiring the proud steppers, risk looking with all one's eyes, fascinated —until the racing actually started. Then one must hurry away, with one's little boys held by the hand, lest, by some chance, the tabernacle of the sky should crash downward, *then,* upon the callous.

And there was always of course the sin that mocked and raged, not be looked upon when it was ruby red, lest one be deceived thereby. To thwart *that* sin, *any* steps seemed justified. So there were pledges—"Do you, Dickie Rowe, age eight, now solemnly undertake to touch no spirituous liquors for the period of six months?" Dutifully, Dickie did. . . . And then the snow came, snow, the first in many years, the last, most likely, for years to come. And Dickie's people gathered snow in great tumblers, and over the snow poured much heavy cream, and over all that, oh, delicately given, some drops of *spiritus frumenti.* . . . And what did Dickie do? He made shift with vanilla extract (since that was not officially alcoholic) as best he could—*"and let this be a lesson to you,"* quoth Senior, *"not to go about making commitments without first talking to your papa."*

So the saving grain of salt worked then as always. And again: "For of course," the lady said, reminiscing, looking back near sixty years to the nineties, "of course one always arranged to invite one's young lady visitors to be here for the two weeks of the 'Revival' "—one could always be sure of plenty of nice entertainment for young visitors at the time of a "Revival."

Church-going was in fact one of the main social activities the year round, for everybody. For the young, too prone to frivolity, it was thought of as specially useful. How often has one heard reports of all this, in fond memory! There would be a little Negro boy at the back door of a young lady's house, knocking, a little boy bearing a note to the young lady herself, addressed with opulent flourishes—and in the note, a "date"—as one now would say: "Mr. John Smith presents his compliments and requests the honor of accompanying Miss Mary Jones to church on Wednesday evening."

* * * *

All along, we were strong for "missions," and the Orient bore heavily upon us. There is a legend, which, whether it is accurate or not, shows well how the wind blew hereabout in reference to our concern for earth's distant places. There was a lady speaking, a returned missionary, telling her experiences in China. "And do you know, my dear people," she asked, "oh, do you know that in that fine Methodist School for girls, the plumbing fixtures are altogether antiquated and inadequate?" The information was received as almost insupportably dolorous, as truly it was. Yet it is interesting, in view of everything, that in the Marshallville Schools at the time there was no plumbing fixtures at all, no, not one.

There was little actual money in Marshallville, but society was plainly strong, with a dearth of the superfluities of life, perhaps, but with a superfluity of the necessities. On first Monday nights, when the stewards met, there was often supper, and in winter it was often *oyster*-supper. Oyster and ice cream Church-benefit suppers came frequently till the idea developed, somehow, that such occasions were not proper, and then the benefit-suppers became indoor "free" picnics to which all the guests brought a contribution of food.

Particularly lavish were the mid-day luncheons at which the Church women entertained themselves at the *all-day* meeting they attended periodically, a relic of the former *week* of prayer. There is an old letter describing one of these occasions. The writer described the food, suggesting the menu of a Roman banquet—and "that attended to," the writer reported, "we listened to a superb talk by a returned missionary on the harrowing poverty, want, and famine that always weigh down the people she has been serving—oh, speed that devout woman's noble work!"

*   *   *   *

The minister assigned to Marshallville at the turn of the century was a zealot, to be sure. He held revivals, reprobated the complacent virtuous-liver along with the complacent evil-liver, he held sun-rise prayer meetings, he lured sedate parents to church via their children, who were promised candy if papa and mama really got there.

The Methodist mind in those days assumed a contact with the Infinite that it would hardly assume currently. The Pastor and indeed several of the congregation, including a prominent lay-woman, did not hesitate from time to time through direct personal warnings, to prophesy eternal Hell for people whose ways seemed to them unacceptable—people who talked callously of missions or failed to come to Sunday School, or did any one of many other things. A number of sinners, so trodden upon, took heavy offense and turned, surely; but most of them apparently took the dark tidings lightly.

Either because custom was fixed in the matter or because ladies were somehow in general thought sinless, or for some other reason, the securely virtuous seem to have limited their rebukes to gentlemen only. Surely, legend has little to tell of Jennie Doe's having been accosted often upon the sidewalks by Richard Rowe, offering the distressing intelligence that only a little more from her and she would be damned beyond any possible help.

But this zealot was a superior man, able and sincere, a representative of an exalted tradition; and there were no lazy bones in him. There is a story that once when there was no money for the preacher in the Church treasury, the preacher said that he could no longer, then, buy groceries.

*   *   *   *

It was during 1910 that the agitation for a new church-building first took definite form. A few vigorous Methodists protested the despoiling of the old church. Among these were some people who had lately moved in from Ohio, and who were already conscious of the value that the strong-pulsing society there was beginning to attach to any authentic memorial of "old" America. The doomed white wooden building, rectangular and besteepled, was of course ancient only by frontier standards, but it looked like a proper church for a village that had its cultural roots in an era prior to the Revolution. Its partisans pointed all of this out, that it was indeed not *much* too small, that it could be added to, sumptuously equipped, and even endowed for what a new building would cost.

But the truth is that in Marshallville, as well as in many other places, there was an impulse for what passed as style, and people were actually wishing for something new and, as they conceived, up-to-date—which is to say, though they hardly understood the matter, they wished a building that would be in general more suggestive of the twelfth century than of the eighteenth! They got what they wished, and the old building, sold for certain pieces of silver to the grandson of the man who gave the land it stood on, was by the purchaser, without bell, book, or candle, wrecked and rebuilt as a huge shed on his farm.

It was during 1920 that the Church last tried any one for conduct "unbecoming a Church member" in this case, drunkenness and other charges. From the Kelsey trial in 1847, for wearing the wrong spectacles, these ordeals had been enacted less and less often—against girls for dancing or furbelow-wearing, against boys for circus going, against gentlemen for drinking. One of these tipplers, a minor Church official, commanded, about 1900, to apologize for his error in open Sunday School, executed the command and was then and there absolved. The "trial" Committee of 1920 reported as follows:

The accused pleads guilty, and throws himself on the mercy of the Church. He is penitent, and promises he will do better, if given another chance. The Committee recommends he be given this chance. He also asks the prayers of the church, to aid him in his struggle to do better. . . .

*   *   *   *

The minister of 1933-35 was committed to the idea—one often shared by Jonathan Edwards and John Wesley, among others— that if a man lacked a definite memory of the *beginning* of his conversion, he had quite possibly never been converted at all. Several of the pillars of his Church, vague when subjected to his questioning, found themselves classed as little better than the wicked. All of that was troublesome. . . . This evangel was convinced that what he most needed to improve his ministry was a trip to Palestine; and his pertinacity to that end was rewarded when several members of his congregation in early 1934 financed such a trip for him and his wife. A clear result of the trip was a number of picture "slides" of Jerusalem, the Dead Sea, and other scenes in Palestine which he exhibited at church services from time to time.

The minister who headed the Church, 1939-41, had been born during the 1860's in Ohio of a family with pro-Southern sympathies, and he was married to a Georgia woman. During the 1930's, he had ministered to the "Northern" Methodist Church in Fitzgerald, but he was in thorough accord with the Marshallville Church in its consistent, though at length futile, opposition to the national unification of Methodists.

This outlander, in certain ways one of the most vigorous "natives" ever to occupy this pulpit, was a proper successor to Fielding's Parson Adams and Goldsmith's Dr. Primrose, a man too bedazzled by high music and by higher ideals of the Great Brotherhood to fret himself conventionally about fiscal detail. He was a reader and a student, particularly of history. He preached well. He emphasized, with the competent help of his gifted wife and daughter, the musical aspect of the Church. He rendered his Quarterly Conferences, via box-supper methods, into bright social occasions. He recruited some of his young men parishioners as junior-stewards.

But he consorted with people at bowling alleys; he was sometimes apparently casual about some of his official duties; and, like the lilies of the field, he did not trouble himself greatly for the morrow. He went from here to Talbotton, and he was there retired from active preaching. Later he earned his Master's degree in history at the University of Georgia, and he died in 1948, at something over sixty, at his home in Macon. He was buried in the cemetery at Marshallville. Justly or not, he had idealized this place as the most authentic relic he had encountered of the old decentralized America that had existed before 1860; and he remarked shortly before his death that he would rather take off from here, for Heaven, than from any other place known to him.

But the idyllic state of affairs that seemed to this indigenous foreigner blessed had come to seem not blessed to the fast-moving, industrialized civilization of America at large. His concern as to what destination was wished—expressed once when somebody remarked that the town was not getting anywhere—was not a concern generally shared. It was evident, certainly by all material standards, that the community, though still vital, was relatively as compared with its neighbor communities vastly less vital than it had been in 1900.

Many now of the old fervid and ably-generous Methodists were long dead, and others were living elsewhere, and it began to seem that the Church that had walked alone for so long a time was going to be obliged to walk again with some other Church, was going to have to become again a "part-time" station. But thanks in part surely to the happy presence of the "new" wise and venerable minister who was assigned to us in 1949, this crisis was successfully lived-over.

For it is not the number of members nor the money represented that must at last justify a Church. God does not, as Milton declared long ago, need either man's work, nor his own gifts. What He does need, and what man needs, no individual man, of himself, can ever wholly typify. But the chief business surely of any minister or indeed of anybody else, is with what wisdom and humility he can achieve to try to typify this elusive, this hard-to-name and impossible entity.

வ§ஜ்

Shakespeare–A Thumbnail Sketch

WILLIAM SHAKESPEARE was born in April, 1564, in Stratford, England. The nation had at the time a population of something over 4,000,000; London, something less than 200,000; and Stratford about 2,000. Only seventy-two years before, Columbus had discovered America, and there were as yet no English settlements west of the Atlantic. Only six years earlier, Elizabeth, at the age of 24, had ascended to a throne sadly askew from its recent contrary slantings, first the intensely Protestant slantings of her brother, Edward VI, and later the intensely Romish slantings of her sister, Mary.

Shakespeare's father, John, was a brisk and ambitious man of ordinary origin, but his mother, Mary Arden, had family connections that were exalted, and, perhaps incidentally, Roman Catholic. William attended the village school, studying Latin almost exclusively, and, in off times, he worked in his father's wool shop. Among the sights of Stratford in his youth were the steeple of the church, the stone bridge over the Avon River, and a pretentious residence called New Place. All of these were the work of Sir Hugh Clopton, the legendary great man of the village who had grown up there, gone to London to achieve wealth and fame, and finally returned home to do what he could for the town that had bred him. All of that had been long ago, and Sir Hugh Clopton was resolved to dust before William Shakespeare was so much as thought of; but it is none the less possible, in view of Shakespeare's later procedure, that Sir Hugh, through the tales that William heard of him during his youth, was among the most important of all the influences ever brought to bear upon the greatest gift that Stratford, or nearly any other place, has ever offered to mankind.

From *The Georgia Education Journal*, April, 1938.

At eighteen, William Shakespeare married Anne Hathaway, eight years older than himself and the daughter of a recently dead neighboring farmer, long a friend of the Shakespeare family. The circumstances of the marriage are not known, but the fact is that shortly *after* it William and Anne found themselves parents.

There is no record of the next five or six years of Shakespeare's life. He may have remained in Stratford working with his father, he may have taught school there or elsewhere, he may have joined a troupe of roving actors. Most likely he taught school. But before he was 25 he was in London, notable enough in theatrical circles to excite the enmity of playwrights and actors already well established. That is saying a great deal, for, from the time that Shakespeare was ten or twelve till the time of his death at 52—say for forty years—the English theater was among the most distinguished in all history—this, quite excluding Shakespeare's own contribution to it.

At the beginning of his career in London Shakespeare was as much an actor as a playwright, but as time went on he composed more and acted less. Technically he followed the styles of the moment, as faddish as a producer in Hollywood. If historical plays were the fashion, he wrote them; if comedies were the fashion, he wrote comedies. The point was not so much *what* he wrote as it was *how* he wrote. There was a craze for English history—the nation was prosperous and aggressive and patriotism was irresistible; so Shakespeare dug into the old records for his plots. There was a craze for Italy—Renaissance Italy was reputedly a splendiferous thing and England was splendiferous, too; so Shakespeare lifted what he would from the flood of Italian story books then inundating London. Ancient Greece and Rome were also spoken of as fine, and England, ready to identify itself with any fine thing it could hear tell of, fell eager for talk of Greece and Rome; so Shakespeare read through Plutarch's Lives of Greek and Roman worthies and took what he would. And he re-shaped old and forgotten plays, emphasizing this, depressing that, rephrasing where he wished. But all of these things were one thing when Shakespeare took hold of them and a thousand quite different things when he finished. Even his non-dramatic sonnets, as exalted as any other poetry, anywhere, were made on a pattern already quite familiar. Elizabethan England knew when it was pleased, and the world since then has known, too, and nobody has cared very much about whether Shakespeare did or did not devise his own stories.

In spite of Shakespeare's immediate and unexcelled popularity it is possible to trace a growing power in what he wrote. At first, somebody has said, he should be thought of as in the Workshop, as a sort of prentice, writing, in the main, plays which have never been as highly esteemed as other plays which he wrote later—in the main, historical plays. Next, the same critic has said, Shakespeare was in the world—he had learned his trade and he wrote under the exhilaration of knowing that he was valued by his contemporaries, and particularly valued by the people whose judgment he most prized. This was the period of the great comedies.

But the same forces that had eventuated in so much blithe excellence, once set in motion were more or less bound to push on. Whether so bound or not, they did in Shakespeare's case push on to something that was the reverse of blithe. He observed himself an acknowledged paragon; and the same discernment, the same faculty of analysis that had brought him to that position now took him further. If *he* were a paragon, he must have reasoned, what of the great run of humanity that passed as being, and indeed was, he was forced to see, *inferior* to him? If one capable of being bound in a nut shell with room to spare was yet a sort of giant, relatively, with reference to his fellows, what of those fellows, what of *their* dimensions? It is a pretty shattering contemplation, and in its direction lies pure madness. Then Shakespeare was in the Depths, and the great tragedies ensued, a heart-breaking procession of them, from Hamlet through Macbeth and Othello and King Lear down to Antony and Cleopatra— in the lowest depths, just short of being irrecoverably lost in darkness.

And then, when he was in his mid-forties a thing happened, and the consummate man was saved. He suddenly knew that all of this was foolish, that it was thought only, and speculation, and *not* reality, thought and speculation, a function merely, of real humanity, traitorously setting up as master of its creator. That was a reverse state of things indeed and he would not abide it. For thought and speculation, he knew to be not so mighty after all; and he set them into their just category as toys, as far-ranging kites perhaps, which are to be let go of when they threaten to raise up their creator only to plunge him to destruction. That much he knew, and he would go back to Stratford where people all knew that much already without the pain of having had to learn it—back to Stratford where people were simple and kind and loyal to one another, where they regarded one another as individuals, quite concretely, not as detachable units in an abstract conception of mankind at large. That, he concluded, was the true wisdom, and he would recapture it as he had had it in his boyhood. And he did recapture it; and he was then, as the phrase goes, On the Heights. In the workshop, in the world, in the depths, and on the heights.

With Prospero in the *Tempest* he had rid himself of all his power, however great that looked for its source to anything other than what was simple. And with Miranda in the *Tempest* he had achieved the boon of realizing again the basic goodness of humanity. "O brave new world," he makes Miranda say, "that has such people in it." But he was living back in Stratford before he learned that saving wisdom wholly, living in Hugh Clopton's house, planning village conquests, buying land here and there, projecting—who knows—perhaps another steeple for the village church, higher than Sir Hugh's steeple, perhaps another bridge to arch the clement river—mighty works of more interest to him, quite possibly, than Juliet and Beatrice and Hamlet and Lear and Caliban all rolled into one.

His life was itself a play of grand meaning, be sure of that, but he could doubtless not even himself have handled that huge theme with entire adequacy. And it is sure that nobody else has so handled it. Matthew Arnold once made a trial of suggesting that theme in a sonnet, and the result, if not *all* that one might wish for, is none the less very noble. This is Arnold's sonnet:

> Others abide our question. Thou art free.
> We ask and ask—thou smilest and art free.
> Out-topping knowledge. For the loftiest hill
> Who to the stars uncrowns his majesty,
> Planting his steadfast footsteps in the sea,
> Making the heaven of heavens his dwelling place,
> Spares but the cloudy border of his base
> To the foiled searching of mortality;
> And thou, who didst the stars and sunbeams know,
> Self-schooled, self-scanned, self-honored, self-secure,
> Didst tread on earth unguessed at—Better so!
> All pains the immortal spirit must endure
> All weakness which impairs, all griefs which bow,
> Find their sole speech in that victorious brow.

Poems

Happy Birthday to You

To count the ways I love you, dearest child,
Could time be given me for counting—oh, I
Might shape a world in that eternity
Yet fail to number to the end the ways piled
On ways of this boundless cherishing! Mild
Is this cherishing, yet governing all, so high
And holy are its ways, they justify
The mad dream of Whale and minnows reconciled.

For you are twelve today and I, alas,
My child, am more than twelve, out of any reason.
Yet well we know, we two, though it come to pass
That season shall no longer follow season
And all sureties crumble, we know we spoke
Once, together, a covenant nothing will revoke.

From *The Georgia Review*, XI (Fall, 1957), 264.

M. B. F.*

For no cause one can ever state
But truly, just as light is true—
Light turning darkness aureate—
This lady moved in light not old or new

But timeless. And creatures mostly blind,
By timeless miracle would see
When she passed by—the sodden mind
Would stand exultant, wise, and free.

*Mary Barrington Frederick (Mrs. D. B.) of Marshallville, Georgia

Mister Hugh*

I cry Amen, power, might and glory too
And wisdom and thanksgiving for the old bond
Between us, dipping many an opulent frond
Of handy pine for the incomparable Hugh.
For we swore young to make our Georgia true
To the ultimate Symbol, well beyond
Sane men's aspiring to, it seems, unparagoned
Anywhere at all this side the heavenly blue.

That way, we'd save the worlds, for virtue seen,
We'd heard, must needs be followed. But years have passed
And though still we've met few angels with their sheen
Of garments, we keep and will keep to the last
Quick love and long hope and a restive clod
For nasty fools who suck their teeth at God.

*Hugh Hodgson, Head of the Department of Music, University of Georgia, 1928-1960.

Sad Tidings

If all the lights men burn were only one light
And, the sun being down, no moon nor stars would come
And all would be darkness throughout Christendom
But for that one great beacon, through the night
Men would adore it, each a sworn neophyte,
Sworn to cherish it and ruthlessly to drum
To stark perdition with hot opprobrium
The knave or fool not honoring it aright.

But *God* being three, we've hardly one light only,
And yet my news-sheets cry there's mostly one.
For Press, Press says, exults in being lonely
In wit, in virtue lonely like God's ghostly Son.
This makes my insides churn, for well I know
Our sovereign Press for a slimy So-and-So.

Axiom

If anything is equal, precisely so,
To any other thing, if x equals y,
For example, or a is truly b, why
The equations are identical on come or go.
That's sure—or how would the great fixed stars that flow
Volatile about the cosmos ever play
Their courses, how would little pebbles fly
From sling-shots, or pretty maids stand in a row?

There is a saying, God is love, that lifted Job
In sorrow, a senseless, timeless, sovereign word
For this or anybody else's globe,
Opening all skies when it is rightly heard
And filling the wide air for any man who loves
With bright infinitudes of heavenly doves!

Barber Shop Chord

A hair-cut please—ah no, no manicure.
Yes, shine them if you must—and please don't whack
Too much from out the top—one then leans back
Humble and contrite, hoping to endure.

Now next me mounts King Babbitt, suave, secure.
A man among men, conscious of no lack
Of power, he barks his crisp desire that Jack
Trim him up speedily *en cynosure.*

The leashed but greedy shears leap for their prey
While Jack conciliates as best he can:
"It's getting thin around the temples here, I'll say."
"Yes, getting thin," concedes the mighty man.

And over his brash face come weakly, smiles
Levelled past earth, on ivory peristyles.

From *Vanderbilt Masquerader,* X (December, 1933), 14. This was a special issue of the student magazine, devoted to the work of the Fugitive poets, the Agrarians, and student poets of the younger Vanderbilt generation. John Wade contributed four poems to this issue, which begins with a full page congratulatory telegram from Louis Untermeyer and carries cartoons by "Gaston Werm" (Charles Bissell) and the late Avery Handly.

A True Friend

We have a dog named Harvey; he is sweet.
He loves us all, us three, John, Julia, Anne.
When weather's hot, with his tail for a little fan
He cools us well all over, head to feet,
And beds us down at night without a sheet,
Drips water on us from a punctured can,
And says, "Don't swelter now, but be a man
Like me, oblivious of cold and heat."

Of cold too? So he said—and if frost came
And sleet and snow and blustering wind, he'd stoke
Great fires to keep us warm. He would not blame
Us weaklings if the hard freeze made us choke,
But bring us steaming bowls of oyster-stew
Made by a recipe his grandmother knew.

Initiation

Last night when tea was done at Cousin Pearl's
We all played cards, but Claude, her better half,
And Walter Clark, who said they'd talk and laugh,
Ten being present, plus the little girls.

Soon Walter yawned from muffled boredom's furls,
"It's late, Claude says we must go home"—his chaff
Of course, but puzzling as a cryptograph
To primish youngsters blinking through their curls,

And driven beyond escaping to conclude
A grown man false, or father downright rude.
For me, I thanked my stars that being maturer
We daily rear our trust on Something surer.

But Walter jested: "More and more, we see
Every dependable illusory."

Also from *The Vanderbilt Masquerader.*

Index